Eleventh Edition

Drug Dosages in Children

Eleventh Edition

Drug Dosages in Children

Meharban Singh
MD, FAMS, FIAP, FIMSA, FNNF, Hony. FAAP

Former Professor and Head
Department of Pediatrics and Neonatal Division
WHO Collaborating Center for Training and
Research in Newborn Care
All India Institute of Medical Sciences, New Delhi

Ashok K Deorari
MD, Diplomate NB, FAMS, FNNF

Principal and Dean
Himalayan Institute of Medical Sciences
Jolly Grant, Dehradun, Uttrakhand

Former Professor and Head
Department of Pediatrics and Neonatal Division
WHO Collaborating Center for Training and
Research in Newborn Care
All India Institute of Medical Sciences, New Delhi

CBSPD

CBS Publishers & Distributors Pvt Ltd

New Delhi • Bengaluru • Chennai • Kochi • Kolkata • Lucknow • Mumbai
Hyderabad • Jharkhand • Nagpur • Patna • Pune • Uttarakhand

Eleventh Edition

Drug Dosages in Children

ISBN: 978-93-5466-877-7

Eleventh Edition: 2024

First Edition: 1986
Second Edition: 1990
Third Edition: 1993
Fourth Edition: 1997
Fifth Edition: 2001
Sixth Edition: 2004
Seventh Edition: 2007
Eighth Edition: 2011
CBS Reprint: 2015
Ninth Edition: 2015
Tenth Edition: 2020
Reprint: 2020[1], 2023, 2024

Disclaimer

Science and technology are constantly changing fields. New research and experience broaden the scope of information and knowledge. The authors have tried their best in giving information available to them while preparing the material for this book. Although, all efforts have been made to ensure optimum accuracy of the material, yet it is quite possible some errors might have been left uncorrected. The publisher, the printer and the authors will not be held responsible for any inadvertent errors, omissions or inaccuracies.

Published by Satish Kumar Jain and produced by Varun Jain for

CBS Publishers & Distributors Pvt Ltd

4819/XI Prahlad Street, 24 Ansari Road, Daryaganj, New Delhi 110 002, India
Ph: 011-23289259, 23266838 Website: www.cbspd.com; e-mail: delhi@cbspd.com

Corporate Office: 204 FIE, Industrial Area, Patparganj, Delhi 110 092, India
Ph: 011-49344934 Fax: 011-49344935 e-mail: publishing@cbspd.com; publicity@cbspd.com

Branches

- **Bengaluru:** Seema House 2975, 17th Cross, K.R. Road, Banasankari 2nd Stage, Bengaluru 560 070, Karnataka, India
  Ph: +91-80-26771678/79 Fax: +91-80-26771680 e-mail: bangalore@cbspd.com
- **Chennai:** 7, Subbaraya Street, Shenoy Nagar, Chennai 600 030, Tamil Nadu, India
  Ph: +91-44-26680620, 26681266 Fax: +91-44-42032115 e-mail: chennai@cbspd.com
- **Kochi:** 42/1325, 1326, Power House Road, Opposite KSEB, Power House, Ernakulum 682 018, Kochi, Kerala, India
  Ph: +91-484-4059061–65 Fax: +91-484-4059065 e-mail: kochi@cbspd.com
- **Kolkata:** 147, Hind Ceramics Compound, 1st Floor, Nilgunj Road, Belghoria, Kolkata 700 056, West Bengal, India
  Ph: +91-33-25330055/56 e-mail: kolkata@cbspd.com
- **Lucknow:** Basement, Khushuma Complex, 7 Meerabai Marg (behind Jawahar Bhawan), Lucknow 226 001, UP, India
  Ph: +91-522-4000032 e-mail: tiwari.lucknow@cbspd.com
- **Mumbai:** PWD Shed, Gala No. 25/26, Ramchandra Bhatt Marg, Next JJ Hospital, Gate No. 2, Opp. Union Bank of India, Noorbaug, Mumbai 400 009, Maharashtra, India
  Ph: +91-22-66661880/89 e-mail: mumbai@cbspd.com

Representatives

- **Hyderabad** 0-9885175004
- **Jharkhand** 0-9811541605
- **Nagpur** 0-8692091830
- **Patna** 0-9334159340
- **Pune** 0-9664372571
- **Uttarakhand** 0-9716462459

Printed at: Rahul Print 'O' Pack Press, Okhla Industrial Estate, New Delhi, India

Preface to the Eleventh Edition

We are amazed at the reception and acceptance accorded to the earlier editions of the pocket book. We are indeed satisfied that our efforts have amply served the felt needs of medical students, resident doctors, general practitioners, and consultant pediatricians. This edition has been brought out on the advice of several readers and their suggestions have been incorporated. The book has been updated and expanded. Drugs for malignant disorders have been dropped because a variety of protocols are being followed by different oncologists. Several newer formulations including antiretroviral agents, antacids, antimalarials, and antibiotics have been included. The standard or usual adult doses of most of the drugs are also provided to serve the felt needs of GPs and family physicians. The previous style and format has been maintained. Index has been provided to facilitate retrieval of information with ease and speed. We do hope that the book shall continue to enjoy the patronage of physicians dealing with care of sick children as well as adults.

We greatly appreciate the assistance and suggestions provided by faculty colleagues, residents and DM fellows across India. The contributions made by Drs Rakesh Kumar, Deepshikha Jain, Manju Kedarnath, Sanobar Wasim (HIMS, Dehradun), Nihar Ranjan Mishra, Subhankar Sarkar (AIIMS, Kalyani), Prateek Panda, Mayank Priyadarshi (AIIMS, Rishikesh), Krishan Mohan Gulla, Krithika IK (AIIMS, Bhubaneshwar), Rohan Malik, Rajni Sharma, Narendra Bagri, Kanaram Jat, Mohsin Raj Mantoo, Sukanya Priyadarshini (AIIMS, New Delhi) are gratefully acknowledged. We would like to take this opportunity to thank Mr YN Arjuna Senior Vice President—Publishing, Editorial and Publicity, Mrs Ritu Chawla GM—Production and Mr Vikrant Sharma for composing and inserting the manuscript in the word processor and to our friend Mr Satish Kumar Jain, CMD for his enthusiasm and commitment to publish the eleventh edition of the book in an improved style and format. We sincerely hope that the updated and revised edition of the popular pocket book would continue to serve the felt needs of medical students, residents, family physicians and consultant pediatricians.

New Delhi
August 15, 2024

Meharban Singh
Ashok K Deorari

Preface to the First Edition

There is no simple formula to calculate the dosages of drugs for children and most physicians lack confidence to write a prescription for infants. The dose varies with the age, weight, surface area, nature of the disease process and functional maturity of the child. The knowledge regarding precise dosage is essential because margin of drug safety is low in infants and administration of medications in suboptimal doses is associated with unsatisfactory outcome. Due to several reasons, the adult dose cannot be modified for use in children. The pocket book has been designed to serve as a ready reckoner of drug dosages to young residents, practising pediatricians and family physicians and we hope it will instill confidence in their prescriptions and reduce incidence of avoidable side effects of drugs.

The book provides brief information regarding the pharmacokinetics and pharmacodynamics of drugs with special emphasis on advantages and disadvantages of various routes of administration, drug absorption, distribution, bioavailability, tissue binding and its metabolism and excretion. The drugs have been listed alphabetically giving daily dosages per unit body weight, frequency and route of administration. Certain important cautions and contraindications in respect to selected drugs have been provided to prevent therapeutic misadventures. To improve the practical utility of the booklet, trade names of formulations from standard pharmaceutical companies along with their formulations and strengths are appended in parentheses.

The authors are thankful to Shri Anil Bhutani for typing the manuscript. The credit for prompt publication of this manual is shared by our publisher and friend Shri Narinder K. Sagar.

New Delhi
October 2, 1986

Meharban Singh
Ashok K Deorari

List of Banned Drugs

According to the recommendations of US Food and Drug Administration (FDA) and World Health Organization (WHO), the following drugs have been globally banned or withdrawn because of the risk of serious adverse effects. The MOH, Government of India has banned over 300 "fixed drug combinations" and several cough mixtures are unsafe and associated with serious adverse effects. The complete list of drugs banned by Health Ministry in India is given in a gazette notification (cdsco.gov.in).

Alipidem	Inhaled insulin
Amidopyrine	Levamisole
Analgin (dipyrone)	Lynestrenol
Aprotinin	Methaqualone
Astemizole	Nimesulide
Atenolol	Nitrofurazone
Capreomycin	Pemoline
Cetrimide	Phenacetin
Cisapride	Phenolphthalein
Deanxit	Phenyl butazone
Diethylstilbestrol	Phenyl propranolamine
Diloxanide furoate	Pioglitazone
Droperidol	Piperazine citrate
Efalizumab	Proproxyphene hydrochloride
Etritinate	Quiniodochlor
Fenfluramine	Rapacuronium
Furazolidine	Rimonabant
Gatifloxacin	Rofecoxib

(Contd.)

(*Contd.*)

Rosiglitazone	Thioridazine
Sibutramine	Ticrynafen
Tegaserod	Travalfloxacin
Terfenadine	Ximelagastran
Thalidomide	Zimelidine

Immunization Schedule Recommended by IAP

Age	*Vaccine*	*Doses*
	Essential vaccines	
Birth to 2 weeks	BCG OPV HBV	Single dose before discharge 1st dose soon afterbirth 1st dose within 24 hours
6–8 weeks	DTwP or DTaP + Hib + HBV + IPV + PCV 13	1st dose
10–12 weeks	DTwP or DTaP + Hib + HBV + IPV + PCV 13	2nd dose
14–16 weeks	DTwP or DTaP + Hib + HBV + IPV + PCV 13	3rd dose
6 months	Flu vaccine	Two doses 4 weeks apart followed by boosters every year up to 5 yr age
7–8 months	Typhoid conjugated vaccine, single dose	
9 months	MMR vaccine	1st dose
12 months	HAV	Single doses in case of live vaccine
15 months	MMR, PCV 13, varicella	2nd dose

(Contd.)

Immunization Schedule Recommended by IAP *(contd.)*

Age	*Vaccine*	*Doses*
	Essential vaccines	
16–18 months	HAV 2nd + Varicella 2nd + DTwP or DTaP + Hib + HBV + IPV	1st booster
4½–5 years	dTaP + IPV	MMR 3rd dose
9–14 years	HPV (4 and 9 valent vaccines)	2 doses 6 months apart
>14 years	0, 1 or 2, 6 months	
10 years	dTaP	

(Contd.)

Immunization Schedule Recommended by IAP *(contd.)*
Additional vaccines during special situations
IPV (injectable or inactivated polio vaccine) is given to immunocompromised or HIV-positive children. It is being administered routinely as a part of post-polio eradication policy.
Meningococcal vaccine (during an epidemic, Haj pilgrims, sickle cell disease, CSF rhinorrhea).
Pneumococcal polysaccharide vaccine, i.e. PPV 23 (chronic lung and heart disease, splenectomy, nephrotic syndrome, immunocompromised child).
Influenza vaccine (bronchial asthma, immunocompromised child). Initially 2 doses (single dose after the age of 9 years) are given 4 weeks apart after the age of 6 months, followed by yearly boosters at the onset of monsoon and winter.
Anti-rabies "post-exposure" vaccine following animal bites.
Rabies "pre-exposure prophylaxis" is given to high-risk population (children with pets, hostelers), postmen, veterinary doctors, wildlife handlers, and technicians. Three primary doses 1.0 ml IM on day 0, 7 and 21 or 28. A booster dose is given after 1 year and then every 5 years. In immunized subjects, for "post-exposure" protection only two doses are given on days 0 and 3. In these cases, no rabies immune globulins (RIG) are needed.
Cholera vaccine (to control epidemics, visitors to *Kumbh Mela*, Haj pilgrims).
Japanese B encephalitis vaccine (endemic areas, during epidemics) Jeev (Biological Evan Ltd.) is administered (0.5 ml 1–3 years, 1.0 ml 3–10 years Sc) in 2 primary doses 4 weeks apart while Jenvac (Bharat Biotech) 0.5 ml is given as a single dose after the age of one year.
Yellow fever vaccine (travelers to South Africa). A single dose after the age of 6 months provides lifelong immunity. Avoid during pregnancy and infancy.

(Contd.)

Immunization Schedule Recommended by IAP *(contd.)*

BCG: Bacillus Calmette-Guerin vaccine for TB, HBV: Hepatitis B vaccine, DTP: Triple antigen containing vaccines against diphtheria, tetanus and pertussis (whooping cough), DTwP (whole cell pertussis), DTap (acellular pertussis), PCV 13: 13-valent pneumococcal conjugated vaccine, PPV 23: 23-valent pneumococcal polysaccharide vaccine. OPV: Oral polio vaccine (dual vaccine containing polio strains 1 and 3), IPV: Inactivated polio vaccine, MMR: Measles, mumps and rubella vaccine, Tdap: Tetanus toxoid with low dose diphtheria and low dose acellular pertussis vaccine, Td: Dual vaccine with low dose diphtheria vaccine (5 Lf or 2 iu) which can be safely given to adults, TT: Tetanus toxoid,

Hib: *Haemophilus influenzae* type b, HAV: Hepatitis A vaccine

1. The suggested schedule may be modified by the consultant pediatrician as per the local needs.
2. Breastfeeding can be given after oral polio vaccine and it does not interfere with development of satisfactory immunity.
3. Most immunizations can be given in the presence of a minor illness. Paracetamol can be given following a vaccination for relief of local pain and fever, but it may reduce immunogenicity of the vaccine.
4. There is no need to give Hib vaccine (*Haemophilus influenzae* type b vaccine), if it has not been taken by the age of 1½ years.
5. The need and cost-effectiveness of optional vaccines must be explained to the parents before they are recommended.
6. Live vaccines should be avoided in immunocompromised children and symptomatic HIV-positive infants.
7. A number of vaccines can be administered together simultaneously at two different sites or as a combo formulation without interfering with development of protection against different antigens. A live vaccine can be administered after an inactivated vaccine (or *vice versa*) without any minimum recommended interval. However, a minimum interval of 4 weeks is recommended between administration of two live vaccines.
8. When a dose of a vaccine is missed, the remaining doses should be administered at the earliest opportunity while keeping in mind that the vaccine dose already given is valid.
9. Before giving the next dose of vaccine, ask the mother if the child had any significant reaction to the last dose of the vaccine.
10. OPV-related paralytic poliomyelitis is being increasingly reported from developed countries. These countries have changed their strategy and are giving IPV (injectable or inactivated or killed polio vaccine) and dual oral polio vaccine containing polio strains 1 and 3.

Source: Singh M, Care of the Newborn, CBS Publishers & Distributors, New Delhi, Revised 9th edition 2024.

Prescription Abbreviations

Weights and Measures

cc	cubic centimeter
g	gram
kg	kilogram
m^2	meter square
mg	milligram
µg	microgram
ml	milliliter
ng	nanogram
pg	picogram

Latin Abbreviations and their Meanings

a.c. (ante cibum)	before meals
aq. (aqua)	water
b.i.d. or b.d. (bis in die)	twice a day
gtt. (gutta/e)	drop(s)
h (hora)	hourly
h.s. (hora somni)	at bedtime
i.u.	international units
liq.	a liquor
mist. (mistura)	a mixture
o.d. (omne in die)	once a day
omn. hor. (omni hora)	every hour
omn. man. (omni mane)	every morning
p.c. (post cibum)	after food
p.o. (per os)	orally
p.r. (per rectum)	rectally
p.r.n. (pro re nata)	when needed

q (quaque)	every
q.i.d. (quarter in die)	four times a day
q.s. (quantum sufficiat)	a sufficient quantity
℞	take (thou) a recipe
s.o.s. (si opus sit)	as and when required
stat (statim)	immediately
t.d.s. (ter die sumendum)	three times a day
t.i.d. (ter in die)	three times a day
u.d. (ut dictum)	as directed

Abbreviations

BMI	body mass index
C/I	contraindications
Caps	Capsules
CR	controlled release
CSF	cerebrospinal fluid
d	day
div	divided
DT	dispersible tablet
ER	extended release
ES	extra strength
ET	Endotracheal
hr	hour
IM	intramuscular
indic	indications
inf	infusion
inj	injection
IR	immediate release
IT	intrathecal
IV	intravenous
IVIG	intravenous immunoglobulins
MD	mouth dissolving
min	minutes
NG	nasogastric

PEM	protein energy malnutrition
PO (per os)	by mouth or oral
PR	per rectum
SC	subcutaneous
SE	side effects
sec	seconds
SL	sublingual
SR	sustained release
Susp	suspension
Syr	syrup
Tabs	tablets
wk/wks	week/weeks
XR	extended release
XT	extra time

Contents

Chapter

1

Pharmacokinetics and Pharmacodynamics of Drugs

Pharmacokinetics (PK) is the study of drug movements within the body. In order to produce its optimal effect, a drug must be present in an appropriate concentration at its site of action. The various steps involved in the pharmacokinetics of drugs can be remembered by an acronym DADME. The concentration of the drug at the target site depends upon the **D**ose or amount of drug, and release of active ingredient from the pharmaceutical formulation, **A**bsorption from the site of delivery into blood circulation, and **D**istribution into various fluid compartments (VdF) and tissues (VdT) of the body. The transfer of drugs across cell membranes largely depends on their dose or concentration, molecular size and shape, solubility at the site of absorption, degree of ionization and relative lipid solubility. This is followed by **M**etabolization (biotransformation, activation, inactivation) of the drug which mostly occurs in the liver. The water-soluble drug is largely **E**xcreted or eliminated in the urine (and partly in the bile, saliva, sweat, breast milk, feces) while ionized lipid-soluble agents may be stored in the body tissues.

Pharmacodynamics (PD) deals with the biological effects of drugs on various therapeutic targets or receptors. There is increasing awareness that each patient or host is unique because of genetic differences in drug metabolic pathways (Pharmacogenomics) which determines the efficacy of therapeutic agent and risk of the adverse drug reactions (ADRs). In due course of time, the drug therapy is likely to be "fine tuned" to the concept of "personalized prescription" depending upon the genome of the patient.

Factors Modifying Absorption

The drugs in an aqueous solution are more readily absorbed than those given in an oily solution, suspension or solid form because the aqueous formulation mixes more readily with the aqueous phase at the site of absorption. Local conditions at the site of absorption alter solubility particularly in gastrointestinal tract. The concentration of a drug influences its rate of absorption. The circulation at the site of absorption also affects drug absorption. The area of absorbing surface to which a drug is exposed is one of the most important determinants of the rate of drug absorption. The absorbing surface is determined largely by the route of administration (Table 1.1).

Distribution of Drugs

The body can be considered as a series of compartments with varying accessibility to drugs. In the blood, the distribution of a drug is chiefly influenced by its lipid solubility, ionization, pH of blood, available protein binding capacity and differences in the regional blood flow. A water-soluble drug is distributed mostly in the extracellular space and it may not readily pass into cerebrospinal fluid or other body cavities. Lipid-soluble drugs are distributed throughout the intracellular and extracellular spaces.

Selective distribution of drugs occurs due to protein binding in the blood (penicillins, phenylbutazone) and in the tissues (mepacrine). In case of drugs which are not bound to proteins, distribution is confined to the extracellular space and they can be used to measure extracellular fluid volume (inulin, bromide). The drugs that are rapidly absorbed from the gut because of their lipid solubility (unionized) are known to readily diffuse into the CSF and brain. The ionized water-soluble (neostigmine, streptomycin) drugs are poorly absorbed from the gut and they show poor penetration into various body fluids. When meninges are inflamed, the penetration of all drugs into CSF is enhanced.

TABLE 1.1: Routes of administration of drugs and their practical implications

Route	*Absorption pattern*	*Special utility*	*Limitations and precautions*
Intravenous	Potentially immediate effect.	Valuable for emergency use, permits titration of dose, suitable for large volumes and irritating substances which can be administered in a diluted form.	Increased risk and chances of infection, sepsis and tissue necrosis on extravasation. Not suitable for oily and insoluble substances. It is expensive and self and ambulatory medication is not possible.
Intramuscular	Prompt absorption from aqueous solution but slow and sustained absorption from oily preparations.	Suitable for oily vehicles and some irritating substances.	May precipitate abortive polio, cause local necrosis and infection and are contraindicated in patients with a bleeding disorder. Some drugs are locally irritant and have erratic absorption (dilantin, chloramphenicol).
Subcutaneous	Prompt absorption occurs from aqueous solution but absorption is slower compared to intramuscular route.	Suitable for vaccines, insulin and some insoluble suspensions and for implantation of solid pellets.	Self-medication is possible, not suitable for large volumes, local pain and necrosis may occur.
Oral	Variable absorption depending on multiple factors.	Most common, convenient, economical and safe route. The unabsorbed drug acts at the local site.	Requires cooperation of the patient and the caretaker. The bioavailability is erratic because most drugs are metabolized in the liver after absorption and gastric juices may inactivate some drugs.

(*Contd.*)

1

TABLE 1.1: Routes of administration of drugs and their practical implications *(Contd.)*

Route	*Absorption pattern*	*Special utility*	*Limitations and precautions*
Sublingual	Prompt absorption of lipid-soluble drugs.	Relatively fewer molecules are required to produce drug effect because gastro-intestinal tract is bypassed.	Drugs requiring rapid effect on the heart (nitroglycerine, nifedipine) are given through this route.
Rectal	Slower absorption, 50% will pass through liver and then enter systemic circulation.	Useful in children with persistent vomiting and alteration in consciousness in domiciliary practice.	Psychological embarrassment, irritant to mucosa, irregular and incomplete absorption (paraldehyde, paracetamol, diazepam, aminophylline).
Intrathecal	Effective levels are achieved at the site of action.	Produce local effects on meninges and CNS.	Iatrogenic and chemical meningitis can occur. Large volumes cannot be given (gentamicin, human antitetanus serum).
Pulmonary (aerosol, pressurized nebulizer, inhalers and rotacaps)	Prompt local and systemic effects	Direct absorption with avoidance of hepatic transformation and systemic side effects.	Poor ability to regulate dose, cumbersome method in children, irritant to lungs. Particle size of >7 microns will not reach small bronchi and if it is <1 micron, it is likely to be exhaled.

Plasma Proteins and Tissue Binding

Many drugs circulate in the blood in two forms, free (pharmacologically active, diffusible and available for metabolism and excretion), and bound (pharmacologically inert, neither diffusible nor available for metabolism or excretion). The drugs with weak protein binding readily release the active drug as soon as the concentration of free drug falls. Thus, protein binding can be regarded as a mechanism for drug storage. Total plasma concentration (free plus bound drug) of a drug without any regard to the proportion of protein bound component can give a misleading impression, because only the free drug will diffuse into the tissues and other body fluids and provide biological activity. The claims that one penicillin gives higher total plasma concentration as compared to another, are meaningless unless it is known as to what proportion of the drug is in the bound form.

When two drugs having an identical affinity for the same binding site are given, they will compete with each other thus interfering with their bioavailability. In situations with reduced protein binding capacity (malnutrition), the concentration of a free drug may be significantly higher.

Plasma Concentration of Drugs

Plasma concentrations are specially useful and monitored when a drug may have to be taken in near toxic doses (lithium, anticonvulsants, digoxin); there are great individual variations and lack of easily measured response (antidepressants) or a potentially toxic drug is being used in the presence of renal failure (aminoglycosides), to assess compliance (anticonvulsants) and for management of poisoning (salicylates, barbiturates).

The blood is the principal vehicle for distribution of the drug into the various fluid compartments of the body. The concentration of a drug in blood (or plasma) is often related to its concentration in the target tissues. Because of ease of accessibility for samplings, plasma concentration is commonly used as a guide in clinical practice. The blood sample should be collected when a steady state has been achieved and just before the administration of next dose of drug. The relationship between plasma concentration and tissue concentration (pharmacological effect) is closest in the case of drugs that are themselves the sole pharmacologically active compounds (not their metabolites) or drugs that act irreversibly such as monoamine oxidase inhibitors and anticholinesterases.

Half-life of a Drug

The peak plasma concentration of a drug after administration is called C_{max} and the time taken to reach the maximum concentration after its administration is called T_{max}. The period of time required for the concentration of the drug to get reduced to one-half (t½) is called biological half-life which corresponds to the duration of action of a drug. The plasma half-life of a drug depends upon how quickly the drug is eliminated from the plasma. The drug may be eliminated from the body by excretion, protein binding, metabolic inactivation or translocation to another body fluid compartment such as the intracellular fluid. The dosing interval of medications is based on the biological half-life of the drug to ensure sustained effect throughout the day. The drugs with short half-life are administered at frequent intervals while a drug like levothyroxine which has a half-life of 5–7 days is administered as a single daily dose.

Metabolism

Drugs must be eliminated from the body in a reasonable time. Those drugs which are water soluble and relatively lipid insoluble and ionised are usually excreted unchanged by the kidneys. Volatile anesthetics are highly lipid soluble and unionized drugs are reabsorbed by back diffusion from the glomerular filtrate and tend to remain in the body indefinitely unless metabolized and inactivated. Drug metabolism occurs chiefly in the liver and is of two kinds:

1. Conversion to pharmacologically inactive substances.
2. Conversion to pharmacologically active substances, e.g. cortisone, prednisone, imipramine, phenylbutazone and cyclophosphamide.

The amount and nature of drug metabolizing enzymes are genetically determined and the rate of drug metabolism varies greatly between individuals. Drugs are principally metabolized by enzymes in hepatic microsomes (a fraction of the cell endoplasmic reticulum) but also to a lesser extent by enzymes elsewhere in the body and in the blood. Two basic chemical reactions occur:

1. *Nonsynthetic*: The molecule is changed by oxidation, reduction or hydrolysis.
2. *Synthetic*: The molecule is conjugated with other substances, glucuronic acid (glucuronidation), acetic acid (acetylation), and sulphate (ethereal sulphate formation).

Phenobarbitone, phenytoin, phenylbutazone, alcohol, DDT and griseofulvin, to name a few, are enzyme inducers. Enzyme induction by alcohol is a likely explanation for tolerance shown by alcoholics to barbiturates and tolbutamide. While treating epilepsy, enzyme induction has practical implications. Drugs that depress hepatic drug metabolizing enzymes (including drugs that interfere with liver function) will potentiate the effect of certain drugs. Phenytoin metabolism is inhibited by coumarin anticoagulants, isoniazid and phenylbutazone so that phenytoin toxicity may occur when these drugs are being administered concomitantly.

Excretion

Renal excretion: The renal excretion depends upon the extent of plasma protein binding of a drug, glomerular filtration rate, amount of back diffusion from glomerular filtration (influenced by urine pH) especially when a drug is lipid soluble, active renal tubular reabsorption and active renal tubular secretion. Renal plasma flow is 12 ml/min at birth and reaches adult level of 140 ml/min by one year of age. Similarly, glomerular filteration rate (GFR) is 2–4 ml/min at birth, increases to 8–20 ml/min by 2 to 3 days and reaches adult level of 120 ml/min by 3 to 5 mon.

Biliary excretion: Many drugs excreted in the bile are often reabsorbed (enterohepatic circulation) into the circulation thus prolonging their half-life. They are eventually excreted in the urine. High concentration of a chemotherapeutic agent is mandatory for treating infections of the biliary tract including typhoid carriers. The drugs that achieve significant concentrations in the bile include penicillins, rifampicin, erythromycin and tetracyclines.

Pulmonary excretion: Volatile lipid-soluble anesthetics and metabolites are excreted through the lungs.

Excretion/secretion in the milk: Unionized lipid-soluble drugs readily diffuse from blood to breast milk; but since the pH of the blood and milk are different (blood 7.4, milk 7.0), the total concentration of the drug is not identical in the two fluids. *In general, whatever is safely tolerated by the nursing mother, is generally safe for her suckling infant*. However, the ingestion of following drugs by the nursing mother contraindicates breastfeeding: Antithyroid drugs (except propylthiouracil), radioactive pharmaceuticals, anticancer drugs or cytotoxic agents, phenelzine, phenindione, amiodarone, tamoxifen, lithium carbonate, bromocriptine, and drugs of abuse. In most other situations when transmammary medication occurs in a suckling infant, it is best to stop the intake of offending agent to the mother and replace it by a safer alternative.

Calculation of Dose

The dose of a drug can be calculated on the basis of body weight or surface area (SA), the latter being more appropriate because it is proportional to the metabolic rate. However, because of convenience, the dose of drug is usually calculated on the basis of body weight. Because of their higher metabolic rate, children generally require higher dose per unit body weight compared to adults. There is no reliable formula for calculation of drug dosages in infants and if the proper dose of a drug is not known, it must be ascertained because the risk of intolerance is grave in infants. When available, experimentally determined or clinically established doses should be used. No method of calculation of dose provides for the individual variations in response. *The fixed dose combinations* (FDCs) *should be avoided in children due to difficulty in administration of correct dose of each component and greater risk of toxicity*. Based on adult dose, various formulae are available to calculate the dose of drugs in children.

1. $\frac{\text{Weight of the child in kg}}{60} \times \text{adult dose}$
2. $\frac{\text{SA of the child in M}^2}{1.8} \times \text{adult dose}$
3. SA of the child in $M^2 \times 60$ = % of adult dose
4. Clark's rule: Adult dose × (weight in lbs ÷ 150)
5. Young's rule: Adult dose × (age in yrs + 12 ÷ age in yrs)
6. Fried's rule: Adult dose × (age in months ÷ 150)
7. Webster rule: Adult dose × age in yrs + 1 ÷ age in yrs + 7.

In obese children, dosing per unit body weight may create problems because they have a slow metabolic rate with reduced drug clearance. *Therefore, it is recommended to calculate the dose in obese children on the basis of their ideal body weight for their age.*

Influence of Age, Sex and Disease

Age: Preterm babies are likely to be intolerant to many drugs because the organs responsible for disposing off the drugs from the body are less efficient. Newborn babies have relatively lower renal blood flow and glomerular filtration rate than adults. A wide variety of enzyme reactions are less developed specially in the prematures. Excretion of many antibiotics is delayed. Total plasma protein and albumin concentrations are lower in the newborn than in older children. Thus binding capacity of drugs is lower so that more of the drug is free and available for diffusion into the tissues. The older children are more tolerant than adults to digitalis but tolerance to atropine and morphine is either low or normal.

Sex: Females are believed to be more liable to be excited follow- ing intake of morphine and respond poorly to antidepressant drugs. As such there are no clinically important qualitative sex differences in action of drugs but there are wide individual variations.

Diseases: Adequate knowledge regarding both the drug and the disease is essential for safe and rational therapy. Hepatic and renal insufficiency often results in defective metabolism or excretion and necessitates modification of drug dosages. Patients with malfunctioning of respiratory system are intolerant to drugs which are known to depress respiration (opiates and barbiturates). Asthmatic attack may be precipitated by cholinergic drugs, release of histamine or by blockage of beta-receptors. Myocardial damage makes a patient intolerant to therapeutic doses of digitalis and sympathomimetics. Hepatic porphyria may be precipitated by certain drugs and chemicals either by induction of hepatic ALA-synthetase enzyme or by the haem-containing drug oxidizing enzymes, cytochrome P450, e.g. phenobarbitone, sulfonamides, hydantoin, methyldopa, chloroquine, pentazocine, phenylbutazone and oral contraceptives.

In patients with shock, the drugs injected subcutaneously may not be absorbed owing to intense peripheral vasoconstriction and when shock resolves, there is pronounced effect of previously administered drug. Therefore, drugs should preferably be administered intravenously in children with shock. In patients with congestive heart failure, sodium-containing drugs like sodium salicylate, sodium penicillins and sodium-containing antacids should be avoided. A number of drugs and chemicals lead to intravascular hemolysis in patients with G-6-PD deficiency. The list of banned drugs includes primaquine, pamaquine, pentaquine, plasmoquine, sulfonamides, furazolidone, antipyrine, para-aminosalicylic acid (PAS), naphthalene, methylene blue, phenylhydrazine, probenecid and fava beans.

Pharmaceutical Formulations and Biological Availability

When a drug is prescribed, the patient does not receive the drug alone but a complex mixture along with other excipients which are added to allow the drug to be offered in a convenient, stable and easily administered form. Majority of physicians tend to ignore pharmaceutical formulations and additives or excipients as an important factor producing variable or unexpected response to drugs. The particle size (surface area of a tablet exposed to solution), diluting substances, tablet size and the pressure used in the tableting machines can affect the biological availability of the drug.

Drug Dosages in Patients with Renal Failure

The drugs may accumulate in the body due to failure of renal excretion or they may exacerbate renal damage. Problems of safety arise especially in patients with renal failure who must be treated with drugs that are potentially toxic and which are eliminated by the kidneys. Creatinine clearance is the best guide for relationship of half-life of a drug to renal failure. If the creatinine clearance is halved, the half-life of a drug is doubled and if it is reduced to 25 percent, the half-life of the drug is quadrupled and so forth.

a. *Drugs eliminated by the kidneys:* Aminoglycosides, amphotericin B, and sulfonamides.
b. *Drugs eliminated by nonrenal mechanisms:* Chlortetracycline, erythromycin, chloramphenicol and nalidixic acid. Metabolites of these drugs may accumulate in patients with renal failure but they are safely tolerated.
c. *Drugs intermediate between (a) and (b) above:* Penicillins, cephalosporins and cotrimoxazole.

The measurement of plasma concentration of drugs is useful and desirable in patients with renal failure. The maintenance dosages of the drugs in group (a) should be reduced to about 25 percent and in case of less toxic members of group (c) to about 50 percent of the recommended dose. The priming or loading doses should be avoided in children with renal dysfunction. The interval between doses should be increased on the basis of a crude formula: Drug interval (hr) between two doses = plasma creatinine mg/dl × 8. Based on plasma creatinine and creatinine clearance values, charts can be consulted for identifying the fractional dose of the drug required in children with renal failure of varying severity.

Drugs and the Liver

Many drugs are metabolized in the liver. The metabolites may be pharmacologically active (cortisone, chloral hydrate, phenylbutazone, cyclophosphamide) or inactive (most drugs). In patients with hepatic disease, the drugs may thus become either more or less active. The drugs may interfere with hepatic functions in the following ways:

- *Interference with bilirubin metabolism:* Novobiocin inhibits bilirubin conjugation while C-17 steroid derivatives interfere with bilirubin excretion into the hepatic canaliculi. The androgens and anabolic steroids, estrogens and progestins interfere with bilirubin excretion into the hepatic canaliculi and cause reversible cholestatic jaundice.
- *Direct liver cell injury:* Carbon tetrachloride, DDT, paracetamol, arsenicals, iron, anticancer drugs and chloroform can cause hepatocellular damage.
- *Allergy or hypersensitivity or idiosyncratic reaction:*
  - Hepatitis-like reaction. Hydralazine, INH, pyrazinamide, ethionamide, NSAIDs, MAO inhibitors, etc.
  - Cholestatic injury. It is may be dose related (steroids) or allergic (phenothiazines).
  - Combined hepatocellular and cholestatic damage. Sulfonamides, PAS, and erythromycin estolate.

Prescribing in Hepatic Disease

Whenever possible it is recommended to use alternative drugs which can be safely given to children with hepatic dysfunction.

Fever: Use acetylsalicylic acid and paracetamol. NSAIDs should be avoided.

Sedation: Use diazepam or pethidine and avoid paraldehyde.

Antidepressants: Tricyclics are safer as compared to MAO inhibitors. Anticonvulsants should be used with caution.

Diuretics: It is desirable to use potassium-sparing (spironolactone) diuretics. Severe hypokalemia with worsening of hepatic status may occur with commonly used diuretics (thiazides, furosemide).

Steroids: Cortisone and prednisone may be ineffective in conventional doses because they are converted into active form (hydrocortisone and prednisolone) by the liver. Anabolic steroids and sex hormones should be used with caution because they are normally metabolized to inactive forms in the liver.

Antibiotics and chemotherapeutic agents: Antitubercular drugs should be used with caution. Penicillins and its semisynthetic derivatives, aminoglycosides and cotrimoxazole are safely tolerated by children with hepatic dysfunction.

Drug Therapy in Children with Protein–Energy Malnutrition

Malnourished children have a high incidence of intercurrent infections necessitating frequent use of drugs. The nutritional status is known to alter the biological functions in children. It is essential to know the pharmacokinetics and pharmacodynamics of drugs in malnourished children in order to ensure rational use of drugs. Due to frequent association of hypoproteinemia, the levels of free drugs are likely to be higher in children with protein–energy malnutrition (PEM). In addition, clearance of drugs by kidneys and their biotransformation by liver may be decreased. Calculation of drug dosage on the basis of body weight may be erroneous because they are likely to have relatively large surface area per unit body mass. It is advisable to calculate drug dosage on the basis of body surface area in malnourished children. The biological functions recover in a period of 4 to 6 wk following nutritional rehabilitation. Therefore, drug administration should be revised when the child has recovered. Scanty information is available regarding the pharmacokinetics of drugs in malnutrition but some drugs need special consideration when used in children with PEM.

Malnourished children should not be digitalized as they are sensitive to digitalis and its derivatives. Instead, a diuretic should be used alone while treating congestive cardiac failure. Due to decreased biotransformation in the liver, glucuronide and sulfate pathways get saturated at lower plasma concentrations of paracetamol thus posing an increased risk of toxicity. The absorption of chloramphenicol is not altered by the nutritional status but there is a slower rate of its biotransformation by the liver. Accordingly, children with severe PEM should receive two-thirds of the recommended dose of chloramphenicol. Bioavailability of intramuscular penicillin is not altered, except in children with gross edema. It appears that in kwashiorkor, the renal clearance of penicillin is decreased and it should be administered at longer intervals. Chloroquine is bound to plasma protein to a greater extent in children with kwashiorkor than in normal children and, therefore, reduced amount of free drug is available. Nevertheless, modification in the dosages of chloroquine is not required because of its slower biotransformation in patients with kwashiorkor.

Oral Medications

Most medications are given orally and most children are fussy to take medicines because of their unpleasant taste. It needs a lot of patience and tact on the part of the mother or nurse to give them medicines. Medicines are absorbed better when given on empty stomach or in-between the meals (one hr before taking food or two hr after food) but they are preferably administered after or along meals to reduce gastric side effects and improve their tolerance (Table 1.2).

Drops formulations are preferred in young infants because small volume of the medicine need to be administered. In preschool children, syrup or suspension formulation is usually given. Dispersible tablets or mouth dissolving tablets can be given to children above 2 to 3 yr of age. Most school-going children should be able to swallow tablets or capsules but at times even an adolescent child may refuse to take a tablet. Some children are extremely prone to vomit when a medicine is given to them. Mother should hold the infant in her lap in a semi-upright position while giving medicine to him. Medicine can be given with a spoon or preferably with a plastic dropper. The exact amount to be administered should be measured with a plastic syringe or by the graduated dispenser provided by the manufacturer. Medicine should not be poured on the dorsum of the tongue but instead it should be spilled between the side of

TABLE 1.2: Drugs that should be administered on empty stomach or in-between meals

- **Antibiotics:** Penicillin G, ampicillin, ceftibuten, cloxacillin, dicloxacillin, erythromycin, azithromycin, tetracycline, cotrimoxazole, levofloxacin, antitubercular drugs especially isoniazid and rifampin.
- **Antifungal agents:** Itraconazole, ketoconazole.
- **Antiviral agents:** Dianosine, didanosine, efavirenz, indinavir, amprenavir, zidovudine.
- **Cardiovascular agents:** Digoxin, captopril, nifedipine, diltiazem, sotalol.
- **Miscellaneous drugs:** Thyroxine, omeprazole, lansoprazole, ranitidine, sucralfate, antiemetics, d-penicillamine, iron*, bisphosphonates, sildenafil, bethanechol, proton pump inhibitors, bisacodyl, etidronate, risedronate, zafirlukast, methotrexate.

*Should preferably be taken in-between the meals or at bedtime.

the tongue and the cheek. No medicine should be mixed in the milk or food because the child may stop taking the milk or food which was laced with the medicine. The medicine or crushed tablet can be mixed in honey or fruit juice.

The toddlers create the greatest fuss in taking medicines and need to be handled with understanding and firmness. The attention is diverted and child is held firmly while giving the medicine. In a struggling child, due care should be exercised to prevent choking and aspiration. *If the medicine is vomited out immediately or within 5 min after the administration, it should be readministered.* The older child should be dealt with understanding and explanation that the medicine will make him feel better and he will be able to get better or go to school sooner.

Drug Prescription

The prescription should clearly mention the name of the patient, age, sex, weight and diagnosis. The dosing matrix should provide the name and concentration of the formulation, exact dose, frequency of administration, whether taken on empty stomach or after food, duration of therapy, etc. It is recommended to use the calibrated measuring device provided by the manufacturer or preferably a calibrated dropper or a plastic syringe to ensure precise dosing of the medication. A sample prescription for dosing matrix for Ronit 5 yr old boy weighing 16 kg with diagnosis of congenital hypothyroidism and acute respiratory infection with asthmatic bronchitis is shown in Table 1.3.

Adverse Effects of Drugs

It must be remembered that most diseases recover spontaneously and no drug is entirely safe and virtually every drug has side effects including a placebo. We should try to avoid medications unless they are unavoidable and use those drugs which have withstood the test of time.

- *Overdose:* Absolute excessive intake or relative excessive accumulation due to defective metabolism.
- *Intolerance:* Due to low threshold to normal pharmacological action.

TABLE 1.3: A sample prescription matrix

Medicines	*Empty stomach*	*After breakfast*	*After lunch*	*Evening*	*After dinner*	*Duration*
Tab thyronorm 50 µg	✓					Lifelong
Syrup crocin DS 250 mg/5 ml		✓	✓		✓	2 days, then sos
Syrup moxclav	✓			✓		5 days
Syrup levolin plus 5 ml		✓	✓		✓	7 days
Syrup rantac 75 mg/5 ml	✓			✓		7 days

Please revert back if there is any adverse reaction or intolerance to any medication.

- *Side effects:* They include undesired and unavoidable effects. The side effect may be an undesirable known therapeutic effect (e.g. drowsiness with phenobarbitone when used as an anticonvulsant) or a side effect on one occasion may be a desired effect in another situation, e.g. atropine for anesthetic premedication to dry the bronchial secretions.
- *Secondary effects:* Indirect consequences like diarrhea and deficiency of vitamins, following prolonged use of broad spectrum antibiotics.
- *Idiosyncrasy:* Inherent qualitatively abnormal reaction to a drug due to genetic abnormality, e.g. porphyria, G-6-PD deficiency and nimesulide.
- *Hypersensitivity reactions:*
  - Anaphylactoid shock. It is common following administration of penicillin and horse serum.
  - Pulmonary reactions. Antigen-antibody reactions causing local liberation of substances, including histamine and SRS-A.
  - Urticarial rashes and angioneurotic edema.
  - Serum sickness syndrome.
- *GI intolerance:* Dyspepsia, nausea, vomiting, abdominal pain, diarrhea, and constipation are the most common adverse reactions due to a variety of oral medications.
- *Blood dyscrasias:* Thrombocytopenia, granulocytopenia, agranulocytosis and aplastic anemia are rare but life-threatening.
- *Hemolysis:* Dose-related pharmacological action on normal cells, e.g. lead, some snake venoms, idiosyncracy, G-6-PD deficiency, and allergy. At times a drug (hapten) may combine with protein in the RBC membrane, i.e. PAS, quinine.
- Non-urticarial skin rashes including Stevens-Johnson syndrome.
- Drug fever
- *Syndrome resembling collagen vascular diseases:* Hydralazine, procainamide and anticonvulsants.
- *Hepatitis and cholestatic jaundice:* INH, rifampicin, erythromycin estolate, NSAIDs and chlorpromazine.

- *Miscellaneous adverse effects:* Severe hematemesis (aspirin, NSAIDs), peripheral neuritis, nephritis and toxic cataract.

Drugs and the Fetus

When a pregnant woman is administered a chemotherapeutic agent, there is unwanted and unavoidable exposure of her unborn child to the same agent. A drug which is apparently safe and well tolerated by the mother, may be harmful and damaging to the fetus. *No drug is entirely safe during first trimester of pregnancy*. While prescribing any medicines to a pregnant woman, it is mandatory to ask oneself several questions. Is medication indicated? Is the disease more dangerous as regards fetal safety compared to the known hazards of the therapeutic agent? Has the drug withstood the test of time? When a nursing mother receives some medications, her suckling infant is likely to receive variable amount of drugs secreted through the breast milk. However, whatever is safely tolerated by the nursing mother, is generally safe for her suckling infant. For a detailed list of fetal and neonatal consequences of maternal medications, please refer to Singh M, *Care of the Newborn*, Ninth Edition-2021, CBS Publishers & Distributors Pvt. Ltd., New Delhi.

Drugs in Lactating Women

TABLE 1.4: Conditions where breastfeeding should be avoided

Do not breastfeed and do not feed expressed breast milk	▪ Infant with classic galactosemia. ▪ Mother is infected with HTLV I or II. ▪ Mother has suspected or confirmed Ebola virus disease. ▪ Mother is using illicit drugs (e.g. phencyclidine or cocaine). ▪ Mother has HIV infection*.
Temporarily do not breastfeed, but may feed expressed breast milk to infant	▪ Mother has untreated active tuberculosis: Mother may resume. breastfeeding once she has been treated appropriately for 2 wk and is documented to be no longer contagious. ▪ Mother has active varicella that developed between 5 days prior to delivery and 2 days following delivery.

(Contd.)

TABLE 1.4: Conditions where breastfeeding should be avoided (*Contd.*)

Temporarily do not breastfeed and do not feed expressed breast milk	▪ Mother has untreated brucellosis. ▪ Mother has an active HSV infection, with lesions present on the breast. ▪ Mother is taking certain medications.

Mother is taking certain medications and vaccines

Live attenuated vaccine	*Psychoactive drugs*	*Drugs of abuse*	*Other drugs*	*Radioactive compounds*
Mpox/Smallpox (ACAM2000) Yellow fever	Citalopram Clomipramine Diazepam Doxepin Fluoxetine Fluvoxamine Lamotrigine Lithium Mirtazapine Nortriptyline Olanzapine Sertraline Venlafaxine	Alcohol Amphetamines Benzodiazepines Cocaine Heroin LSD Methamphetamine MDMA Marijuana Phencyclidine	Amiodarone Antineoplastics Gold salts Iodine Lithium Retinoids	**Temporary Cessation of Breastfeeding** ^{14}C-labeled ^{99m}Tc-labeled I-labeled (^{123}I, ^{125}I or ^{131}I-iodo hippurate) **Prolonged Cessation of Breastfeeding** I-labled (^{23}I- BMIPP, -HSA, -IPPA, -MIBG, -NaI, or -HSA) ^{201}Tl-chloride ^{67}Ga-citrate ^{22}Na, ^{75}Se

*Breastfeeding by HIV-infected women may be appropriate in resource-limited settings if breast milk replacement is not feasible, affordable, or safe.

1

Drugs to be Avoided in Children with G6PD Deficiency

TABLE 1.5: Medicines and other substances unsafe or safe in individuals with G6PD deficiency

Unsafe in moderate to severe G6PD deficiency	*Medicines that are probably safe*
Chlorpropamide Dabrafenib Dapsone Fluoroquinolones (ciprofloxacin, moxifloxacin, norfloxacin, ofloxacin) Methylene blue Nalidixic acid Nitrofurantoin, nifuratel, and nitrofurazone Phenazopyridine Primaquine and tafenoquine Rasburicase and pegloticase Sulfonylureas Fava beans Henna compounds (black and red Egyptian) Naphthalene (mothballs, lavatory deodorant) Phenylhydrazine Isobutyl nitrite, amyl nitrite	Acetaminophen Aminophenazone (NSAIDs) Antihistamine Antipyrine Ascorbic acid Aspirin Benzhexol Chloramphenicol Chloroquine and hydroxychloroquine Colchicine Clotrimazole Diphenhydramine Isoniazid Levodopa (L-Dopa) and levodopa-carbidopa Para-aminosalicylic acid Para-aminobenzoic acid Phenylbutazone Phenytoin Probenecid Procainamide Pyrimethamine Quinine Streptomycin Sulfa-containing drugs Tiaprofenic acid Trimethoprim Tripelennamine Vitamin K

For detailed list of fetal and neonatal consequences of maternal medications, please refer to Singh M, *Care of the Newborn, Ninth Edition-2021*, CBS Publishers & Distributors Pvt. Ltd., New Delhi.

Chapter

2

Analgesics, Antipyretics and Nonsteroidal Anti-Inflammatory Agents

Aceclofenac Minimal anti-inflammatory action; overdosing can produce fulminant hepatic failure. Avoid in children.

Adult dose: 50–100 mg q 12 hr.

C/I: Hepatic and renal dysfunction, coronary artery disease, porphyria, and breastfeeding.
(Aceclo, acefen, acefen p, acenac, dolochek, dolokind, hifenac, movon, moviz, zerodol tab 100 mg, dolokind SR, hifenac SR, zerodol CR tab 200 mg, movon CR cap 200 mg).

Acetylsalicylic acid Anti-inflammatory dose: 80–100 mg/kg/day q 6 hr oral; antiplatelet dose: 3–5 mg/kg/day OD. In acute rheumatic fever, anti-inflammatory doses are given for 4–8 wk depending on clinical response and then tapered off during next 4 wk. In Kawasaki disease, moderate (30–50 mg/kg/day) to high (80–100 mg/kg/day) dose till child becomes afebrile followed by antiplatelet dose for 6–8 wk, if there are no coronary abnormalities and indefinitely in case of persistent coronary abnormalities. *Avoid empty stomach and medication should be stopped one wk prior to surgery.*

Adult dose: 75–100 mg single dose daily for prophylaxis against coronary artery disease and cerebral stroke.

C/I: Bleeding or coagulation disorder, peptic ulcer, surgical procedure, bronchial asthma, patient on anticoagulants, severe hepatic and renal disease. It should be avoided as an antipyretic especially in children with viral infections (influenza, chickenpox) due to risk of Reye's syndrome.

(Aspirin tab 300 mg; colsprin tabs 100 mg, 325 mg, 650 mg; ecospirin 75 mg, 150 mg, 325 mg tabs, disprin, tab 350 mg; nusprin, sprin, zosprin tabs 75 mg and 150 mg, aspin tab 100 mg; aspicot tab 80 mg; mazoral tab 75 mg, aspent tab 60 mg).

Celecoxib It is selective COX-2 inhibitor. It should be used in patients at high risk of peptic ulcer, perforation or gastrointestinal bleeds. It is the only FDA approved selective COX-2 inhibitor recommended for use in juvenile idiopathic arthritis (in children 2–17 yr).

Children 10–25 kg: 50 mg BD, >25 kg: 100 mg BD

Adult dose: 200 mg/day in one or two divided doses.

(Celact, celcib, celib, cobix, colcibra caps 100 mg and 200 mg).

Codeine phosphate For relief of pain 0.5–1.0 mg/kg/dose q 4–6 hr oral. Antitussive dose is 0.2 mg/kg/dose. Avoid below 2 yr.

Adult dose: 30 mg q 6 hr.

C/I: Liver disease, ventilatory failure, respiratory depression, obstructive airway disease, bronchial asthma, convulsive disorders, head injury, coma, and raised intracranial pressure.

(Codifos tab 10 mg, codeine sulfate tab 15 mg, codeine linctus: codeine sulfate 15 mg and menthol 0.2 mg per 5 ml; Mit's linctus codeinae CO: codeine phosphate 10 mg and chlorpheniramine maleate 4 mg per 5 ml; phensedyl cough linctus: codeine phosphate 10 mg and chlorpheniramine maleate 4 mg per 5 ml; corex: codeine phosphate 10 mg and chlorpheniramine maleate 4 mg and menthol 0.1 mg per 5 ml).

Diclofenac sodium 1–3 mg/kg/day (maximum 150 mg) q 8 hr oral or IM. Commonly used for post-traumatic and postinflammatory conditions, and renal colic.

Adult dose: 50–150 mg/day in 2–3 divided doses, SR tab once daily.

SE: Gastric bleeding, gastric ulcer.

(Voveran, relaxyl, diclonac, doflex, fensaide, monovac tab 50 mg; diclomaximum tabs 25 mg, 50 mg; voveran DT 46.5 mg, voveran SR 75 mg and 100 mg, diclonac SR, doflex SR, fensaide SR, relaxyl SR tab 100 mg, inj diclonac, voveran 25 mg/ml in

3 ml ampoule, inj diclomax, fensaide 75 mg per 3 ml ampoule; actimol, diclomol, enzoflam tab: diclofenac sodium 50 mg, paracetamol 500 mg, chymoral plus tab: chymotrypsin 50000 units, diclofenac potassium 50 mg.

Etodolac 10–20 mg/kg/day. Children 6–16 yr the dose of extended release is as follows: 20–30 kg 400 mg OD, 31–45 kg 600 mg OD 46–70 kg 800 mg OD, over 70 kg 1000 mg OD

Adult dose: 200–400 mg every 6–8 hr up to maximum of 1000 mg/day. Extended release (ER) tab 400–1000 mg is given once a day. (Lodin, etova, etios, etobest, etocare, etogesic, etolar tabs fast acting or extended release (ER) 200 mg, 400 mg, 600 mg. Etogesic-P, etobest-P, etios-P, cutodo-P tabs contain etodolac 400 mg plus paracetamol 500 mg).

Etoricoxib Newer COX-2 inhibitor with a half-life of 22 hr. Avoid below 16 yr of age. Children 16–17 yr: 30 mg OD, increase if necessary to 60 mg OD

Adult dose: 60–120 mg single daily dose.

Indic: Osteoarthritis, rheumatoid arthritis, ankylosing spondylitis, acute gout, chronic back pain.
(Etoll, eflam, etox, ecos, etoday, etorix, etocox, etoshine, alcoxib, etorica, etoxib, eto tabs 60 mg, 90 mg and 120 mg).

Fentanyl citrate It is a synthetic piperidine opioid which is 100 times more potent than morphine. 0.5–5 µg/kg/dose q 1–4 hr IV, may be administered as a continuous infusion 1–5 µg/kg/hr. Titrate dose for the desired effect. Potent narcotic analgesic, 0.1 mg dose provides an equivalent activity to 10 mg of morphine.

Adult dose: 50–100 µg IM or IV.

SE: Rapid IV infusion may cause skeletal muscle and chest wall rigidity, impaired ventilation or respiratory distress/arrest.

For sedation refer to tranquillisers, hypnotics, sedatives and antidepressants.

C/I: Opioid hypersensitivity, bronchial asthma; respiratory depression; myasthenia gravis; concomitant use of MAO inhibitor.

(Inj fendrop, fenilate, fenstud, trofentyl 50 μg per ml in 2 ml amp, 10 ml vial; oralet lozenges 200 μg, 300 μg, 400 μg).

Gabapentin For neuropathic pain 10 mg/kg in a single or two divided doses up to maximum of 300 mg q 12 hr or 24 hr.

Adult dose: 300 mg BD or t.d.s. up to maximum daily dose of 3600 mg per day.

SE: Sedation, dizziness, ataxia, headache and behavioral changes.

Indic: Neuropathic pain, focal epilepsy, restless leg syndrome. (Neurontin 300 mg, 400 mg cap, gabantin, gabapin 100 mg, 300 mg, 400 mg cap and pregabid–50 mg and 75 mg cap. Gabaneuron, gabantin plus, gabantin forte, gabapin- ME tab contain gabapentin 300 mg + methylcobalamin 500 μg).

Ibuprofen As antipyretic/analgesic 5–10 mg/kg/dose q 6–8 hr, maximum 40 mg/kg/24 hr. It is one of the safest traditional NSAID with a favorable toxicity/efficacy profile.

For ductus closure in preterm babies: 10 mg/kg IV followed by 5 mg/kg IV every 24 hr for 2 doses. The same dose can be given orally and the course may be repeated after 48 hr.

Adult dose: 400 to 600 mg q 8 hr or sos.

C/I: Salicylate or NSAID allergy, peptic ulcer disease.

(Ibugesic, brufen, bren, alflam, emflam, ibusynth tabs 200 mg, 400 mg, 600 mg; febrilix, ibugesic and ibusynth susp 100 mg per 5 ml; ibrumac susp 125 mg/5 ml; ibugesic plus, imol and combiflam susp contain ibuprofen 100 mg plus paracetamol 162.5 mg per 5 ml; combiflam tab/anaflam tab: ibuprofen 400 mg + paracetamol 325 mg; anaflam, ibugesic plus, and flexon suspension: ibruprofen 100 mg and paracetamol 125 mg per 5 ml).

Indomethacin 0.5–1 mg/kg twice daily. It has less favorable safety profile. It may be more beneficial in spondyloarthropathies and in management of systemic juvenile idiopathic arthritis.

For ductus closure in premature infants: 0.2 mg/kg/dose IV every 12–24 hrly for 3 doses. (2nd and 3rd doses 0.1 mg/kg, if the 1st dose started before first 48 hr of age).

Prevention of intraventricular hemorrhage: 0.1 mg/kg every 24 hr for 3 doses, beginning at 6–12 hr of age.

Adult dose: 25–50 mg q 8 hr.

C/I: Peptic ulcer, gastrointestinal lesions or bleeding, kidney disease, psychiatric patients.
(Idicin, ducain, indocap cap 25 mg; artisid caps 25 mg and 50 mg; indocap SR 75 mg; inj indocin 1 mg lyophilized powder or plug in a vial).

Mefenamic acid Good efficacy in dysmenorrhea. The analgesic dose is 25 mg/kg/day q 6–8 hr oral. For antipyretic effect, administer 5–8 mg/kg/dose.

C/I: GI inflammation, peptic ulcer disease, aspirin allergy, and seizures.

SE: Colitis, seizures, renal damage, bleeding, and skin rash.

Caution: Give drug with food. Do not use for more than 7 days. Stop therapy, if patient develops diarrhea or skin rash. Avoid in children with seizures.
(Dysmen, ponstan, meftal tabs and caps 250 mg, 500 mg, meftal-P tab 100 mg DT; meftal-P, mefkind-P, mefast, mefacid susp 100 mg per 5 ml, ponstan susp 50 mg per 5 ml; meftal forte contains mefenamic acid 500 mg with paracetamol 450 mg. Dysmen forte contains mefenamic acid 500 mg with paracetamol 500 mg).

Meloxicam A newer congener of piroxicam 0.125 to 0.25 mg/kg/day OD (maximum 7.5 mg/day).

Children above 12 yr; 7.5 mg OD (BW< 50 kg) and 15 mg OD (BW> 50 kg).

Adult dose: 15 mg OD
(Ecwin, metaflam, mobic, M-cam, melonex, muvera tabs 7.5 mg and 15 mg).

Morphine sulfate 0.1–0.2 mg/kg/dose SC, maximum dose 15 mg. It is given IV 2–5 mg/dose for preoperative medication, postoperative pain, restlessness, pulmonary edema and tet spells. For continuous infusion in neonates 5–20 mcg/kg/hr, infants and children 10–30 µg/kg/hr (maximum 100–150 mcg/kg/hr).

Adult dose: 10–30 mg IM or oral q 12 hr.

C/I: Respiratory depression, coma, seizures, bronchial asthma, head injury, raised intracranial pressure, and acute hepatic disease.
(Inj morphine sulfate ampoules 10 mg, 15 mg, 25 mg per ml; morcontin 10 mg, 30 mg, 60 mg, 100 mg CR tabs, duramor, rumorf, vermor tabs 10 mg and 30 mg, rilimorf 10 mg, 20 mg, 60 mg SR tab).

Nabumetone 30 mg/kg/day OD A prodrug which generates active metabolite (6-MNA) inhibiting both COX-1 and 2.

SE: Abdominal cramps and diarrhea.
(Nabuflam 500 mg tab, nilitis 750 mg tab, nilitis-P tab contains nabumetone 500 mg + paracetamol 500 mg).

Naproxen Owing to its strong anti-inflammatory activity and overall favorable toxicity profile, it is commonly used NSAID in juvenile idiopathic arthritis in a dose of 10–15 mg/kg/day q 8–12 hr oral (maximum 1 gm/day).

Adult dose: 250–375 mg q 12 hr. There is no risk of cardiovascular complications.

C/I: Peptic ulcer disease, salicylate or NSAID allergy, and advanced renal disease.

Indic: Musculoskeletal disorders, juvenile idiopathic arthritis, rheumatoid arthritis, osteoarthritis, chikungunya, Caffey disease, migraine, dysmenorrhea, gout.
(Artagen, naprosyn, nalyxan tab 250 mg; naprosyn tab 500 mg, xerobid tab 375 mg, naprosyn suspension 125 mg/5 ml).

Paracetamol (acetaminophen) 10–15 mg/kg/dose oral q 4–6 hr up to maximum of 60 mg/kg/day. Rectal 15 mg/kg/dose, inj 7.5 mg/kg IM per dose.

Intravenous Paracetamol Infusion

Neonate and child <10 kg: 10 mg/kg every 4–6 hr, to be administered over 15 min, max; 30 mg/kg/day.
Child (10–50 kg); 15 mg/kg every 4–6 hr, to be administered over 15 min, max; 60 mg/kg/day. Child (>50 kg); 1 gm every 4–6 hr, to be administered over 15 min, max; 3 gm/day.

Adult dose: 0.5–1 g every 4–6 hr up to maximum of 4 g in 24 hr.

C/I: Hepatic damage and nephropathy.
(Crocin, crocin advance, calpol, dolo, febrex, malidens, metacin, paracin, pyrigesic, P-500, pacimol tab 500 mg; crocin, calpol, dolo, cofamol, acticin, dolopar, febrex, P-650, tab 650 mg; syrup 125 mg per 5 ml; crocin pain relief contains paracetamol 650 mg and caffeine 50 mg, crocin DS, calpol, pyrigesic DS, P-250, cofamol, dolopar, febrex syrup 250 mg/5 ml; crocin, calpol, pyrigesic, fevago drops 100 mg per ml; anamol rectal suppository 125 mg and 250 mg; paracetamol suppository 80 mg and 170 mg, Junimol-RDS 80 mg, 170 mg, 250 mg suppository; inj febrinil, mol, neomol, fevastin, aeknil 150 mg per ml for IM).

Pentazocine hydrochloride For postoperative and moderately severe pain in burns, trauma, fracture, cancer, etc. 0.5–1.0 mg/kg/day q 4 hr oral, IM and IV. 30–60 mg IM is equivalent to 10 mg of morphine. Orally 50 mg equals 60 mg of codeine.

Adult dose: 30–60 mg IM or SC; 30 mg IV; given every 3–4 hr. Maximum dose 360 mg/day. Oral 25–50 mg 3–4 times a day.

C/I: Head injury, raised intracranial tension, porphyria, and respiratory depression.
(Fortwin tab 25 mg, expergesic, foracet, fortagesic tab: pentazocin 15 mg with paracetamol 500 mg, fortwin, fortstar, susevin ampoule 30 mg/ml).

Pethidine hydrochloride (meperidine hydrochloride) 1–2 mg/kg/dose IM or IV.

Caution: Diziness, constipation, seizures.
(Inj pethidine hydrochloride and demerol ampoule 25 mg/ml, 50 mg per ml and 100 mg/2 ml; 50 mg, 100 mg pethidine tabs).

Piroxicam 0.2–0.3 mg/kg/day single daily dose oral. It is not the first choice for any underlying inflammatory condition because of relatively higher toxicity.

Adult dose: 20 mg per dose q 4–6 hr.

C/I: Aspirin/NSAID allergy, active peptic ulcer, inflammatory bowel disease.

(Piricam, pirox, dolonex caps 10 mg, 20 mg; brexic DT, pirox DT, piny DT, amida, biocam, dolocare 20 mg; dolonex, pirox 20 mg/ml inj in 1 ml and 2 ml amp).

Tolmetin sodium 20–30 mg/kg/day q 6–8 hr oral. Least favourable toxic effect and efficacy profile. Avoid below 2 yr of age.

Adult dose: 400 mg q 8 hr (maximum 1800 mg/d).
(Tolectin tabs 200 mg, 600 mg; cap 400 mg.)

Tramadol hydrochloride It acts on opiate receptors in the CNS without producing any respiratory depression. Usually indicated for mild to moderate short-lasting pain due to diagnostic procedures, trauma or surgery. Children: 1–2 mg/kg 4–6 hrly (maximum 400 mg/24 hr). Avoid below 14 yr.

Adult dose: 50–100 mg q 8 hr up to maximum of 400 mg/day.

Caution: Seizures, renal and hepatic impairment.
(Contramal, domadol, tramazac, urgendol cap 50 mg, tab DT 50 mg, tab SR 100 mg, injection 50 mg/ml in 1 ml and 2 ml vials for IM and slow IV use. Tram-P, Atdol plus, Anatram-P tab contain tramadol 50 mg and paracetamol 500 mg).

Triptans They are tryptamine-based drugs used to abort the attack of migraines and cluster headaches. Rizatriptan oral, sumatriptan and zolmitriptan oral and nasal spray are commonly used triptans for migraines in children. They are effective to abort the attack if taken as soon as possible after onset of aura or headache. Tryptans are serotonin agonists and helps in reducing cerebral blood flow.

Rizatriptan (age 6–17 yr): 5 mg for <40 kg and 10 mg for children >40 kg. Sumatriptan (age 6–17 yr) 25 mg for 6–9 yr, 50 mg for 10–11 yr and 100 mg 12–17 yr. Nasal spray 10–20 mg one dose (above 12 yr). Zolmitriptan (12–17 yr) oral 2.5, 5 mg; nasal spray 5 mg (above 12 yr).

C/I: Coronary artery disease, hypertension, heart attack or stroke, Raynaud's disease.

Adult dose: Sumatriptan 25, 50 or 100 mg single dose p.o.
(Sumatriptan tabs 25, 50, 100 mg, nasal spray 5 mg and 20 mg/ACT).

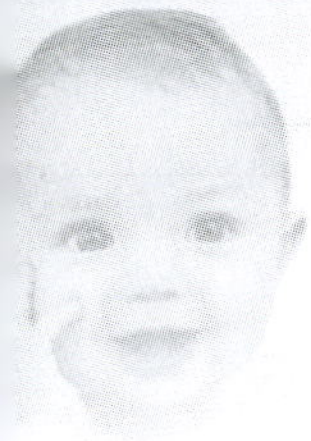

Chapter

3

Antacids

It includes substances that reduce or neutralize acidity of the stomach to relieve dyspepsia, nausea, indigestion, heart burn, flatulence and symptoms of gastroesophageal reflux like regurgitation, bitter taste, persistent dry cough, heart burn in supine position, burps or eructations. There are three classes of drugs that relieve gastric acidity.

1. **Over-the-counter drugs** They neutralize acid and/or provide a protective covering over the lining of stomach. They include eno (sodium bicarbonate + citric acid), alka-seltzer (acetylsalicylic acid, sodium bicarbonate, anhydrous citric acid), maalox plus and mylanta (magnesium hydroxide + aluminium hydroxide + simethicone), tums (calcium carbonate + sucrose), rolaids (calcium carbonate + magnesium hydroxide), gelusil (aluminium hydroxide, magnesium hydroxide, simethicone), milk of magnesia, aludrox (aluminium hydroxide anhydrous), sucrafil (sucralfate), sucrafil-D (sucralfate with domperidone), gaviscon and riflux forte (sodium alginate + sodium bicarbonate + calcium carbonate) tab and susp.

   Indic: Acidity, dyspepsia, heart burn, burps and flatulence.

   SE: Excessive intake may lead to nausea, vomiting, constipation, hypercalcemia, kidney stones, hypophosphatemia, alkalosis, osteoporosis, aluminium toxicity.

2. **H_2-receptor antagonists (H_2RA)** They include the group of medicines that reduce the amount of acid produced in the stomach by blocking the histamine H_2 receptors in the

parietal cells of the stomach. They have a plasma half-life between 1 and 4 hr. The list includes ranitidine, cimetidine, famotidine and nizatidine. They have been surpassed by proton pump inhibitors which are more effective and faster in promoting healing of esophagitis, gastritis and duodenal ulcer.

SE: Headache, dizziness, constipation, diarrhea, skin rash, dry mouth, runny nose, insomnia and gynecomastia.

3. **Proton pump inhibitors (PPIs)** They include a group of drugs that are credited with a pronounced and long-lasting reduction of acid production in the stomach. They work by irreversibly blocking an enzyme called H^+/K^+ ATPase which controls acid production. They need to be protected from gastric acid by either enteric coated microspheres or capsules. They are best taken 30 min before breakfast. They do not provide immediate relief and it takes 2 to 8 days for their maximum effect. The plasma half-life of PPIs is only 60–90 min but they covalently bind to the proton pump and effectively reduce gastric acid secretion up to 24 hr. The list includes omeprazole, pantoprazole, lansoprazole, esomeprazole, rabeprazole, dexlansoprazole. For children lanzoprazole is available as an orally dispersible tablet and esomprazole as granules. BD dosing may be used for GERD with refractory symptoms and for *H. pylori* eradication therapy.

   Indic: Indigestion, heart burn, *H. pylori* infection, Barrett's esophagitis, duodenal ulcer, gastroesophageal reflux disease (GERD), hiatus hernia, Zollinger–Ellison syndrome.

   SE: Prolonged use is associated with risk of dizziness, light headedness, sweating, shortness of breath or wheezing, chest or shoulder pain, hypocalcemia, hypomagnesemia, cyanocobalmin deficiency, features of gastrointestinal infections including nausea and bloating.

   Clostridium difficile infection. They reduce the absorption of ketoconazole and increase the absorption and toxicity of digoxin.

4. **Lifestyle changes and dietary modifications**
   a. *Acidity, heart burn and acid reflux:*
   Avoid: Obesity, intake of fried and oily foods, carbonated drinks, tea, coffee, NSAIDs, chocolates, citrus fruits, garlic, onions, spicy food, mint, processed cheese, red meat, intake of alcohol, smoking, lying down immediately after taking food, etc.
   Promote: Intake of plenty of water, cold milk, yogurt, egg white, honey, grilled or broiled lean meat, oat meal, ginger, apple cider in water, green vegetables, bananas, melon, and apple. Eat meals 2 to 3 hr before sleeping, raise the head end of bed by 6 inches, sleep by turning on the left side which reduces acid reflux.
   b. *Flatulence and gas:* Avoid intake of milk, vegetables of cruciferous family (cauliflower, cabbage, mustard green, radish, turnips, knol khol, broccoli), lentils with hard covering, carbonated drinks and excessive carbohydrates. Eat slowly and mindfully (avoid gulping the food), take enough insoluble fiber, drink plenty of water, exercise and walk daily, avoid lying down immediately after eating. The over-the-counter useful medicines include simethicone, activated charcoal, pepto-bismol and lactase enzyme.
5. ***H. pylori*** **protocols**
   a. *Triple therapy*
   PPI (standard dose) BD, amoxicillin 1.0 g BD and clarithromycin 0.5 g BD for14 days.
   b. *Sequential therapy*
   1–5 days: PPI (standard dose) BD and amoxicillin 1.0 g BD
   6–10 days: PPI (standard dose) BD, metronidazole 0.5 g BD and clarithromycin 0.5 g BD

Cimetidine It is an H2-receptor antagonist (H2RA) 20–40 mg/kg/day q 6 hrly. The double dose is given in patients with gastroesophageal reflux disease (GERD) and peptic ulcer. The parenteral dose is 5–10 mg/kg every 6–8 hr IM or IV.

Adult dose: 150–400 mg 4 times/day with meals. The parenteral dose is 300 mg IM or IV slowly q 6–8 hr.
(Tagamet, tagamet-HB, cimetidine, cimetiget, tymidin, ulciban, C Met, cimetin tabs 200 mg and 400 mg).

Dexlansoprazole It is a proton pump inhibitor and not recommended in children below 18 yr.

Adult dose: 30 to 60 mg OD
(DDR, lantas-DX, dexolan, dexlanzol, dexsofighter, deltone, duabit, lanfil DX 30 and 60 mg caps).

Esomeprazole It is a proton pump inhibitor. 1.0 to 1.5 mg/kg/day in a single or two divided doses.
For erosive esophagitis 12–17 yr, same dose as adults, 1 to 11 yr >20 kg 10 to 20 mg OD for 8 wk, <20 kg 10 mg OD for 8 wk. 1 mon to 1 yr >7.5 kg 10 mg OD for 6 wk, 5–7.5 kg 5 mg OD for 6 wk, 3 to 5 kg 2.5 mg OD for 6 wk. Use with caution the lower mentioned dose for GERD in children younger than 1 mon.

Adult dose: 20–40 mg OD or BD half an hr before food. Granules are available in 10 mg and 20 mg strength. Erosive esophagitis 20 to 40 mg once a day for 4–8 wk, GERD 20 mg once a day for 4–8 wk.
Inj 20–40 mg IV infusion slowly over 10–30 min.
(Nexium, sompraz, raciper, somifiz, esomac, esodoc, izra, neksium tabs 20 mg and 40 mg. Granules 10 mg and 20 mg esomac granules, nexpro granules, esole delayed release granules, cap sompraz IT contain esomeprazole 40 mg + itopride 150 mg).

Famotidine It is an H_2-receptor antagonist. 1–2 mg/kg/day q 8–12 hr. The tablet should be chewed well before swallowing.

Adult dose: 20 mg BD or 40 mg OD at bedtime for 4–8 wk.
Parenteral dose 20 mg q 12 hr intravenously.
(Pepcid, famtac, famocid, famotin, famodin, acredin, zactane, advantac, blocacid, facid, fadine tabs 20 mg and 40 mg. Injection formulation 10 mg/ml and 20 mg/ml).

3 **Lansoprazole** It is a proton pump inhibitor. 1.0–1.5 mg/kg/day q 12–24 hr.

Pediatric dose >30 kg 30 mg OD <30 kg, 15 mg OD. Dose under 1 yr of age is not well defined. Lansoprazole is available as an orally dispersible tablet.

For the 15 mg tablet: Place it in the oral syringe and add 4 ml of water.

For the 30 mg tablet: Place it in the oral syringe and add 10 ml of water.

Shake the syringe gently until the tablet dissolves and is mixed well. Give the mixture within 15 min.

Refill the syringe with 2 ml (15 mg tablet) or 5 ml (30 mg tablet) of water and shake it gently. Give the mixture to make sure all of the medicine is administered.

Adult dose: 30 mg single dose at bedtime for 4–8 wk.

(Lanzol Jr DT tab 15 mg and 30 mg, lanzol, prevacid, acilanz, lan tabs and caps 30 mg; delayed release, lanzap, lancid, zapacid, lanzol liquid can be prepared in sodium bicarbonate 3 mg/ml.)

Nizatidine It is an H2-receptor antagonist. 2–4 mg/kg/day q 12 hr.

Adult dose: 150 mg BD or 300 mg OD 30–60 min before meals. Inj 50 mg IM 6–8 hr.

(Axid, axid-AR, tazac tabs, 150 mg and 300 mg, axid oral solution 15 mg/ml in 120 ml and 480 ml bottles).

Omeprazole It is a proton pump inhibitor. 2.0–2.5 mg/kg/day single or two divided doses.

Adult dose: 20 mg OD or BD with a maximum daily dose of 80 mg for 4–8 wk. Inj 40 mg OD slowly over 20–30 min intravenously.

(Zegerid, prilosec, losec, omez, omey, acimax, acichek tabs and caps 10 mg, 20 mg, 40 mg. Injection 40 mg/10 ml vial).

Pantoprazole It is a proton pump inhibitor. Children 15–40 kg: 20 mg OD, >40 kg: 40 mg OD

Adult dose: 40 mg OD morning or bedtime for 4–8 wk. Inj 80 mg once or twice daily slow infusion over 5–15 min IV.

(Pan, pantop, zipant, protera, protonex, pacid 20 mg and 40 mg tabs).

Rabeprazole It is a proton pump inhibitor. 0.5–1.0 mg/kg/day in a single or two divided doses. It is more effective than ranitidine.

Adult dose: 20–40 mg in a single or two doses for 4–8 wk.
(R-PPI 20, rabeloc, rabicip, razo, acera, acistal, rabekind, aciphex tabs 20 mg and 40 mg).

Ranitidine hydrochloride It is histamine-2 blocker. 1–5 mon: 1.0 mg/kg q 8 hr, 6 mon and above: 2–4 mg/kg q 12 hr. In GERD, the dose is double. The IV dose is one half of adult dose. The experience for its use in children is limited.

Adult dose: 75–150 mg twice daily or 300 mg at bedtime for 4–6 wk. The IV dose is 50 mg q 6 hr.
(Zantac, rantac, rantop, ranitin, histac, aciloc liquid 75 mg/5 ml, tabs 150 mg and 300 mg; histac evt (effervescent) tab 150 mg, inj 50 mg/2 ml ampoule).

Chapter

4

Anthelmintics

Albendazole Broad-spectrum anthelmintic useful for treatment of pinworms, roundworms, and hookworms. 200 mg single dose for children between 1 and 2 yr, 400 mg single dose for children above 2 yr. Repeat dose after 2 wk for pinworms and roundworms. For treatment of strongyloidosis, taeniasis and *H. nana* infestation, administer 400 mg once daily for 3 days. For giardiasis, 400 mg daily for 5 days and for hydatid disease 400 mg twice daily with fatty meals for 28 days. Therapy may be repeated after 14 days interval for a total of 3 cycles for eradication of hydatid cysts. For neurocysticercosis, give 15 mg/kg/d in 2 divided doses for 7 to 30 days along with corticosteroids and an anticonvulsant for 5 days to reduce cerebral edema. Albendazole is started on day 3 of steroid therapy. A second course may be given after an interval of 2 wk.

Adult dose: 400 mg single dose for pinworms and roundworms, repeat the dose after 2 wk.

Indic: Roundworms, hookworms, nematodes, whipworms *(Trichuris trichiura), Giardia intestinalis, H. nana*, tapeworms, threadworms *(Enterobius vermicularis), Strongyloides stercoralis*, neurocysticercosis, filariasis, cutaneous larva migrans and hydatid cysts.

C/I: Ocular and intraventricular cysticercosis.

(ABZ, albendazole, albendol, albezole, bandy, noworm, alminth, anthel, bendex, combantrin, dispel, emanthal, nemozole, vermitel, wormin-A, zentel, zuwarm tabs 200 mg, 400 mg; susp 200 mg per 5 ml in 10 ml and 50 ml bottles.

Diethylcarbamazine citrate 6 mg/kg/day q 8 hr oral for 3–4 wk for filariasis. The course may be repeated after 6 mon. 10 mg/kg/day q 8 hr oral for tropical eosinophilia and visceral larva migrans for one mon, 15 mg/kg/day single dose for 4 days for Loeffler's pneumonia due to ascariasis.

Adult dose: 100 mg 3 times a day for 21 days.

Indic: Filariasis, tropical eosinophilia and visceral larva migrans, Loeffler's pneumonia due to ascariasis.

C/I: Onchocerciasis.

(Banocide, hetrazan, trozan, eofil tabs 50 mg, 100 mg; banocide syrup 50 mg, 120 mg per 5 ml; hetrazan syrup 120 mg per 5 ml).

Ivermectin 0.2 mg/kg single dose. The dose may be repeated after 2 wk.

Adult dose: 12 mg single dose, may repeat after 3–12 mon.

Indic: Scabies, lice, visceral larva migrans, filariasis, onchocerciasis and strongyloidosis.

C/I: Avoid below 15 kg (<5 yr).

(Iverin, ivermectol, scavista, vermin tabs 3 mg DT, 6 mg DT and 12 mg; ivermect, vermectin, ascapil, scabicaro tabs 6 mg and 12 mg).

Levamisole 2.5–3.0 mg/kg in <12 yr and 150 mg in 12–18 yr as a single dose. Repeat after 7 days in case of severe infection.

Adult dose: 300 mg OD for 1–2 days.

Indic: Roundworm, hookworm infection.

C/I: Caution in patients with rheumatoid arthritis, Sjögren syndrome, epilepsy and liver disease.

(Dewormis, dicaris, vermisol, vapal tabs 50 mg, 150 mg, 50 mg/5 ml syr.)

4 **Mebendazole** 100 mg twice a day for 3 days for ascaris; whipworms and hookworms; 100 mg (50 mg in infants <10

kg) single dose to be repeated after 2 wk for pinworms (all household members above the age of 2 yr should be treated simultaneously to eradicate threadworms); 200 mg twice daily for 3 days for tapeworms and mixed infections. Repeat after 2–4 wk. For hydatid cyst, 30 mg/kg/day q 8 hr oral for 4 wk. For trichinosis, 200 mg b.i.d. for 4 days.

Adult dose: Same schedule as in children above 2 yr.

Indic: Roundworms, pinworms, threadworms, whipworms, hookworms, tapeworms, echinococcus and mixed infestations. (Mebex, mendazole, idibend, mebazole, kit kat, wormin, eben, zumin tab 100 mg; susp 100 mg per 5 ml).

Niclosamide 1.0 gm empty stomach followed by another dose after 1 hr. Give a brisk purgative after 2 hr of last dose. Give half the dose to children below 6 yr of age. For dwarf tapeworm, single dose as above on day 1, half the dose once a day for 6 days.

Adult dose: 2 gm on day 1, followed by 1.0 gm daily for 6 days.

Indic: Taenia saginata, taenia solium, diphyllobothrium latum, and hymenolepis nana.
(Niclosan, niclocide, niclosal, niclosig tab 500 mg).

Nitazoxanide 1–4 yr: 100 mg BD for 3 days, 4–12 yr: 200 mg BD for 3 days.

Adult dose: 500 mg b.i.d. for 3 days.

Indic: Giardia lamblia, E. histolytica, Cryptosporidium parvum.

C/I: Give with food. Avoid in diabetics.
(Nitcol, nitacure, nitarid, nizonide, nitasafe, nitoxin, zimdax tabs 200 mg DT, 500 mg; susp 100 mg per 5 ml).

Oxamniquine For >20 kg child 15 mg/kg single dose, and children <20 kg, 1.0 mg/kg single dose oral up to maximum dose of 1.0 gm single dose. Repeat after 2 wk. For hookworm, 10 mg/kg/dose oral once a day for 3 days.

Adult dose: 1 gm single dose.

Indic: Schistosoma mansoni infections. Praziquantel is usually preferred.

C/I: History of seizures, hypersensitive reaction, liver dysfunction. (Available as generic name and vansil 250 mg tab).

Paromomycin sulfate It is an aminoglycoside. For tapeworms, 10 mg/kg/dose (maximum 500 mg) q 15 min 4 doses and for *H. nana* 45 mg/kg/dose once a day PO for 7 days. 25 mg/kg/d q 8 hr for 10 days for giardiasis, 10 mg/kg/dose (maximum 500 mg) q 8 hr for 7 days for eradication of cysts of *E. histolytica*. 11 mg/kg/day IM for 21 days for visceral leishmaniasis.

Adult dose: 500 mg 3 times a day is given for 10 days in giardiasis. It can be given during pregnancy and lactation.

Indic: Amebiasis, giardiasis, cryptosporidiosis, tapeworm infestation, visceral leishmaniasis, and drug resistant tuberculosis.

C/I: Intestinal obstruction and ulcerative bowel lesions.
(Humatin cap 250 mg)

Praziquantel 50 mg/kg/day q 8 hr oral for 15 days with steroids to counteract raised intracranial tension during treatment of neurocysticercosis. Dermal cysticercosis 60 mg/kg/day in 3 divided doses for 6 days. Single dose 5–10 mg/kg for tapeworms, 25 mg/kg for *H. nana*, 20 mg/kg/dose PO q 8–12 hr for 1 day for schistosomiasis. For liver fluke infestation, 75 mg/kg/dose q 8 hr for 2 days.

Adult dose: 75 mg/kg/d divided 3 times per day for 1–2 days.

Indic: All species of Schistosoma, liver flukes *Clonorchis sinensis*/ *Opisthorchis viverrini*, neurocysticercosis.

C/I: Ocular and intraventricular cysticercosis.
(Cysticide tab 500 mg, prazine, biltricide, biltree, cest tabs 600 mg).

Pyrantel pamoate 11 mg/kg single dose oral with maximum of 1.0 gm single dose. Repeat after 2 wk. For hookworm, 10 mg/kg/dose oral once a day for 3 days.

Adult dose: For hookworm, 500 mg single dose. In severe *Necator americanus* infection 500 mg daily may be given for 3 days.

Indic: Roundworms, hookworms, pinworms, *Strongyloides stercoralis*, and mixed infestations.

C/I: Liver dysfunction.
(Nemocid, antiminth, expent, pyrmoate, pyranthel tabs 250 mg; susp 250 mg per 5 ml).

Tetramisole 2.5 to 5 mg/kg single dose oral (avoid below 2 yr of age).

Adult dose: 150 to 200 mg single dose.

Indic: Roundworms, hookworms infestations.

SE: Agranulocytosis, liver dysfunction and allergic reaction.
(Anthelban, nitrotan, solaskil syp (25 mg/5 ml); naphtamine, tetra deworm, T-misol tabs 50 mg, 100 mg, 200 mg pyrmoate, pyranthel tab 250 mg; susp 250 mg per 5 ml).

Thiabendazole 50 mg/kg/day PO q 12 hr up to a maximum dose of 3 g/day for 2 days for strongyloides, intestinal nematodes 2 days, cutaneous larva migrans 2–5 days, visceral larva migrans 5–7 days and trichinosis 2–4 days.

Adult dose: 500–1250 mg BD or t.d.s. Recommended maximum daily dose is 3000 mg.

Indic: Roundworms, hookworms, strongyloidiasis, aspergillosis, visceral larva migrans.

SE: GI disturbances, cholestasis, keratoconjunctivitis sicca, xerostomia, headache, giddiness.
(Mintezol, thiabendazole, equizole tabs 500 mg; susp 500 mg/5 ml).

Triclabendazole 10 mg/kg is given in BD doses for one day in children above 6 yr of age.

Adult dose: 250 mg 12 hrly for 2 doses.

Indic: Fascioliasis (liver fluke).

C/I: Hypersensitivity to benzimidazole derivatives, caution in children with renal and hepatic impairment.
(Egaten tab 250 mg).

Chapter

5

Antiarrhythmic Agents

Adenosine For paroxysmal supraventricular tachycardia (PSVT) in children, the initial dose is 0.1 mg/kg (maximum 6 mg) as a rapid IV bolus (preferably given via antecubital vein or central vein, using a three-way stopcock followed by a 10 ml of normal saline flush). If no effect is seen within 1–2 min, the next dose is increased to 0.2 mg/kg (maximum 12 mg). Maximum single dose in children is 0.3 mg/kg or 12 mg.

Adult dose: For PSVT 6 mg IV rapid bolus followed by NS flush. If no effect within 1–2 min, administer 12 mg rapid IV bolus which may be repeated after 1–2 min if required, followed each time by NS flush. For pharmacologic cardiac stress imaging, adenosine is given as IV infusion at a rate of 140 μg/kg/min for 6 min during which the nuclear tracer is given. For fractional flow reserve testing in coronary artery disease, adenosine is given as IV infusion 140 μg/kg/min for a duration of 3 min.

Indic: Paroxysmal supraventricular tachycardia (PSVT), pharmacologic cardiac stress testing.

C/I: Sick sinus syndrome, 2nd or 3rd degree AV block, known hypersensitivity to components of injection, and bronchial asthma.

Caution: Adenosine may precipitate pre-excited atrial fibrillation in patients of WPW syndrome. All patients need to have continuous ECG monitoring as well as availability of equipment and personnel for cardiac resuscitation.

(Adenoject, adenoz, adenocor, carnosine 6 mg per 2 ml ampoule).

Amiodarone It is useful for ongoing ventricular tachyarrhythmias. Loading dose 5 mg/kg (maximum 300 mg/dose) IV over 20–60 min (preferably given slowly over 60 min to avoid hypotension), may repeat 1–2 doses up to maximum of 15 mg/kg total dose. For ventricular fibrillation/ventricular tachycardia refractory to DCCV during ACLS, amiodarone can be given IV as a rapid bolus of 5–15 mg/kg (maximum 300 mg).

For long term management of tachyarrhythmias or during atrial arrhythmias: Oral loading dose 10–15 mg/kg/day q 12 hr for 4 to 14 days, reduce to 5 mg/kg/day once daily for several weeks. If there is no recurrence of arrhythmia, reduce the dose to lowest effective level usually 2.5 mg/kg/day.

Adult dose: IV loading 150 mg over the first 10 min (15 mg/min), followed by 360 mg over the next 6 hr (1 mg/min) and then 0.5 mg/min infusion for next 18 hr or until switched to oral formulation. Oral dose 800–1600 mg/day is required for 1 to 3 wk. Maintenance dose 400 mg OD.

Indic: Ventricular tachycardia, ventricular fibrillation, atrial fibrillation.

C/I: Known hypersensitivity to amiodarone, sick sinus syndrome, baseline 2nd or 3rd degree AV block, severe hypotension/shock.

Caution: May precipitate pre-excited atrial fibrillation in patients with WPW syndrome. It is usually not preferred for chronic maintenance therapy unless no alternative is available.

(Cordarone, amiodar, ritebeat, tachyra tabs 100 mg, 200 mg; inj cordarone, cardichek, tachyra, aldarone 50 mg/ml in 3 ml ampoules).

Atropine sulfate For symptomatic bradycardia: 0.02 mg/kg/dose SC or IV or through ET (minimum 0.1 mg/dose; maximum: 0.5 mg/dose). May repeat once in 5 min. For organophosphate or carbamate poisoning: 0.05 to 0.1 mg/kg IV which may be repeated every 3–5 min; double the dose in case atropinization not achieved. For pre-anesthesia, 0.02 mg/kg/dose for <5 kg weight and 0.03 mg/kg/dose in >5 kg body weight.

Indic: Heart block, pre-anesthetic medication to reduce respiratory secretions, or as an antidote.

C/I: Thyrotoxicosis, narrow angle glaucoma, obstructive uropathy, tachycardia secondary to cardiac insufficiency and obstructive gastrointestinal lesions.

Caution: Routine use of atropine during cardiac resuscitation is no longer recommended in advanced cardiac life support (ACLS) guidelines. Increase in heart rate and blood pressure may precipitate myocardial ischemia.
(Inj atropine sulfate IP, atro, atron 0.60 mg per ml ampoule).

Disopyramide phosphate 10–30 mg/kg/day q 6 hr, children 1–4 yr 10–20 mg/kg/day q 6 hr, children 4–12 yr 10–15 mg/kg/day q 6 h and adolescents 12–18 yr 6–15 mg/kg/day. Intravenous loading dose is 5 mg/kg followed by maintenance therapy orally. The dose can be repeated IV after 30 min, if arrhythmia is not reverted, occasionally used as infusion at a rate of 0.4 mg/kg/hr following IV loading dose.

Adult dose: Immediate release: 200–300 mg followed by 150 mg q 6 h. Controlled release: 200–300 mg q 12 hr. Maximum adult dose 400 mg q 6 hr (immediate release formulation).

Indic: Ventricular arrhythmias, hypertrophic obstructive cardiomyopathy.
(Norpace caps 100 mg, 150 mg; regubeat cap 100 mg; inj rhythmodan 10 mg per ml).

Lignocaine (lidocaine) hydrochloride For ventricular fibrillations or pulseless VT: 1 mg/kg per dose as IV bolus, followed by IV infusion of 20–50 μg/kg/min. Endotracheal dose 2–3 mg/kg/dose followed by 5 ml NS flush and 5 assisted manual ventilations. For local anesthesia: use <2% solutions for cutaneous infiltration. Do not exceed 5 mg/kg/dose.

Adult dose: 1.0–1.5 mg/kg, repeat 0.5–0.75 mg/kg q 5–10 min up to maximum dose of 3 mg/kg, followed by continuous infusion @ 1–4 mg/min.

Indic: Acute treatment of ventricular arrhythmias.

C/I: Adam-Stokes syndrome, WPW syndrome, baseline higher degrees of atrioventricular or intraventricular conduction defects.

(Inj gesicard, biocaine, lignocaine, xylocaine, xylocard 2% 50 ml vial, 1 ml = 21.33 mg).

Phenytoin sodium 1.25 mg/kg IV q 5 min up to a total of 15 mg/kg or until arrhythmia reverts or hypotension develops, followed by maintenance IV/PO dose of 5–10 mg/kg/d q 12 hr. Maximum loading dose is 1.5 g.

Indic: Ventricular arrhythmias especially due to digitalis. For other indications refer to *see* Anticonvulsants.

(Epsolin, episol, eptoin injection 50 mg per ml in 2 ml ampoule).

Procainamide hydrochloride 10–15 mg/kg loading dose IV over 30–60 min (maximum 500 mg) or 2–6 mg/kg/dose IV loading dose (maximum 100 mg) infused over > 5 min and repeated q 10–30 min as needed. Maintenance 20–80 µg/kg/min as constant IV infusion. Oral dose 15–50 mg/kg/day q 3–6 hr.

Adult dose: IV maximum loading dose 1000 mg followed by infusion at the rate of 1–4 mg/min.

SE: Proarrhythmia, thrombocytopenia, Coombs' positive hemolytic anemia, and lupus-like syndrome. Monitor QTc during therapy.

Indic: Ventricular arrhythmias, pre-excited atrial fibrillation, stable monomorphic ventricular tachycardia.

C/I: Heart block, myasthenia gravis, SLE, torsades de pointes.

(Pronestyl tab 250 mg, Inj 100 mg/ml in 10 ml vial).

Propafenone Direct membrane stabilizer useful for treatment of ventricular arrhythmia. No data is available on pediatric dosing.

Adult dose: 150 mg t.d.s., dose can be gradually increased every 3–4 days up to maximum dose of 300 mg t.d.s.

Indic: Life threatening ventricular arrhythmias, atrial fibrillations without structural heart disease.

C/I: Conduction disorders (sinoatrial or AV or intraventricular), usually known as Brugada syndrome, heart failure, severe hypotension/shock.

(Rhythmonorm, rythmol tab 150 mg).

Propranolol hydrochloride 0.01–0.15 mg/kg/dose slowly IV over 10 min (maximum dose: 1 mg in infants, 3 mg in children). Oral 0.5–1.0 mg/kg/day q 6–8 hr, up to maximum daily dose of 60 mg.

For tetralogy spells: 0.15–0.25 mg/kg/dose IV (maximum 1 mg) over 10 min. May repeat the dose if required.

Adult dose: 10–20 mg q 6 hr PO.

Indic: Ventricular arrhythmias, prophylaxis for angina and migraine, hypertension, infantile hemangioma, tachycardia, hyperthyroidism, erythromelalgia, essential tremors, portal hypertension.

SE: Bradyarrhythmias, bronchospasm, hypotension, fatigue, hypoglycemia.
(Ciplar, provanol, corbeta, betacap, betapro, inderal tabs 10 mg, 40 mg, 80 mg; Inj ciplar, pranosal 1 mg per ml ampoule).

Quinidine sulfate Give 2 mg/kg test dose followed by 15–60 mg/kg/day q 6 hr oral.

Adult dose: 200–400 mg/day q 6 to 8 hr. Maximum adult daily dose: 2400 mg/day.

Indic: Paroxysmal atrial tachycardia, atrial flutter, atrial fibrillation, ventricular tachyarrhythmias, and ventricular ectopics.

C/I: Congestive heart failure, heart block and hypotension.

SE: QT prolongation and drug proarrhythmia, cardiac arrhythmias, dizziness, headache, diarrhea/GI upset.
(Quinidine tab 200 mg, natcardine tab 100 mg, inj quinidine 80 mg/ml).

Verapamil 4–8 mg/kg/day, divided q 8 hr oral, 0.1–0.2 mg/kg IV over 2 min in infants and 0.1–0.3 mg/kg IV over 2 min in children.

Indic: Control of ventricular rate in PSVT, atrial fibrillation and flutter.

Adult dose: 5–10 mg IV, 80–120 mg/dose q 6–8 hr PO.

C/I: Cardiogenic shock, and heart block.

(Veramil, veratril, veraprim, calaptin, vasopten, isoptin tabs 40 mg, 80 mg; Inj calaptin 5 mg per 2 ml ampoule).

Chapter

6

Antibiotics and Chemotherapeutic Agents

Various terms are used to describe drug-resistant bacteria which are emerging as a major issue for rational and effective use of antibiotics. They include multidrug resistant (MDR), extensively drug resistant (XDR), pan drug resistant (PDR), extended spectrum β-lactamases (ESBLs), carbapenem-resistant enterobacteriaceae (CRE), ESBL producing Gram-negative bacteria, methicillin-resistant *S. aureus* (MRSA) and vancomycin-resistant enterococci. The acronym "ESKAPE" is used to describe six bacterial pathogens because of their ability to 'escape' the effect of commonly used antibiotics by development of various evolutionary mechanisms. They include ***E**nterococcus faecium*, ***S**. aureus*, ***K**lebsiella pneumoniae*, ***A**cinetobacter baumanii*, ***P**seudomonas aeruginosa* and ***E**nterobacter* species.

AMINOGLYCOSIDES

Amikacin sulfate 15–20 mg/kg/day IV, higher dose may be considered in patients with cystic fibrosis. Intravenous infusion to be given over 1 hr. Adjust the dose in patients with renal failure.

Adult dose: 15 mg/kg/day q 12 hr (maximum 1.5 g/day).

For drug-resistant TB, 15 mg/kg single daily dose IM 5–7 days per wk.

(Inj Amicin, alfakim, amikamac, amistar, biocin, ivimicin, mikacin, nikacin, novacin 2 ml vials 100 mg, 250 mg and 500 mg). Amikacin 250 mg/ml injection contains 12.88 mg of sodium in each 2 ml vial.

Gentamicin sulfate 5.0–7.5 mg/kg/day IM, cystic fibrosis 7–10 mg/kg/day IV q 8–12 hr. In ambulatory cases, 4 mg/kg IM single dose per day is effective.

For cystic fibrosis inhaled dose <5 yr: 40 mg BD, 5–12 yr: 80 mg BD, >12 yr: 160 mg BD.

Adult dose: 250 mg per day q 8–12 hr IM, IV.

C/I: Myasthenia gravis; previous toxic reaction to aminoglycoside. (Inj genticyn, biogaracin, lyramycin, garamycin, genkind gentasporin, gentaryl, ingen, lupigenta, merigenta, ranbiotic, zenta 5 ml, 2 ml ampoules 40 mg/ml, 10 mg/ml).

Kanamycin sulfate 15–30 mg/kg/day q 8–12 hr IM, IV given over 30–60 min. MDR tuberculosis 15 mg/kg/day. In some cases, dose up to 30 mg/kg/day has been recommended.

Adult dose: 0.5–1 g daily q 12 hr, maximum 1.5 g/day.
(Inj Kancin 500 mg, 1 g per vial; inj efficin, kanamac, kancin, neokanyn 500 mg, 750 mg, 1 g per vial).

Neomycin sulfate 0.25–1 g/day q 6 hr oral. Oral neomycin is used for preparation of bowel before surgery, hepatic encephalopathy.

Adult dose: 1.0–3.0 gm q 16 hr for 5–6 days.
(Neomycin sulphate tabs 350, 500 mg).

Netilmicin sulfate Children: 5.0–7.5 mg/kg/day q 8–12 hr IM or IV. Infants: 7.5–10 mg/kg/day. <1 wk age: 3 mg/kg q 12 hr.

Adult dose: Non-life-threatening infection: 4–6 mg/kg/d; life-threatening infection: 7.5 mg/kg/day.
(Inj netromycin 10 mg, 25 mg, 50 mg, 100 mg per ml amp; inj neticin 200 mg, 300 mg vials; inj netilmac, netmicin, netspan, netromaximum 50 mg, 300 mg vials)

Streptomycin sulfate 20–40 mg/kg/day q 12 hr or single daily dose IM.

Adult dose: 0.75–1 g daily IM, maximum dose 1 g/day.

C/I: Hypersensitivity reaction to the drug, ear disease.
(Inj Ambistryn-S, cipstryn, streptomac, isos, streptoma 0.75 g, 1.0 g vials)

Tobramycin 3–5 mg/kg/day IV, IM q 8–12 hr. For cystic fibrosis inhaled dose <6 yr: 150 mg BD, >6 yr: 300 mg BD.

Adult dose: 3–5 mg/kg/day q 6–8 hr.
(Inj tobacin, tobazest, tobraneg, tocin, bactob 20 mg, 40 mg, 80 mg in 2 ml vials).

Paromomycin 25–30 mg/kg/day q 8 hr oral. Alternative to neomycin for hepatic encephalopathy. Useful for intestinal amebiasis.

Adult dose: 4.0 g/d q 6 hr for 5–7 days.
(Paromycin, humantin cap 250 mg).

CEPHALOSPORINS

Cefaclor 20–40 mg/kg/day q 8 hr oral (maximum dose 2 g/day). Use higher dose for acute otitis media.

Adult dose: 250–500 mg q 8 hr (maximum dose 4 g/day).
(Keflor, distaclor, vercef caps 250 mg, 500 mg; keflor, halocef, distaclor dispersible tabs 125 mg, 250 mg; keflor drops 50 mg per ml; acticlor, halocef, uniclor susp 125 mg per 5 ml).

Cefadroxil 30–50 mg/kg/day q 12 hr oral.

Adult dose: 1–2 g/day q 12–24 hr.

C/I: Hypersensitivity to cephalosporin.
(Cefadur, cefadrox, kefloxin, cefadur, lydoxil cap 500 mg; acudrox, cefoxid DT, odoxil tabs 500 mg, 1 g; cefadrox DT, vepan kid 125 mg; cedrox DT, cefoxid DT, vepan kid 250 mg; cefadrox, bidroxil, cefduxodoxil syrup 125 mg per 5 ml; syrup acudrox, lydroxil 125 mg, 250 mg per 5 ml; droxyl syrup 250 mg per 5 ml).

Cefazolin sodium 50–100 mg/kg/day IM, IV q 6 hr. Intravenous infusion is given over 5–10 min.

Adult dose: 500 mg–1 g IV or IM q 6–8 hr.

Caution: Safety not established in newborn babies.
(Inj azolin, cezolin, cefadin, ciprid, orizolin, reflin, sefazol 250 mg, 500 mg, 1 g vials).

Cefdinir 14 mg/kg/day single or two divided doses. Effective coverage of Gram-positive and Gram-negative organisms with β-lactamase stability.

Adult dose: 300–600 mg daily q 12–24 hr.

C/I: Hypersensitivity to penicillins or cephalosporins.
(Aldinir, adcef, adinir, cednir, cefdiel, zefdinir, zifnir, zinir, rtist, sefdin, dry syrup 125 mg per 5 ml, cap 300 mg, zinir–LB tabs 100 mg DT, 150 mg DT and tab 300 mg).

Cefditoren pivoxil It is a semisynthetic cephalosporin for oral administration. 3 mg/kg/dose q 8 hr for 5 days for eradication of Group A *Staphylococcus haemolyticus*. It is broad spectral against Gram-positive and Gram-negative bacteria except *Pseudomonas aeruginosa* and *S. typhi*.

Adult dose: 200 mg q 2–3 hr/day.
(Cefdicare, cefditoren, ceflorin, spectoren, taxitorin, torocef-O, zostum-O tabs 50 mg DT and 200 mg, susp 100 mg per 5 ml).

Cefepime Children >2 mon: 100 mg/kg/day IV q 12 hr, meningitis, febrile neutropenia, serious infections, cystic fibrosis: 150 mg/kg/day IV q 8 hr, <2 mon: 60 mg/kg/day.

Adult dose: 1 gm q 12 hr IV or IM.

Indic: Broad spectrum activity against Gram-positive and Gram-negative aerobic bacteria. *Its antipseudomonal activity is similar to that of ceftazidime*.
(Inj ceficad, megapime, maxicef, magnora, novapime, pimera, sefdin 250 mg, 500 mg, 1 g vials; cepime, forpar, micropime 1 gm vials).

Cefixime 8 mg/kg/day oral once or twice a day. For enteric fever, 20 mg/kg/day q 12 hr or 24 hr.

Adult dose: 200–400 mg daily q 12–24 hr.
(Taxim-o, zifi, cefi, zofix, omnatax-o, ziprax, cefolac, biotax-o, fixx, extacef tabs, 50 mg DT, 100 mg DT; 200 mg DT, 400 mg; syrup taxim-o, zifi, zofix, ziprax, hifen, topcef, ceftas, biotax-o, brutacef, brutacef DS, 50 mg and 100 mg per 5 ml).

Cefoperazone 100–150 mg/kg/day in 2–3 doses IV. Not recommended in meningitis, because of poor penetration through brain membranes.

Adult dose: 1–2 g IV or IM q 12 hr; maximum 8 g/day.

Caution: It does not cross the blood–brain barrier.

(Inj magnamycin, cefomycin, cefrazo, 3 cef novo 1.5 g, cefkem, cefazone 1 g, 2 g vials; myticef 250 mg, 500 mg, 1 g, 2 g vials).

Cefoperazone with sulbactum sodium It has extended spectrum activity against ESBL organisms. Each vial contains equal amount of both. Dose is 40–80 mg/kg/day q 6–12 hr. For serious infections, up to 160 mg/kg/day can be given. (Dose is mentioned in terms of cefoperazone.)

Maximum dose of sulbactam is 80 mg/kg/day (maximum dose 4 g). If more than 80 mg/kg/day of cefoperazone activity is required, additional cefoperazone should be administered.

Adult dose: 2–4 g/day IV or IM q 12 hr (maximum 8 g/day).
(Inj lactagard, cefkem, cefozen, ceftop, magnazone, cefaguard, ceforex, ciso-DS, kefchek, fytobact, kephazon S, kyzone, magnex 500 mg, 1 g, 2 g vials; inj sanbax, sulcef, zosul 1 g vial; precize, sulbacef 1 g, 1.5 g, 2 g vials).

Cefotaxime sodium 100–150 mg/kg/day q 6–8 hr. For meningitis, use 200 mg/kg/day q 6 hr.

Adult dose: 1–2 g IM or IV q 12 hr; maximum 12 g/day q 6–8 hr.

C/I: Cephalosporin hypersensitivity.
(Inj claforan, biotax, c-tax, lyforan, novatax, omnatax, sifotaxim, taxim, evacef, cefotax 250 mg, 500 mg, 1 g per vial; inj duotax contains cefotaxime 500 mg and 250 mg sulbactam).

Cefpirome 30–60 mg/kg/day q 12 hr IV. Higher dose in severe infections. Active against *Pseudomonas*, Gram-positive organisms including methicillin sensitive staphylococci, coagulase negative staphylococci and *Enterococcus faecalis*.

Adult dose: 1–2 g q 12 hr IV.

Indic: Sepsis, skin and soft tissue infections, infections in immunocompromised host, and severe pneumonia.
(Inj cefor, cefrom, forgen, omnirom, refzil 250 mg, 500 mg, 1000 mg; inj ceforth, bacirom 250 mg, 1 g; inj cef 1 g).

Cefpodoxime proxetil 10 mg/kg/day orally q 12 hr, maximum 400 mg/day, administered with food.

Adult dose: 100–200 mg q 12 hr oral.

Indic: Covers both Gram-positive and Gram-negative bacteria including *S. typhi*.
(Cepodem XP, cefoprox, cepocor, cefective, cefantib, monotax-cefakind, acepod, cefetil, ceftyl, doxcef, gudcef, kefpod tabs 100 mg, 200 mg; monocef-o, monotax-o, microcef, cepodem XP DT 50 mg; syrup 50 mg and 100 mg per 5 ml).

Cefprozil It is a second-generation cephalosporin. 5–30 mg/kg/day q 12 hr. Broad coverage of Gram-positive and Gram negative organisms with β-lactamase stability.

Adult dose: 250–500 mg q 12 hr for 10 days, maximum dose 1 g/day.

Caution: Avoid below 6 mon.
(Refzil-o, orprozil, zemetril tabs 250 and 500 mg, susp 125 mg and 250 mg per 5 ml).

Ceftazidime with tazobactam 100–150 mg/kg/day q 8 hr IV, IM. For meningitis, 150 mg/kg/day q 8 hr.

Adult dose: 2–6 g daily in 2–3 divided doses, maximum 6 g/day.

Indic: Specific for *Pseudomonas aeruginosa*.
(Inj fortum, ceftidin, cefzid, cefazid, tazid, tizime, zytaz, zidime 250 mg, 500 mg, 1 g vials; gebizid TZ, bizid TZ, czid TZ, forzid TZ each vial contains 1 g ceftazidime and 125 mg tazobactam).

Ceftazidime-Avibactam Indicated in complicated intra-abdominal infections, complicated UTI, pneumonia in adult and pediatric patients (aged ≥3 mon) caused by Gram-negative microorganisms
<3 mon: Safety and efficacy not established
3 mon to <6 mon: 50 mg/kg (ceftazidime 40 mg/kg and avibactam 10 mg/kg) IV q 8 hr for 5–14 days
6 mon to <2 yr: 62.5 mg/kg (ceftazidime 50 mg/kg and avibactam 12.5 mg/kg) IV q 8 hr for 5–14 days
2 yr to <18 yr: 62.5 mg/kg (ceftazidime 50 mg/kg and avibactam 12.5 mg/kg) IV q 8 hr for 5–14 days; not to exceed 2.5 g/dose (ceftazidime 2 g and avibactam 0.5 g).

Adult dose: 2.5 g (2 g ceftazidime and 0.5 g avibactam) IV q 8 hr.

C/I: Hypersensitivity to any of the components.

(Cefazid AV, cipcza, tivibact, threezid AV, zeftabac, zavicefta –2.5 gm vials contains equivalent to 2.0 g of ceftazidime pentahydrate/sodium carbonate powder and 0.5 g of avibactam sodium)

Ceftibuten 9 mg/kg/day orally once a day.

Adult dose: 400 mg once daily.

Indic: Wide coverage against Gram-positive and Gram-negative organisms except *Pseudomonas aeruginosa*, *Enterococcus* and *Enterobacter*.
(Procadax cap 400 mg; susp 90 mg per 5 ml).

Ceftizoxime 100–200 mg/kg/day IM, IV q 6–8 hr in severe infection. Use 30–60 mg/kg/day in less severe infections.

Adult dose: 1–2 g q 8–12 hr by deep IM or slow IV. In severe infections, use up to 6 g daily.

Indic: Wide coverage and excellent for anaerobes. Crosses blood–brain barrier.
(Inj cefizox, eldcef, epocelin, traxi, trizox, unizox, zatef 250 mg, 1 g vials).

Ceftriaxone sodium 50–75 mg/kg/day IV q 12–24 hr. For meningitis, use 100 mg/kg/day q 12 hr (maximum dose 4 g). 25–50 mg/kg (maximum 125 mg) IM or IV single dose can be given for treatment of gonococcal ophthalmia neonatorum. For prophylaxis against *N. meningitidis*, 125 mg IM single dose can be given to all contacts.

Adult dose: 1 g daily by deep IM or slow IV; 2–4 g daily in severe infections.

C/I: Penicillin or cephalosporin hypersensitivity.
(Inj monocef, acuzon, axone, cefaxone, torocef, becef, ciplacef, cefzone, torocef, gentrax, oframax, powercef, monotax, cefakit, ceftil, ceftrax, zone 125 mg, 250 mg, 500 mg, 1 g vials).

Ceftriaxone with sulbactam sodium Sulbactam is a beta-lactamase inhibitor which reduces resistance and enhances the activity of ceftriaxone against bacteria.
(Inj cefjoy, xtum, sactum, ceftriax-S, cefzone-S, acuzon plus, cefbact-S –1500 contains 1000 mg ceftriaxone and 500 mg

sulbactam; inj sactum–750, xtum–750 contains 500 mg ceftriaxone and 250 mg sulbactam).

Cefuroxime axetil 100–150 mg/kg/day q 6–8 hr IV and IM. Oral dose 20–30 mg/kg/day q 12 hr. For enteric fever, 40 mg/kg/day q 12 hr oral. Give with or after food.

Adult dose: 750 mg 8 hr IM or IV; severe infections 1.5 g q 8 hr; oral dose 250–500 mg twice daily.
(Ceftum, pulmocef, cefasyn, ceroxitum, ketstar, forcef, cefexl, cefoxim, cetil, zocef, zefu, cefakind tabs 125 mg, 250 mg, 500 mg; ceftum, cefoxim, zocef, zefu, kefstar, cefakind, fastclav, furoxil, ceroxim syrup 125 mg per 5 ml. Inj cefogen, supacef, ceftum altacef 250 mg, 750 mg, 1.5 g vials; inj furoxil 250 mg, 750 mg vials).

Cephalexin 25–100 mg/kg/day q 6–8 hr oral.

Adult dose: 250–500 mg every 6 hr (maximum 4 g/day).

C/I: Pencillin and cephalosporin hypersensitivity.
(Cephaxin, sepexin, ceff, sporidex, phexin, solexin, monacef caps 250 mg, 500 mg; cephaxin, sepexin, ceff, sporidex syrup 125 mg per 5 ml; cepen, keflex 250 mg/5 ml ; sporidex, alcephin, ceff drops 100 mg per ml; sporidex DT 125 mg, 250 mg tabs, ceff kid tab 125 mg, ceff DT 250 mg).

Cefdinir 7 to 14 mg/kg in two divided doses, up to a maximum dose of 600 mg per day. Good activity against Gram-positive cocci, β-lactamase producing organisms.

Adult dose: 300 mg BD

C/I: Penicillin or cephalosporin hypersensitivity
(Adcef, biocef, cefdiel, kefnir, maxicef, rtist tabs 150 mg, 300 mg; susp 125 mg per 5 ml)

Cefetamet pivoxil 10 to 20 mg/kg/day in two to three divided doses, maximum of 1–1.5 g/day. Good activity against Gram-negative organisms.

Adult dose: 500 mg BD or TDS

C/I: Penicillin or cephalosporin hypersensitivity.
(Altamet, cepime, kuzet, recocef, pryzm tabs 250 mg, 500 mg).

Ceftaroline fosamil 8 mg/kg every 8 hrly in children from 2 mon to <2 yr of age. In children and adolescents aged 2 yr and older, 12 mg/kg q 8 h is recommended for ≤33 kg, and 400 mg q 8 h or 600 mg q 12 h for >33 kg. Used in treatment of complicated skin and soft tissue infections as well as for community acquired pneumonia (CAP).

Adult dose: 600 mg infused IV over 60 min every 12 hr for 5–14 days; dose to be adjusted if creatinine clearance is <50 ml/min.

C/I: Penicillin or cephalosporin hypersensitivity.

(Inj cinforo, teflaro 600 mg/vial)

Newer cephalosporins like ceftaroline, ceftolazone-tazobactam combination, cefotetan, cefoxitin are currently not available in India.

FLUOROQUINOLONES

Ciprofloxacin 20–40 mg/kg/day q 12 hr oral or 10–20 mg/kg/day q 12 hr IV (maximum 800 mg/day). 20 mg/kg single dose for contacts of *N. meningitidis*.

Adult dose: 250–750 mg q 12 hr oral; 100–400 mg q 12 hr by intravenous infusion. 500 mg single oral dose for contacts of *N. meningitidis.*

Caution: It should be reserved for children where anticipated or cultured pathogens are resistant to all other antibiotics.
(Cifran, ciplox, ciprobid, cify, celox tabs 100 mg, 250 mg, 500 mg, 750 mg; alcipro, biocip, ciproflox, ciprolet, ciprowin, quinobact, strox, supraflox tabs 250 mg, 500 mg; disquin DT 250 mg, ciprolar, avilox susp 125 mg and 250 mg per 5 ml, inj cifran 100 mg per 50 ml, inj ciplox 200 mg per 100 ml, ciplox eye drops 0.3% w/v).

Levofloxacin It is levo-isomer of ofloxacin. 10 mg/kg single dose daily oral or IV with maximum daily dose 500 mg.

Adult dose: 500 mg daily.

Indic: Effective against Gram-positive and Gram-negative infections and MDR TB. No coverage against *Pseudomonas aeruginosa.* 6

Caution: Avoid concurrent use of antacids.
(Levoflox, lotor, levocide, levoday, fynal tabs, L-250, L-CIN, 250 mg, 500 mg; levoflox, levomer, levota, lotor, loxof, emrok, fynal 5 mg per ml for IV infusion).

Moxifloxacin Indications include acute bacterial sinusitis, chronic bronchitis, community-acquired pneumonia, skin and soft tissue infection. 7.5–10 mg/kg single daily dose. Its use is currently restricted to multi-drug-resistant tuberculosis.

Adult dose: Oral 400 mg OD for 7–14 days, IV: 400 mg OD infused over 60 min for 7–14 days, ophthalmic solution 0.5% 1 drop in each eye 8 hrly.
(Avilox, maxnum, rapidox, kindmax, mofil, mahaflox, mcin, moximoc, moxiflox cap/tab; avilox, hycomin, mahaflox 400 mg/100 ml infusion; apdrops, bflox, 4 quin eye drops, cellumox eye oint 0.5%).

Nalidixic acid 50 mg/kg/day q 6–8 hr oral. Not recommended in infants below 3 mon. UTI prophylaxis: 30 mg/kg/day q 12 hr or 15 mg/kg/day q 6 hr.

Adult dose: 1 g every 6 hr.

Caution: Avoid in children with history of seizures, G-6-PD deficiency. May produce pseudotumor cerebri. Serious adverse effects include erythema multiforme, Stevens-Johnson syndrome.

C/I: Epilepsy, porphyrias, age <3 mon.
(Gramoneg, bactomet, nalidys, negadix, dix, riadix, rex tabs 200 mg, 300 mg, 500 mg; susp 200/300 mg per 5 ml).

Norfloxacin 10–15 mg/kg/day q 12 hr oral.

Adult dose: 400 mg q 12 hr.
(Norflox, norilet, alflox, norbid DT 100 mg; norflox, alfox, norbactin, norin, norilet, biofloxin, norbid tabs 200 mg, 400 mg and 800 mg; flox, bacigyl, normet, tamflox susp 100 mg per 5 ml).

6 **Ofloxacin** 15 mg/kg/day oral q 12 hr 5–10 mg/kg/day q 12 hr IV.

Adult dose: 400–800 mg daily; give every 12 hr in divided doses, if >400 mg/day.
(Tarivid, zanocin, oflox, ofla, zenflox, uneek, floxur tabs 200 mg, 400 mg; ofromax, zanocin, oflin tab 100 mg; zenflox, ofla, orivid, zo, oflomac, oflox, uneek, bioff, diof, oflotas, susp 50 mg/5 ml, zenflox forte, oflomac forte, duflox, zanocin, ofla susp 100 mg per 5 ml, inj oflox, tarivid 200 mg, 400 mg per 100 ml).

Pefloxacin 12 mg/kg/day oral q 12 hr. It has effective coverage against most Gram-negative and Gram-positive organisms including *S. aureus* and *S. typhi*.

Adult dose: 400 mg q 12 hr; may use an initial loading dose of 800 mg orally, IV 400 mg over 1 hr as infusion, q 12 hr.

Caution: Adjust dose in hepatic insufficiency.
(Peflox, pelox, ifipef, pebact, pefbid, proflox, qucin tabs 200 mg, 400 mg, 600 mg; pefbid, pelox, peflobid, rolox, inj 400 mg per 100 ml).

Sparfloxacin 4 mg/kg single dose oral per day. It provides effective coverage against both Gram-negative and Gram-positive organisms. Dose 100–300 mg/day in 2 divided doses.

Adult dose: 200–400 mg daily q 12–24 hr.
(Spardac, sparx, sparlox, sparkind, sparflow tabs 100 mg DT and 200 mg; spaeflo, sparbact, spardac, sparcin, sparfio, sparzid tabs 200 mg).

LINCOSAMIDES

Clindamycin hydrochloride 20–30 mg/kg/day q 6–8 hr oral, 20–40 mg/kg/day q 6–8 hr IV. Dilute appropriately for slow infusion over 30 min. Useful for MRSA, anaerobic infections, *P. carinii* pneumonia and toxoplasma encephalitis.

Adult dose: 150–450 mg q 6–8 hr.

Caution: Pseudomembranous colitis. Avoid co-administration with erythromycin.
(Dalcinex, dalacin-c, camyda, clincin caps 150 mg, 300 mg; inj dalacin, camyda, climycin 150 mg per ml in 2 ml, 4 ml ampoules; erytop, cleargel and clindapene (1%) gel for acne).

Lincomycin 30–60 mg/kg/day q 8 hr oral. 10–20 mg/kg/day q 8–12 hr IM, IV.

Adult dose: 250–500 mg q 6–8 hr oral; 600 mg single dose IM, 600 mg q 8–12 hr IV.

Caution: Pseudomembranous colitis, TEN syndrome, **DRESS** syndrome (**D**rug **R**eaction with **E**osinophilia and **S**ystemic **S**ymptoms).
(Lynx, lincosa, lincosin, lysin caps 250 mg, 500 mg; syrup 125 mg per ml; inj prolinc 300 mg per ml as 1 ml, 2 ml amp).

MACROLIDES

Azithromycin 10 mg/kg/day single dose empty stomach oral on day 1 and then 5 mg/kg/day during next 4 days. A single dose of 30 mg/kg can be given. Avoid administration in infants below 6 mon. Enteric fever: 20 mg/kg/day for 7–14 days.

Cholera: 20 mg/kg single dose.

Adult dose: 500 mg once daily for 3 days; or 500 mg on day 1, then 250 mg daily on day 2 to 5; total dose 1.5 g. Genital chancroid: 1 g single dose.

Indic: Gram-positive infections, typhoid fever, campylobacter enteritis, cat-scratch disease, atypical pneumonia, and cholera.

SE: Prolongation of QT interval, torsades de pointes (tdp) and liver dysfunction. The drugs which are known to cause tdp include ciprofloxacin, disopyramide, dofetilide, flecainide, fluconazole, levofloxacin, procainamide and sotalol.
(Azithral, azikem, azee, aziwin, aziwok, azithro, zathrin, zithrox, azivent, zithrocin tabs 100 mg, 250 mg, 500 mg; azirin, azivax, azithrolin, salazor, ziazi tab 500 mg; syrup 100 mg and 200 mg per 5 ml).

Clarithromycin 15 mg/kg/day q 12 hr oral. Efficacy and safety in infants below 6 mon not evaluated.

Adult dose: 250 mg q 12 hr for 7 days; in severe infections up to 500 mg q 12 hr for 14 days.

Indic: H. pylori, Chlamydia, Mycoplasma, atypical mycobacteria, *M. marinum* infection from sea water.

C/I: Previous history of arrhythmia or long QT syndrome. (Claribid, clarigard, clarigen, crixan, crivax, synclar, larit, clarocin, clarimac, maclar, klarim tabs 250 mg and 500 mg; crivax, maclar DT 125 mg; syrup 125 mg and 250 mg per 5 ml; clarmac DS, ifyclar DS 250 mg per 5 ml; crixal gel for acne).

Erythromycin 30–50 mg/kg/day q 6 hr oral. 5 mg/kg/dose IV as infusion over 8 hr with normal saline or Ringer's lactate or intermittent bolus over 20–60 min every 6 to 8 hr.

For gut motility in children 10–15 mg/kg/day in 3–4 divided doses per oral.

Adult dose: 250 mg q 6 hr; initial dose may be 250 or 500 mg.

Indic: Gram-positive infections and *Arcanobacterium haemolyticum*, chlamydial infection, Legionnaire's disease, Lyme disease, lymphogranuloma venereum, pertussis, nongonococcal urethritis, chancroid.

Erythromycin in neonates may cause hypertrophic pyloric stenosis.

(Althrocin, e-mycin, eltocin, erythrocin, emthrocin, erytop, thromycin, erysafe tabs 100 mg, 125 mg, 250 mg and 500 mg; syrup 100 mg and 125 mg per 5 ml; inj erythromycin 1 g vial with 20 ml diluent; acnederm, erysil, gery, medisoft skin cream for acne, ophthalmic solution 0.5%).

Roxithromycin 5–8 mg/kg/day q 12 hr.

Adult dose: 150 mg q 12 hr.

C/I: Concomitant use with ergotamine alkaloids.

(Roxid, rulide, roxikin, droxyrol, roximol, roxem, xyrox, roxeptin tabs 50 mg, 150 mg; apirox, astrox, biorox, roxone, roxycan, roxera tabs 150 mg; biorox, roxid, troxy, xyrox syrup 50 mg per 5 ml).

PENICILLINS

Amoxycillin For milder infections 25–50 mg/kg/day q 8–12 hr oral; 80–100 mg/kg/day q 6 hr oral in enteric fever and otitis media and other severe infections.

Adult dose: 250–500 mg q 6–8 hr.

(Amoxil, amoclox, almox, novamox, mox, lamoxy, amoxybid, amoxyvan, comoxyl, genmox, idimox, moxilium, cidomex, wymox caps 250 and 500 mg, DT 125 mg, 250 mg; syrup 125 mg per 5 ml; drops 100 mg per ml).

Amoxycillin with clavulanic acid 25–50 mg/kg/day (amoxycillin base) q 8 to 12 hr oral, 50–100 mg/kg/day (amoxycillin base) q 6–8 hr IV. Note IV dose is higher than oral dose.

Adult dose: 250–500 mg of amoxycillin q 8 hr; 1.2 g q 6–8 hr IV infusion.

Indic: Wide spectrum with good coverage of beta-lactamase producing strains of *S. pneumoniae, H. influenzae, B. catarrhalis* and *S. aureus.*

SE: It may cause severe skin rash in patients with infectious mononucleosis.

C/I: Jaundice, hepatic dysfunction, penicillin allergy.

(Augmentin, advent, moxclav, moxkind-CV, abclox-CV, enhancin, novaclav, megaclav, flamiclav, augpen, clavam, clamp tabs 375 mg (250 mg amoxycillin + 125 mg clavulanate), 625 mg (500 mg amoxycillin + 125 clavulanate); 1000 mg (875 mg amoxycillin + 125 mg clavulanate), syrup 156 mg per 5 ml (125 mg of amoxycillin + 31.5 mg clavulanate); augmentin duo, moxclav BD, enhancin BD, advent, nuclav duo, curam duo and augpen HS syrup (200 mg amoxycillin + 28.5 mg clavulanate per 5 ml); augpen, augmentin DDS, moxclav DS, advent forte susp (400 mg amoxycillin + 57 mg clavulanate per 5 ml), moxclav drops 91.4 mg/ml (amoxycillin 80 mg + clavulanate 11.4 mg). Inj clavam, acuclav 150 mg (amoxycillin 125 mg), Inj 300 mg (amoxycillin 250 mg), 600 mg (amoxycillin 500 mg); 1.2 g (amoxycillin 1 g), inj augpen 300 mg).

Ampicillin sodium trihydrate 100–200 mg/kg/day q 4–6 hr IV or oral, 200–400 mg/kg/day q 4 hr for meningitis. For enteric fever, 200 mg/kg/day q 6 hr oral.

Adult dose: 250–500 mg q 6 hr.

(Ampipen, aristocillin, broadicillin, campicillin, biocillin, rosicillin, ampilin, bacipen, synthocilin, piracillin, broadil caps 250 mg and 500 mg; dispersible tabs 125 mg; 250 mg; syrup 125 mg per 5 ml; drops 100 mg per ml; inj 250 mg, 500 mg per vial).

Ampicillin with sulbactam 100–200 mg/kg/day (ampicillin base) q 6 hr IV. A combination of ampicillin and sulbactam (penicillanic acid sulfone) a new semisynthetic beta-lactam sulfone.

(Inj ampitum, betamp, cinclox, sulbacin containing 1 g ampicillin and 0.5 g sulbactam; saltum, betamp tab 375 mg containing ampicillin 250 mg).

Carbenicillin 30–50 mg/kg/day in 6 hrly oral dose. Parenteral preparation has been banned in US. Useful against *Pseudomonas aeruginosa* and indole-positive *Proteus* sp.

Adult dose: 382 mg tab 1–2 tab q 6 hrly.

Caution: Do not mix with gentamicin and it may cause hypokalemia.

(Geocillin tab 382 mg; inj carbelin, biopence, pyopen 1 g, 5 g per vial).

Cloxacillin 50–100 mg/kg/day IV or oral (1 hr before or 2 hr after food) for staphylococcal infection. 200 mg/kg/day q 4 hr for meningitis (maximum dose 4 g/day).

Adult dose: 250–500 mg q 6 hr oral or IV.

(Klox, bioclox, baciclox, broadiclox, clopen, cloxacillin, supriclox, aclox caps 250 and 500 mg; syrup 125 mg per 5 ml; novaclox, clamp cap containing cloxacillin 250 mg, ampicillin 250 mg; duoclox syrup contains ampicillin 125 mg and cloxacillin 125 mg; ampilox LB syrup containing ampicillin 125 mg, clox 125 mg and *Lactobacillus sporogenes* 60 million; inj klox, bioclox 250 mg, 500 mg per vial).

Penicillin G aqueous 100,000–200,000 units/kg IV (over 15–30 min), IM q 4–6 hr. For severe infections like meningitis and endocarditis, 2,50,000–4,00,000 units IV, IM q 4 hr (not to exceed 12 million units per day). For prophylaxis of rheumatic fever and pneumococcal infections, 200,000 units (125 mg) twice a day. Administer 30 min before or 2 hr after meals.

Neonates 50,000–1,00,000 units/kg/day in 2 divided doses, 1–2 lakh units/kg/day in 2 divided doses in case of meningitis.

Adult dose: 200,000–400,000 units q 8 hr or 800,000 units q 12 hr.

Caution: Sodium and potassium content is 1.68 mEq of cation per million units, large bolus injections may cause seizures.

C/I: Hypersensitivity to penicillin.

(Pentids tabs 2,00,000 units (125 mg), 4,00,000 units, 8,00,000 units; inj benzyl penicillin 5,00,000–10,00,000 units per vial).

Penicillin G benzathine 0.6 mega units IM 3 wkly below 6 yr of age and 1.2 mega units IM every 3 wk after 6 yr of age for secondary prophylaxis against rheumatic fever.

(Penidure LA 6, LA 12, LA 24; benzathine penicillin G; pencom, longacillin 0.6 million, 1.2 million, 2.4 million units per vial).

Penicillin V (phenoxymethyl penicillin) Infants 62.5–125 mg/dose, children <5 yr 125 mg/dose, 6–12 yr 250 mg/dose administered q 6 hr 30 min before or 2 hr after food. For rheumatic prophylaxis, 250 mg orally twice daily. *250 mg is equivalent to 4,00,000 units.*

(Kaypen tabs 125 mg, 250 mg; penivoral tabs 55 mg, 130 mg).

Piperacillin 200–300 mg/kg/day q 4 to 6 hr IV, IM.

Adult dose: 3–4 gm every 4–6 hr.

C/I: Infectious mononucleosis; penicillin or cephalosporin allergy.

(Inj piprapen, pipracil 1.0 g, 2.0 g, 4.0 g vials).

Piperacillin with tazobactam 300–400 mg/kg/day q 6–8 hr. Broad spectrum antibiotic active against Gram-positive and Gram-negative aerobic and anaerobic bacteria.

Adult dose: 4–5 g by slow IV injection or infusion q 8 hr.

(Inj zosyn, biopiper tz, elpip tz, tazact, maxotaz, piptaz, revotaz, tazotum, tazopip containing piperacillin 4 g, tazobactam 500 mg).

Procaine penicillin G 25,000–50,000 units/kg/day single dose IM. Neonates 50,000 units/kg/day IM.

(Inj procaine penicillin 4,00,000 units per vial).

Ticarcillin with clavulanic acid 200–300 mg/kg/day of ticarcillin q 6–8 hr IV over 15–30 min or IM.

Adult dose: 1 vial (3 g ticarcillin) q 4–6 hr by IV infusion.

6 (Inj timentin, ticarnic, cidal, megacillin, tacidal, pzobact 3.1 g contains ticarcillin 3 g + clavulanate 100 mg).

CARBAPENEMS

They are structurally similar to penicillins but the sulfur atom in position 1 has been replaced with a carbon atom. They are effective against beta-lactamase producing enterobacteriaceae like *Klebsiella pneumoniae, E. coli, Citrobacter* sp, *Acinobacter* sp; *Pseudomonas aeruginosa* and *Alcaligenes* sp. They are not effective against MRSA (methicillin-resistant *Staphylococcus aureus*) and NDM-1 (New Delhi metallo-beta-lactamase 1) strains. They can be administered only intravenously.

Doripenem

Adult dose: 500 mg IV 8 hrly, safety and efficacy in children not studied.
(Carbador, dorobac, doribax, dorigen, dorikem, dormax, icupen, inarem, sudopen 500 mg vial).

Ertapenem

3 mon–13 yr: 15 mg/kg/dose IV BD. Effective against Gram-positive and Gram-negative aerobic and anaerobic bacteria.

Adult dose: 1 g OD IV.

Side effect: DRESS (Drug rash, eosinophilia, and systemic symptoms) pruritus, diarrhea, vomiting, nausea.
(Forstal, invanz, eczas, ertafic, ertamac, ertacrit, gerta, mypenem, zivatar as 1 g vial).

Faropenem Oral formulation is available, but it is not yet approved for use in children.

Adult dose: 150–300 mg t.d.s.

SE: Nausea, vomiting, diarrhea, skin rash, sweating, headache, myalgias.
(Duonem, farobact, faronac, farozet, faronem, orpenem tabs 150 mg, 200 mg, 300 mg).

Imipenem/cilastatin 60–100 mg/kg/day of imipenem q 6 hr IV. Broad spectrum beta-lactam antibiotic for aerobic and anaerobic Gram-positive and Gram-negative bacteria.

Caution: Use with caution in children with epilepsy.

Adult dose: 250 mg–1 g IV q 6–8 hr; maximum daily dose 2 g.

Indic: Drug of choice for extended spectrum beta-lactamase producing microorganisms (ESBL).
(Imicrit, carbinem, cilaxter, cilanem, iminen, imecila, zienam, I-nem contains 250 mg or 500 mg each of imipenam and cilastatin).

Meropenem 60 mg/kg/day q 8 hr IV. For neonatal sepsis, 20 mg/kg/dose q 12 hr, meningitis 40 mg/kg/dose q 8 hr.

Adult dose: 500 mg–1 g q 8 hr slow IV infusion.

Indic: Drug of choice for extended spectrum beta-lactamase producing microorganisms (ESBL).
(Inj. merobact, mero, menoper, merocrit, meroten, penam, aeropen, meronem, esblanem, venomen, romen 250 mg, 500 mg, 1000 mg vials; merosure, mero 125 mg, 1 g vials).

The complete list of beta-lactamase resistant antibiotics includes 3rd and 4th generation cephalosporins, carbapenems, aztreonam, beta lactamase-resistant penicillins (methicillin, naficillin, oxacillin, cloxacillin, dicloxacillin) and combo penicillins (containing clavulanic acid or sulbactam).

SULPHAS

Sulfonamides 100–150 mg/kg/day q 8 hr oral. For prophylaxis against meningococcal infection: 500 mg every 24 hr for 2 days for infants below 1 yr and 500 mg every 12 hr for 2 days for older children. Triple sulfa or sulfasoxazole should be preferred because they are short acting and least toxic.

Adult dose: 500 mg q 6 hr (maximum 4–6 g/day).

Adverse effects: Hypersensitivity reactions, such as skin rash, Stevens-Johnson syndrome, vasculitis, serum sickness, drug fever, anaphylaxis, and angioedema.

C/I: Hypersensitivity to sulfa drugs.
(Sulphamethizole, sulfasoxazole, triple sulpha, orisul tab 500 mg).

6 **Trimethoprim-sulfamethoxazole (co-trimoxazole)** 5–8 mg/kg of TMP or 25–50 mg/kg of SMZ/day q 12 hr oral or IV. 10 mg/

kg/day q 12 hr of TMP for typhoid fever and 20 mg/kg/day of TMP q 6–8 hr for *Pneumocystis jirovecii* infection. For prophylaxis against *Pneumocystis carinii*, 5 mg/kg of TMP either single dose or two divided doses daily for 3 consecutive days in a wk or every alternate day. Single dose 1–3 mg/kg/day of TMP for UTI prophylaxis.

Adult dose: 2 tabs (80 mg/400 mg strength) twice daily; in severe infections give 3 tabs twice daily.

C/I: Age <6 wk; hypersensitivity to sulfa, G-6-PD deficiency.
(Septran, bactrim, colizole, supristol, methoxaprim, oriprim, ciplin, sevoprim tab TMP 80 mg, SMZ 400 mg, cotrimoxazole–DS, sumetrol–DS 400 mg or double strength tab; septran, bactrim, sevoprim, pediatric tab TMP 20 mg, SMZ 100 mg; susp TMP 40 mg and SMZ 200 mg per 5 ml; TMP 160 mg and SMZ 800 mg per 3 ml ampoule for IM or IV).

MISCELLANEOUS ANTIMICROBIALS

Aztreonam 90–120 mg/kg/day q 6–8 hr IV or IM administered by IV bolus over 3–5 min or intermittent infusion over 20–60 min. Bactericidal against enterobacteriaceae and *Pseudomonas aeruginosa* but a little or no activity against Gram-positive aerobic bacteria or anaerobic bacteria. Crosses blood–brain barrier and is beta-lactamase stable. Does not cause oto- or nephrotoxicity.

Adult dose: 1 g q 8 hr or 2 g q 12 hr; maximum 8 g/day IM or IV.

Adverse effects: Diarrhea, vomiting, rarely toxic epidermal necrolysis (TEN).

Caution: Not recommended <1 wk age.
(Inj azactam, azenam, trezam, zonam 250 mg, 500 mg, 1 g, 2 g vials).

Chloramphenicol 50–75 mg/kg/day q 8 hr oral. 100 mg/kg/day q 6 hr IV in severe cases. Infants <2 wk age: 25 mg/kg/day; 2 wk – 1 yr: 50 mg/kg/day.

Adult dose: 50–100 mg/kg/day q 6 hr.

Caution: Monitor blood levels in neonates and maintain between 15 μg and 30 μg/ml.

C/I: Blood dyscrasias, premature infants below 14 days of age, porphyria, hypersensitivity.

Intravenous chloramphenicol use has been associated with development of life-threatening grey baby syndrome. This phenomenon occurs in newborn infants because they do not have fully functional liver enzymes, i.e. UDP-glucuronyl transferase and therefore chloramphenicol remains unmetabolized in the body.

(Chloromycetin, chloramphenicol, chlorocin, chloraxin, paraxin, zitronam, reclor, enteromycetin, vitamycetin caps 250 mg, 500 mg; susp 125 mg per 5 ml; inj enteromycetin, paraxin vial 1 g and 2 g per 10 ml).

Colistimethate sulfate/colistin 50,000 to 75,000 i.u./kg/day q 8 hr IV for treatment of Gram-negative bacteria including *Pseudomonas aeruginosa*, *Enterobacter*, and *Klebsiella*.

Adverse effects: Nephrotoxicity.

(Inj xylistin, promistin, colymonas, colimed, colinem, nicolistin, remergin 1, 2, 4 million i.u. per vial).

Colistin sodium 2.5–5 mg/kg/day q 6 to 8 hr oral. Use with caution in children below 12 yr.

Adult dose: 25–100 mg q 8 hr.

Adverse effects: Nephrotoxicity, and neurotoxicity.

(Walamycin, colistop, colistin susp 12.5 mg per 5 ml; Walamycin-DS, colistop-DS susp 25 mg per 5 ml).

Daptomycin Used in complicated skin soft tissue infection, and *Staphylococcus* bacteremia.

Adult dose: 4 mg/kg/day infused over 30 min for 7–14 days.

Staphylococcus aureus bacteremia 6 mg/kg/day infused over 30 min for 2–6 wk.

SE: GI side effects like nausea, vomiting, diarrhea, dyspepsis, loose stools and abdominal pain, electrolyte imbalance and rarely DRESS syndrome and anaphylaxis, *Clostridium difficile*-associated diarrhea and colitis. Dose needs to be modified in renal failure. Safety and efficacy in children not proven yet.

(Cubicin, dapmicin, daptocure, emarsa, IV dapt: Available in powder format 350 mg to be constituted with normal saline and infused).

Doxycycline hyclate 2–5 mg/kg/day q 12 hr oral. It is more soluble in water than doxycycline hydrochloride. Avoid in children below 8 yr of age due to risk of staining of teeth and growth retardation. Tick-borne rickettsia 2.2 mg/kg/dose q 12 hr.

Adult dose: 200 mg on day 1, then 100 mg daily; 50 mg daily for 6–12 wk for treatment of acne.

Indic: Chronic bronchitis, brucellosis, chlamydia, mycoplasma, anthrax, lyme disease, granuloma inguinale, rickettsia, ehrlichiosis, cholera, and *Cutibacterium acnes*. It is also indicated for short-term (<6 wk) malaria prophylaxis in a dose of 1.5 mg/kg (children above 8 yr) and 100 mg OD in adults, starting 2 days before travel, during stay and 4 wk after leaving the malarious area.

C/I: Below 8 yr, pregnancy and lactation.

SE: Diarrhea, stomach upset, nausea, and itching.
(Cedox DT, biodoxi, doxy-1, doxypal, doxytas, revidox, vibramycin, avidoxy, adoxa, lupidox, monodox, oracea, lydox, vivocycline, Dox-T, minicyclinen, ovadox, nudoxy, tetradox, vibazine DT tabs 100 mg; 200 mg; solomycin tabs 50 mg and 100 mg; minocycline syrup 25 mg, 50 mg per 5 ml).

Fosfomycin Antiseptic, bacterial cell wall synthesis inhibitor. Used when other common antibiotics cannot be used. Dose for acute cystitis or uncomplicated UTI- 6-11 yr: 2 g single dose, ≥12 yr: 3 g single dose, complicated UTI-3 g every 2–3 days, total 3 doses.

C/I: Hypersensitivity to fosfomycin or any of the components.
(Fosirol, fonyl, crifos, fosfotas, fosfocin, novefos, fosfofic inj 4 gm/vial, sachets-3 g, 4 g, 8 g)

Linezolid 20 mg/kg/day q 12 hr IV or oral.

Adult dose: 600 mg IV or oral q 12 hr.

Caution: Give IV injection over 30–120 min, protect from light.

SE: Lactic acidosis, seizures, hepatic and renal dysfunction, long-term use is associated with bone marrow suppression.

Indic: Treatment of infections caused by vancomycin-resistant enterococci, and methicillin-resistant *S. aureus*.

(Linox, linospan, lizolid, linid, linzid, lizbid, zolimaximum tab 600 mg, lizoforce, linospan, LNZ, lizomac suspension 100 mg/5 ml, inj linox 200 mg in 100 ml vial; inj alzolid, linosept, linozid, lizoforce, lizolid 200 mg, 600 mg in 100 or 300 ml vials).

Minocycline Initial dose 4 mg/kg followed by 4 mg/kg/day q 12 hr. Avoid in children below 8 yr of age.

Adult dose: 100 mg once or twice daily.

SE: Vertigo, lupus-like syndrome, autoimmune hepatitis.

C/I: Renal failure.

(Cynomycin, carlocin, divaine, minima, minolox, minotag, minoz tabs and caps 50 mg, 100 mg).

Nitrofurantoin 5–7 mg/kg/day q 6 hr oral with meals. Prophylactic dose for UTI 1–2 mg/kg/day as single dose at bedtime.

Adult dose: 50–100 mg q 6 hr.

C/I: Impaired renal function; G-6-PD deficiency, age <1 mon.

SE: Fever, skin rash, hypersensitivity pneumonitis.

(Furadantin, martifur, niftas, niftran, uribid, urinif, urifast, utifur, nifty-SR, tabs 50 mg and 100 mg; susp 25 mg per 5 ml).

Polymyxin B Infants-IM: up to 40,000 units/kg/day divided q 6 hr if renal function is normal, IV: up to 40,000 units/kg/day divided q 12 hr; Intrathecal: 20,000 units/day for 3–4 days; followed with 25,000 units day for at least 2 wk after CSF cultures are negative and CSF (glucose) has returned to normal.

Children-IM: 25,000–30,000 units/kg/day q 12 hr, IV: 15,000–25,000 units/kg/day q 12 hr; not to exceed 25,000 units/kg/day, Intrathecal: 50,000 day for 3–4 days; then every day for at least 2 wk after CSF cultures are negative and normal for glucose content.

Adult dose: Total daily dose not to exceed 2,000,000 units/day.

C/I: Concurrent nephrotoxic and neurotoxic drugs, hypersensitivity reaction.
(Aerosporin, biofer, biomyxin-B, polinac -B, polium-B, polymix-B- 500000 i.u./vial).

Rifaximin Children above 12 yr, 200 mg BD or t.d.s. for 3 to 7 days useful for traveller's diarrhea and hepatic encephalopathy.

Adult dose: 400–550 mg BD or t.d.s.
(Rifagut, rixmin, sibofix, torifx, zimigut tabs 200 mg, 400 mg and 550 mg; rifaximin syr 100 mg per 5 ml).

Teicoplanin It is a novel glycopeptide. 10 mg/kg q 12 hr for 3 doses and then 10 mg/kg/day q 24 hr IM or IV (bolus or slow infusion). It is bactericidal to most Gram-positive cocci and bacilli. As compared to vancomycin, teicoplanin has longer half life, can be given in a single dose IM. Catheter related phlebitis is uncommon. It can cross blood–brain barrier.

Adult dose: 6 mg/kg on day 1 followed by 3 mg/kg or *Adult dose* of 400 mg q 12 hr for 3 doses and then 400 mg daily.

Caution: Decrease the dose from 4th day onwards in patients with renal failure.
(Inj targocid, tecoplan, ticocin, ticonin, ticovan, zincoplanin 200 mg, 400 mg vials).

Tigecycline It is a derivative of minocycline belonging to a new class of antibiotics called glycylcyclines. 1.5 mg/kg as single dose (maximum 100 mg). Maintenance 1 mg/kg/day as IV infusion over 30–60 min. Effective against MRSA, Gram-negative MDR, Acinetobacter ESBL, and carbapenem-resistant *S. aureus*. Safety not established in children.

Adult dose: 100 mg as a single dose or 50 mg q 12 hr IV.

Caution: Hepatotoxicity.
(Inj tigifen, tgkem, tiganex, tigifec, tigez, tygacil, tigebax, tigilyn, tigimax, zutig, egytig, divercil 50 mg).

Tetracycline hydrochloride 25–50 mg/kg/day q 6 hr oral. Avoid in children below 8 yr because of risk of growth retardation and permanent staining of teeth. There is no place for tetracycline syrup in pediatric therapy. Avoid administration with food.

Adult dose: 1–2 gm daily in 4 divided doses.

C/I: Avoid <8 yr age; SLE, and hypersensitivity.

SE: GI disturbances, *Clostridium difficile*-induced diarrhea (pseudomembranous colitis), and candidiasis.
(Tetracyl, arcycline, lupiterra, achromycin (tetracycline) caps 250 mg, 500 mg; terramycin (oxytetracycline) cap 250 mg; inj achromycin 250 mg and 500 mg IV, inj achromycin 100 mg IM).

Vancomycin hydrochloride 40 mg/kg/day q 6 hr by IV infusion over 60 min or longer. 60 mg/kg/day q 6 hr for CNS infection. In pseudomembranous colitis, 40–50 mg/kg/day q 6–8 hr oral.

Adult dose: 500 mg q 6 hr or 1 g q 12 hr.

Caution: Flushing of face and neck ("red man" syndrome or flushing syndrome) if infusion is given rapidly. It occurs due to anaphylactoid reaction caused by degranulation of mast cells. It resolves spontaneously by reducing the rate of infusion.

SE: Anaphylaxis, ototoxicity, thrombocytopenia, hypotension, renal dysfunction.

Indic: Pencillinase-resistant staphylococcal and pneumococcal infections, and antibiotic-associated diarrhea.
(Inj forstaf, vancogen, vancocin, vancorin, vancotech, vanlid, vancomate, vanconis, vanking, valcosa 500 mg per vial; vanco-CP, vansafe CP, vantox CP 500 mg, 1 g in 10 ml vials; vancocin CP cap, 125 mg).

Chapter

7

Anticoagulants

Acenocoumarol 2 mon–1 yr: 0.2 mg/day, 1–5 yr: 0.09 mg/day, 6–10 yr: 0.07 mg/day, 11–18 yr: 0.06 mg/day single dose oral, administered at the same time daily. Maintain INR 2–3 times of normal.

SE: Skin necrosis, hemorrhage, priapism and hepatotoxicity.

Adult dose: Initial loading dose 16–28 mg, followed by 8–10 mg on day 2 and then 2–10 mg/day as maintenance.
(Acitrom tab 0.5 mg, 1 mg, 2 mg, 3 mg, 4 mg; sintrom tab 1 mg, 2 mg, 4 mg).

Heparin for thrombosis treatment 75 iu/kg IV bolus over 10 min followed by 28 i.u./kg/hr for <1 yr, 20 i.u./kg/hr for >1 yr as IV infusion. Adjust the dose to maintain anti-Xa activity 0.35–0.7 units/ml or aPTT between 60 and 85 seconds. DVT prophylaxis: 5000 i.u./dose SC q 8–12 hr until ambulatory.

Central line flush and patency The amount is calculated on the basis of volume of the catheter or slightly higher, 10 units/ml every 6–8 hrly.

Peripheral arterial catheters *in situ* Heparin infusion at 1 ml/hr (5 units/ml concentration).

Umbilical artery catheter (UAC) Heparin infusion at a concentration of 0.25–1.0 unit/ml; total heparin dose of 25–200 units/kg/day.

Other uses: Congenital heart defect palliated with systemic to pulmonary artery shunts, antibiotic lock technique for

HD catheter, atrial fibrillation, frostbite, anticoagulation in hemodialysis, ischemic heart disease, mechanical heart valve, peripheral arterial occlusion.

Caution: Keep protamine sulfate ready as an antidote to treat severe life-threatening bleed due to over dose of heparin. Last dose of heparin <30 min: 1 mg protamine/100 i.u. heparin, 30–60 min: 0.5–0.75 mg protamine/100 iu heparin, 60–120 min: 0.375–0.5 mg protamine/100 i.u. heparin, >120 min: 0.25–0.375 mg protamine/100 i.u. heparin.

SE: Major bleeding, thrombocytopenia and osteoporosis.

LOW MOLECULAR WEIGHT HEPARIN (ENOXAPARIN)

Recommended for prophylaxis and treatment of thrombo-embolic disorders specially for prevention of DVT following surgery. Administered with warfarin for inpatient treatment of DVT with or without pulmonary embolism and outpatient acute DVT without pulmonary embolism.

Subcutaneous <2 mon—Prophylaxis: 0.75 mg/kg/dose q 12 hrly; Treatment: 1.5 mg/kg/day q 12 hrly. ≥2 mon to ≥18 yr—Prophylaxis: 0.5 mg/kg/dose q 12 hrly; Treatment: 1 mg/kg/dose q 12 hrly.

Monitoring Maintain anti-factor Xa 0.5–1.0 units/ml in a sample taken 4–6 hr after the subcutaneous injection.

Indic: DIC, purpura fulminans, and thromboembolism.

C/I: Bleeding disorder, and GI ulcer.

SE: Major bleeding, spinal hematoma or epidural intracranial hemorrhage, heparin-induced thrombocytopenia (HIT) and thrombosis in heparin-induced thrombocytopenia (HITT), anemia, transaminitis and hyperkalemia.
(Inj heparin 5 ml vial containing 1000 units and 5000 units per ml, 0.83 mg = 100 units).

Phenindione 0.5 to 4 mg/kg/day q 12 hr oral. Rarely used due to hypersensitivity reactions, warfarin is preferred.

Adult dose: 100 mg on 1st day, 50 mg on 2nd day and then 12.5–50 mg/day q 12 hr.

Indic: Thromboembolism.

(Dindevan tab 50 mg).

Warfarin 0.05 to 0.34 mg/kg/day oral or parenteral. Adjust the dose to maintain desired prolongation of prothrombin time. The INR (international normalized ratio) should be maintained between 2 and 3.

Day 1: Initial loading dose 0.2 mg/kg/day once daily (if baseline INR 1–1.3).

Day 2 to 4: Additional loading doses depend upon patient's INR.

INR 1.1–1.3: Repeat the initial loading dose, INR 1.4–1.9: Dose is 50% of the initial loading dose, INR 3.1–3.5: Dose is 25% of the initial loading dose, INR >3.5: Hold the drug until INR <3.5, then restart at 50% of the previous dose.

Day ≥5: Maintenance dose depends upon patient's INR.

INR 1.1 to 1.4 : Increase the dose by 20% of previous dose, INR 1.5–1.9: Increase the dose by 10% of previous dose, INR 2–3: No change, INR 3.1–3.5: Decrease the dose by 10% of previous dose, INR >3.5: Hold the drug until INR <3.5, then restart at 20% less than the previous dose.

SE: Major hemorrhage, atheromatous embolism/cholesterol embolus syndrome, calciphylaxis (calcium uremic arteriolopathy), decreased bone mineral density, anaphylaxis skin necrosis and increased liver enzymes.

Warnings/precautions Prolonged dietary insufficiencies (vitamin K deficiency), heparin-induced thrombocytopenia, infection, hepatic impairment, renal impairment, thyroid disease, genomic variants in CYP2C9, elective surgery/procedure (discontinue for ~5 days before surgery; may reinstitute warfarin within 24 hr after surgery).

Adult dose: 5 mg daily for 2 days and then 2.5 mg daily single dose. (Uniwarfin, sofarin, warf, coumadin tab 1 mg, 2 mg, 3 mg, 5 mg; inj coumadin 50 mg vial).

Chapter

8

Anticonvulsants

ACTH 30–40 i.u. daily IM or SC for 4 wk followed by gradual tapering doses over next 2 wk.

Indic: Infantile spasms, West syndrome.

C/I: Cushing disease, tuberculosis, and fungal infections. (Inj corticotrophin, synacthen, acthar gel 40 units and 80 units per ml in 2 ml and 5 ml vials; Acton prolongatum 60 units per ml, 5 ml vials).

Brivaracetam (BRV)

It is a third generation antiepileptic racetam derivative and a 4-n-propyle analogue of levetiracetam.

Indic: Brivaracetam is indicated as adjunctive therapy for prevention and treatment of focal-onset seizures in pediatric patients aged 4 yr and older. Its anticonvulsant effects are believed to be due to its highly selective affinity for synaptic vesicle protein 2A (SV2A) in the brain.

Dose: The recommended starting dosage is 1–2 mg/kg/day, maximum dose of 4 mg/kg/day in two divided doses.

Adult dose: 50 mg twice daily, increments of 25 mg can be done, maximum dose 200 mg/day.

C/I: Hypersensitivity to brivaracetam.

Caution: Suicidal behavior and ideation.

Adverse effects: Somnolence, fatigue, dizziness, disturbance in coordination, impaired gait, bronchospasm and angioedema.

(Brevipil, briviact, brivazen, brivadix tabs 10 mg, 25 mg, 50 mg, 75 mg, and 100 mg; oral solution 10 mg/ml; inj 10 mg/ml single-dose 5 ml vial).

Cannabidiol

Indic: Cannabidiol is indicated for the treatment of seizures associated with Lennox-Gastaut syndrome or Dravet syndrome in pediatric patients aged 2 yr and older.

Dose: 2.5 mg/kg/dose twice daily, increase over 1 wk to maintenance dose of 5 mg/kg/dose twice daily. Weekly increase 2.5 mg/kg/dose with maximum 20 mg/kg/day.

C/I: Patients with a known hypersensitivity to cannabidiol or any of the product's components.

Adverse effects: Dry mouth, diarrhea, reduced appetite, drowsiness and fatigue.

(Epidiolex, gabinex, lexas 100 mg/ml oral solution).

Carbamazepine 10–30 mg/kg/day q 8 hr oral (maximum 1000 mg/day). Retard preparation can be given 12 hrly. Therapy should be initiated at 30% to 50% of initial target dose and increased every 5 to 7 days.

Adult dose: 100–200 mg once or twice daily initially, then increase to 400 mg q 8–12 hr. Maximum dose 1.5–2 g daily.

Indic: Partial tonic-clonic seizures, mesial temporal lobe epilepsy syndrome, myoclonus due to subacute sclerosing panencephalitis (SSPE), trigeminal neuralgia, prophylaxis for depressive psychosis and post-herpetic neuralgia.

C/I: Patients on monoamine oxidase inhibitors, AV conduction defects, bone marrow depression and porphyria. Avoid in patients with infantile and juvenile myoclonic epilepsy and absence epilepsy.

(Mazetol, carbatol, tegrital, zeptol tabs 100 mg, 200 mg, 400 mg; syrup mazetol, tegrital 100 mg per 5 ml; mazetol SR, salicarb SR, tegrital CR, zeptol CR, zen retard tabs 200 mg, 400 mg).

Cenobamate

Indic: Cenobamate is indicated for the treatment of focal-onset seizures in pediatric patients aged 4 yr and older.

Dose: The recommended starting dose of cenobamate for pediatric patients with focal-onset seizures is 12.5 mg once daily for 2 wk. The dose can be increased gradually based on response and tolerability, up to a maximum of 200 mg per day.

C/I: Cenobamate is contraindicated in patients with a known hypersensitivity to the drug or to any of its components.

Adverse effects: Somnolence, dizziness, fatigue, diplopia, and headache.

(Xcopri, xenotop tabs 12.5 mg, 25 mg, 50 mg, 100 mg, 150 mg, and 200 mg).

Clobazam 0.1 mg/kg/day initial dose. Usual maintenance dose 0.3–1 mg/kg/day at bedtime or q 12 hr. 1 mg/kg/day q 12 hr for 2–3 days for prophylaxis against febrile seizures.

Adult dose: 10–30 mg daily in 2 divided doses. Maximum daily dose 60 mg.

C/I: Myasthenia gravis, hypersensitivity to benzodiazepines.

Indic: Effective as an add-on drug in complex partial, generalized tonic or tonic-clonic seizures, absence attacks, myoclonic seizures, atonic seizures and Lennox-Gestaut syndrome, prophylaxis for febrile seizures, reflex epilepsy, continuous spike-waves during slow sleep (CSWS).

SE: Constipation, behaviour changes, aggression, sleep disturbances and weight gain.

(Frisium, clozam, cloba, lobazam tabs 5 mg, 10 mg, 20 mg).

Clonazepam 0.01–0.03 mg/kg/day q 8–12 hr oral. Increase every 3 days by 0.25–0.5 mg till a maximum dose of 0.2 mg/kg/day is reached.

Adult dose: Initially 0.5 mg q 12 hr, increase by 0.5 mg/day every 3–7 days till maintenance dose of 4–8 mg/day.

C/I: Significant liver disease, acute narrow angle glaucoma.

Indic: Add-on therapy for atonic, akinetic epilepsy, resistant absence attacks, myoclonus, infantile spasms, and Lennox-Gastaut syndrome.

(Clonotril, rivotril, lonazep, lonacen, zozep, sezolep, ozepam tabs 0.5 mg, 2 mg; melzap, zapiz tabs 0.25 mg, 0.5 mg, 1 mg, 2 mg).

Diazepam In status epilepticus above one mon of age: 0.2–0.5 mg/kg/dose IV, may be repeated at 3–5 min intervals. May administer IM if IV administration not possible but its efficacy is diminished and absorption is erratic. Maximum total dose <5 yr: 5 mg, >5 yr: 10 mg per-rectal dose 0.3–0.5 mg/kg/dose. Rapid IV bolus may cause apnea.

For symptomatic relief of anxiety, sedation and muscle relaxation, oral dose 0.1–0.3 mg/kg/day q 4–8 hr adjusted to clinical response. For neonatal tetanus, 0.5–5.0 mg/kg IV every 2 to 4 hr.

Adult dose: 5–50 mg/day in divided doses.

Flumazenil, a benzodiazepine antagonist, can reverse sedation but it may not reverse respiratory depression.

Indic: Status epilepticus, muscle spasms due to tetanus, febrile seizures, and anxiety states.

Caution: Watch for respiratory depression and hypotension.

C/I: Myasthenia gravis, acute narrow angle glaucoma, and paralytic ileus.

(Valium, placidox, anaxol tabs 2 mg, 5 mg, 10 mg; calmod, paxum tab 5 mg; calmpose tabs 5 mg, 10 mg; susp calmpose 2 mg per 5 ml; inj calmpose, paxum 10 mg per 2 ml ampoule; Direc 2 rectal diazepam 2 mg/ml; Rec-DZ rectal solution 2 mg/2.5 ml and 5 mg/5 ml).

Divalproex sodium

Indic: Treatment of manic episodes associated with bipolar disorder, monotherapy and adjunctive therapy of focal seizure with impaired awareness, typical and atypical absence seizures, prophylaxis of migraine headaches

Dose: The recommended starting dose of divalproex for pediatric patients with epilepsy is 10–15 mg/kg per day, divided into two doses. The dose can be titrated based on response and tolerability with maximum daily dose of 60 mg/kg/day.

C/I: A known hypersensitivity to valproate products or any of the product's components. It is also contraindicated in patients with hepatic disease, mitochondrial disorders, urea cycle disorders, or known mitochondrial DNA depletion syndromes.

Adverse effects: Hepatic and renal dysfunction, "Reye-like" syndrome, bleeding, alopecia, excessive weight gain, aggravation of polycystic ovarian disease.

(Depakote, epival, valcote, valpakine tabs: 125 mg, 250 mg and 500 mg).

Eslicarbazepine

Indic: Monotherapy or adjunctive therapy for the treatment of focal seizures in pediatric patients aged 4 yr and older.

Dose: The recommended starting dose of eslicarbazepine for pediatric patients with focal-onset seizures is 10–20 mg/kg per day, divided into two doses. The dose can be titrated based on response and tolerability, up to a maximum of 60 mg/kg per day, maximum dose being 800–1600 mg/day.

C/I: A known hypersensitivity to the drug or to any of its components.

Adverse effects: Hyponatremia, diplopia, vomiting, fatigue, vertigo, ataxia, blurred vision, and tremors.

(Aptiom, zebinix, esliceptin, zarote, tabs 200 mg, 400 mg, 600 mg, 800 mg).

Ethosuximide 10 mg/kg/day q 12 hr. The dose is increased every wk till control of absence seizures is achieved. Usual maintenance dose 20–40 mg/kg/day q 12 hr, maximum dose <6 yr: 500 mg/day and >6 yr: 1500 mg/day.

Adult dose: Initial dose 500 mg daily, increase by 250 mg every 4–7 days to a maximum dose of 1.0–1.5 g daily.

Indic: Absence attacks.

(Zarontin tab 250 mg; absenz syrup 250 mg per 5 ml).

Fenfluramine

Indic: It is indicated for the treatment of seizures associated with Dravet syndrome (hemicolonic seizures with jerking movements affecting one side of the body) in patients 2 yr of age and older.

Dose: The initial starting and maintenance dosage is 0.1 mg/kg twice daily, which can be increased wkly based on efficacy and tolerability.

Patients not on concomitant stiripentol: The maximum daily maintenance dosage is 0.35 mg/kg twice daily (maximum daily dosage of 26 mg).

Patients taking concomitant stiripentol plus clobazam: The maximum daily maintenance dosage is 0.2 mg/kg twice daily (maximum daily dosage of 17 mg).

C/I: Hypersensitivity to fenfluramine or any of the excipients, within 14 days of the administration of monoamine oxidase inhibitors.

Caution: Serotonin syndrome, a potentially life-threatening condition, may occur with it, particularly with concomitant administration of other serotonergic drugs.

Adverse effects: Decreased appetite, somnolence, sedation, lethargy, hypertension, drooling, salivary hypersecretion.
(Fintepla, cerovel oral solution: 2.2 mg/ml).

Fosphenytoin sodium It is a water-soluble prodrug of phenytoin and 1.5 mg fosphenytoin is equivalent to 1.0 mg phenytoin (expressed as phenytoin equivalents, PE).

Loading dose is 15–20 mg/kg IV. Maintenance 4–6 mg/kg/day IV/IM. Maximum IV infusion rate 3 mg/kg/min.

Adult dose: 15 mg/kg IV at a rate of 100–150 mg/min.

Indic: Status epilepticus, tonic-clonic seizures, and partial seizures.

C/I: Porphyria.
(Inj fosolin 2 ml ampoule, 10 ml vial; inj fosphen 2 ml ampoules containing 50 mg phenytoin equivalent per ml).

Gabapentin Initial dose 15 mg/kg/day q 8 hr, increase over several days to 30–60 mg/kg/day q 8 hr.

Adult dose: Initially 300 mg once daily on day 1, 300 mg q 12 hr on day 2, 300 mg q 8 hr on day 3, then increase by 300 mg increments in 3 divided doses; maximum dose is 800 mg q 8 hr.

Indic: Add on therapy for partial seizures, diabetic neuropathy and postherpetic neuralgia. Avoid below 12 yr.
(Gabapin, neurontin caps 300 mg, 400 mg).

Lacosamide Starting dose 1 mg/kg/day q 12 hr. Usual maintenance dose 2–12 mg/kg/day q 12 hr.

Adult dose: Initial dose 50 mg twice daily, with weekly increments of 100 mg/day. The usual maintenance dose is 200 to 400 mg/day.

Indic: Adjunctive therapy for refractory partial-onset seizures and diabetic neuropathy.

SE: Dizziness, headache, nausea, vomiting, ataxia, tremors, diplopia, fatigue, and somnolence.
(Lacasa, lacosam, lacoset tablets, 50 mg, 100 mg, 150 mg, 200 mg).

Lamotrigine Start with a low dose and increase gradually. Slow dose titration is necessary to reduce incidence of skin rash. Without sodium valproate or other enzyme inducers, 5–10 mg/kg/day q 12 hr p.o.; with sodium valproate 0.5–5 mg/kg/day q 24 hr oral; with enzyme inducing antiepileptic drugs start with 2 mg/kg/day and increase to 5–15 mg/kg/day q 12 hr. Maximum dose 15 mg/kg/day or 400 mg/day.

Adult dose: As a monotherapy 25 mg once daily for 2 wk, then 50 mg daily for 2 wk, then increase by 50–100 mg every 1–2 wk till seizures are controlled; usual dose is 100–200 mg/day. Co-administration with valproate; initially 25 mg on alternate days for 2 wk then 25 mg daily, then increase by 25–50 mg every 1–2 wk till response occurs; usual dose 100– 200 mg per day. When co-administered with enzyme inducing drugs, initial dose is 50 mg daily for 2 wk then 50 mg q 12 hr for 2 wk, then increase by up to 100 mg every 1–2 wk till response occurs; usually 200–400 mg daily q 12 hr. Maximum dose 800 mg/day.

C/I: Significant hepatic disease.

SE: Life-threatening hypersensitivity skin rash, dizziness, diplopia and aseptic meningitis.

Indic: Add-on therapy for partial seizures, Lennox-Gastaut syndrome (LGS), generalized seizures, atypical absence attacks,

atonic seizures and myoclonic seizures. It may be used as a first line drug for treatment of absence seizures with hair loss (Loose Anagen syndrome). It is useful for prevention of mood swings in bipolar disorder in adults.
(Lametec tabs 5 mg, 25 mg; lamitor tabs 25 mg, 50 mg, 100 mg).

Levetiracetam Start with 10 mg/kg/day q 12 hr, increase by 10 mg/kg every 2 wk up to 60 mg/kg/day. It can be given to newborn babies.

Adult dose: 1–3 g/day q 12 hr.

Adverse effects: Dizziness, drowsiness, tiredness, weakness, skin rash, anorexia, stuffy nose, irritable, depression, suicidal tendencies.

Indic: Add-on therapy for refractory partial seizures, generalized tonic-clonic seizures, absence attacks and astatic myoclonic seizures (Loose Anagen syndrome).
(Levroxa, levera, levecetam, levilex, levesam, keppra tabs 250 mg, 500 mg, 750 mg; torleva, levipil, elepsia, levilex tabs 250 mg, 500 mg, 750 mg, 1000 mg; syrup levroxa, levilex, levesam, keppra 100 mg/ml).

Lorazepam 0.05–0.1 mg/kg/dose (maximum 4 mg) over 2–5 min IV or IM, may repeat once after 10–15 min. Use 0.05 mg/kg/dose q 4–8 hr for sedation oral, IM or IV. The risk of hypotension and respiratory depression is low. The duration of effect is longer as compared to diazepam.

Adult dose: For anxiety, 2–3 mg daily in divided doses, for insomnia 1–2 mg at bedtime.

Indic: Uncontrolled status epilepticus, postanoxic myoclonus.

C/I: Narrow angle glaucoma, respiratory depression, and sleep apnea.
(Ativan, calmese, trapex, larpose, lorazine tabs 1 mg, 2 mg; inj calmese 2 mg per ml; inj loripam 10 mg/ml).

Midazolam Status epilepticus 0.2 mg/kg IM or IV bolus followed by 0.1–0.2 mg/kg/hr. For sedation during mechanical ventilation, 0.05–0.15 mg/kg/dose q 1–2 hr or continuous infusion at a rate of 0.2–1.0 μg/kg/min for neonates and 0.5–3.0 μg/kg/min for infants and children. For sedation, 0.05–0.1 mg/kg over 2 min, may repeat 0.05 mg/kg in 2–3 min intervals up to a total dose of 0.2 mg/kg. Onset of action within 1–5 min. Intranasal 0.3 mg/kg (5 mg/ml IV preparation), buccal route 0.3 mg/kg may be used for acute seizure control till intravenous access is established. For other details, refer to sections on Tranquillisers, Hypnotics, Sedatives and Antidepressants.

Adult dose: 0.07–0.08 mg/kg IM and 0.01–0.07 mg/kg IV.

C/I: Respiratory depression, shock, coma, and acute narrow angle glaucoma.

Caution: Avoid co-administration with erythromycin which may increase the depth and duration of sedation.
(Fulsed, mezolam, midosed, shortal 1 mg/ml in 5 ml and 10 ml vials and 5 mg/ml in 1 ml ampoule, zapiz 0.25 mg and 0.5 mg sublingual tabs, insed nasal spray or atomizer provides 0.5 mg midazolam per metered dose, midacip provides 1.25 mg/metered dose.)

Nitrazepam 0.25–1.0 mg/kg/day q 12 hr or single dose oral. Adult dose: 5–10 mg at bedtime.

C/I: Myasthenia gravis, porphyria, and acute narrow angle glaucoma.

Indic: Myoclonus, partial epilepsy, infantile spasms and insomnia.
(Nitravet, nitravan tabs 2.5 mg, 5 mg, 10 mg; nitrosun, nipan tabs 5 mg, 10 mg; hypnotex caps 5 mg, 10 mg).

Oxcarbazepine It is a keto analogue of carbamazepine. Start with 8–10 mg/kg/day BD to a maximum dose of 30 mg/kg/day (up to 1800 mg/day). Increase by increments of 10 mg/kg wkly.

Adult dose: Initially 300 mg q 12 hr, increase wkly by 600 mg/day. Usual dose is 600–2400 mg per day.

Indic: It is a first line drug for treatment of simple and complex partial seizures. Add-on drug for partial and generalized tonic-clonic seizures.

Caution: Avoid <6 yr age; use half of initial dose in renal failure.

SE: Fatigue, headache, dizziness, ataxia, hyponatremia, and skin rashes.
(Oxcarb, trioptal, oxep, oxrate, zenoxa, oleptal, oxetol, selzic, vinlep tabs 150 mg, 300 mg, 450 mg, 600 mg; syrup selzic and oxeptal 300 mg/5 ml).

Paraldehyde 0.1–0.2 ml/kg/per dose deep IM or 0.3 ml/kg/ per dose per rectum mixed with 3:1 coconut oil. Additional dose may be given after 30 min and then q 4–6 hr.

Indic: Uncontrolled status epilepticus.

C/I: Pulmonary and hepatic disease.

Caution: Proctitis and abscess at injection site. Ensure sterility. Use glass syringe as paraldehyde is not compatible with plastics. (Inj paraldehyde ampoule 5 ml, 1 g/ml).

Perampanel
Indic: Focal-onset seizures, with or without secondarily generalized seizures in patients with epilepsy 12 yr of age and older, primary generalized tonic-clonic seizures in patients with epilepsy at 12 yr of age and older.

Dose: Recommended starting dosage is 2 mg once daily taken orally at bedtime. Increase dosage by increments of 2 mg once daily no more frequently than at wkly intervals, to a maintenance dose of 8 to 12 mg/day.

Enzyme-inducing AEDs, including phenytoin, carbamazepine, and oxcarbazepine, cause a 50–67% reduction in its plasma levels. In patients receiving concomitant enzyme-inducing AEDs, the recommended starting dosage is 4 mg once daily taken orally at bedtime.

Caution: Suicidal behavior and ideation.

Adverse effects: Dizziness, somnolence, fatigue, irritability, falls, nausea, weight gain, vertigo, ataxia, headache, vomiting, confusion, abdominal pain, and anxiety.
(Fycompa, perampil, perampa tabs: 2 mg, 4 mg, 6 mg, 8 mg, 10 mg, and 12 mg; oral suspension: 0.5 mg/ml).

Phenobarbitone sodium Loading dose 15–20 mg/kg IV over 15 to 20 min at a rate of 1 mg/kg/min as slow IV bolus. May give additional 5 mg/kg doses every 15–30 min up to maximum total dose of 30 mg/kg. Maintenance dose 3–5 mg/kg/day q 12 hr or single dose at night p.o. or IV. Therapeutic level 15–40 mg/l.

Adult dose: 60–240 mg daily in 2–3 divided doses.

Indic: Neonatal seizures, tonic-clonic partial seizures, status epilepticus, and prophylaxis of febrile convulsions.

C/I: Porphyria, hepatic and renal disease, and severe asthma. (Gardenal, epigard, epikon tabs 30 mg, 60 mg; luminal tabs 30 mg, 100 mg; epilepsal, gardenal syrup 20 mg/5 ml; inj gardenal, phenobarbitone sodium 200 mg/ml ampoule).

Phenytoin sodium Loading dose 15–20 mg/kg slowly IV at a rate of 1 mg/kg/min. IV dose should be diluted in normal saline and not dextrose, given slowly under cardiac monitoring. Avoid IM as absorption is erratic. Maintenance dose 5–8 mg/kg/day q 8–12 hr or single dose oral. Therapeutic level 10–20 mg/l.

Adult dose: 150–300 mg daily in a single or two divided doses, increased as required to 200–400 mg/day.

Indic: Tonic-clonic seizures, partial epilepsy, cardiac arrhythmias, trigeminal neuralgia, epidermolysis bullosa, migraine, and status epilepticus.

C/I: Prophyria, heart block.

SE: Gingival hypertrophy, hirsutism, and ataxia.
(Dilantin and epileptin cap 100 mg; epsolin tab 100 mg; eptoin tabs 50 mg, 100 mg; susp dilantin 125 mg per 5 ml; syrup eptoin 30 mg per 5 ml; inj epsolin 2 ml ampoule 50 mg per ml; injection dilantin 25 mg/ml in 2 ml ampoules).

Prednisolone 2 mg/kg/day q 12 hr for 2–6 wk. Taper it over next 4–12 wk.

Indic: Infantile spasms, epilepsia partialis continua.
(Wysolone, nucort, omnacortil tabs 5 mg, 10 mg, 20 mg, predone, besone syrup 5 mg and 15 mg per 5 ml, kidpred 10 mg/5 ml).

Pregabalin 10 mg/kg/d in 2 divided doses.

Adult dose: 50 mg t.i.d. up to maximum of 300 mg/d.

Indic: Partial-onset seizures, fibromyalgia, postherpetic neuralgia, diabetic neuropathy, spinal cord injury, sciatica, plantar fasciitis.

(Pregalin, pregasafe, pregabid, prebaxe caps 25 mg, 50 mg, 75 mg, 100 mg, 150 mg, 200 mg, 300 mg).

Primidone Newborn: 12–20 mg/kg/day q 6–12 hr, children <8 yr: 10–25 mg/kg/day q 8–12 hr, children >8 yr: 125–1500 mg/day p.o. adjusted to patient's tolerance and response (maximum dose 2 g/24 hr). Therapy should be initiated at 1/3 to 1/2 of initial dose.

Adult dose: Start with 50 mg/d and gradually increase every 2–3 wk up to maximum daily dose of 750 mg.

Indic: Partial and tonic-clonic seizures.

(Mysoline tab 250 mg).

Pyridoxine For pyridoxine dependent seizures: Give 50–100 mg/dose IM or rapid IV, under EEG control. Maintenance dose 50–100 mg/day oral (For formulations, *see* Vitamins section).

Thiopental 5–10 mg/kg loading dose IV over 2–5 min followed by 2–10 mg/kg/hr continuous infusion for uncontrolled status epilepticus, the patient will need mechanical ventilation.

Adult dose: 100–150 mg over 10–15 seconds; repeat if required after 20–30 seconds.

(Inj pentothal 250 mg, 500 mg, 1 g vials; inj anesthal, intraval sodium, thiosol 500 mg, 1 g ampoules or vials).

Topiramate Initial dose 0.5–1.0 mg/kg/day, gradually increased every 2 wk up to 5–10 mg/kg/day q 12 hr or single daily dose. For migraine prophylaxis, give one-half the dose (2 mg/kg single dose per day).

Adult dose: 25 mg daily for 1 wk, increase by 25–50 mg daily at 1–2 wk intervals. Usual dose is 200–400 mg in 2 divided doses; maximum 800 mg/day.

Indic: Add-on therapy for refractory partial seizures, primary generalized tonic-clonic seizures, absence seizures, Lennox-Gastaut syndrome, and West syndrome.

SE: Anorexia, weight loss, dizziness, blurring of vision, glaucoma, metabolic acidosis, ataxia, and renal calculi.

(Topamaximum 25 mg; topex tabs 25 mg, 100 mg, topirol tabs 25 mg, 50 mg, 100 mg).

Rufinamide

Indic: It is indicated for adjunctive treatment of seizures associated with Lennox-Gastaut syndrome (LGS) in pediatric patients 1 yr of age and older.

Dose: The recommended starting dose of rufinamide for pediatric patients with Lennox-Gastaut syndrome is 10 mg/kg per day, divided into two doses. The dose can be titrated based on response and tolerability, up to a maximum of 45 mg/kg per day, not to exceed 3200 mg per day, in two divided doses.

C/I: Patients with a known hypersensitivity to the drug or to any of its components.

Caution: Use caution, when administering rufinamide with other drugs that shorten the QT interval.

Adverse effects: Headache, dizziness, fatigue, somnolence, and nausea.

(Banzel, inovelon, irufamide, rufinade, film-coated tablets: 200 mg (pink), 400 mg (pink), oral suspension: 40 mg/ml).

Stiripentol

Indic: It is indicated for the treatment of seizures associated with Dravet syndrome in patients 2 yr of age and older taking clobazam.

Dose: 50 mg/kg/day, orally administered in 2 or 3 divided doses. The dose can be titrated based on response and tolerability, up to a maximum of 100 mg/kg per day. Capsules must be swallowed whole with a glass of water during a meal. Capsules should not be broken or opened.

Caution: Suicidal behavior and ideation, neutropenia and thrombocytopenia. Blood counts should be obtained prior to starting treatment and then every 6 mon.

Adverse effects: Somnolence, decreased appetite, agitation, ataxia, decreased weight, hypotonia, nausea, tremor, dysarthria, and insomnia.
(Diacomit caps 250 mg and 500 mg).

Valproate sodium Initial dose 10–15 mg/kg/day q 8–12 hr oral, can increase up to maximum of 60 mg/kg/day (increments of 5–10 mg/kg/day at wkly intervals). Therapeutic level 50–100 mg/l. In status epilepticus, 20 mg/kg loading dose followed by 5–10 mg/kg/dose q 8 hr. Infuse over one hr up to a maximum of 20 mg/min.

Adult dose: 600 mg daily in 2 divided doses, increase by 200 mg at wkly intervals. The usual adult dose is 1–2 g daily up to a maximum of 5 g.

Indic: Broad spectrum for majority of epilepsies, e.g. generalized tonic-clonic partial seizures, absence attacks, myoclonic, atonic, frequent febrile seizures, Lennox-Gastaut syndrome, West syndrome and juvenile myoclonic epilepsy.

C/I: Active liver disease, urea cycle disorders.

SE: Hepatic and renal dysfunction, "Reye-like" syndrome, bleeding, alopecia, excessive weight gain, aggravation of polycystic ovarian disease, and false positive urine sugar test.
(Encorate chrono, epilex chrono, manoval, magprol CR, torvate chrono tab 200 mg; valparin chrono, cinaval chrono tabs 200 mg, 300 mg, 400 mg, 500 mg; valprol CR 200 mg, 300 mg, 500 mg; syrup valparin, epilex 200 mg per 5 ml; injection encorate 100 mg/ml for IV infusion as 5 ml vial).

Vigabatrin It is a structural analogue of gamma-aminobutyric acid (GABA) which irreversibly inhibits the enzyme GABA transaminase. Initial dose 50–150 mg/kg/day. The dose is gradually increased by 30 mg/kg every 5 days. Stop if there is no response in 2 wk.

Adult dose: 1.0 g daily q 12 hr. Increase gradually at wkly interval up to 3.0 g per day q 12 hr.

Indic: Add-on drug for resistant partial seizures, infantile spasms especially due to tuberous sclerosis and Lennox-Gastaut syndrome. It can be combined with valproate and intravenous immunoglobulins (IVIG). May be used as a first-line drug for infantile spasms along with steroids.

SE: Weight gain, hyperkinesia, visual field defects and retinopathy.

(Sabril and vegarin tab 500 mg; viganext, viby 500 mg sachets).

Zonisamide 4–8 mg/kg/day q 12 hr. Avoid below 16 yr.

Adult dose: 50 mg daily q 12 hr. Increase by 50 mg/day at wkly intervals. Usual dose is 200–600 mg/day q 12 hr.

Indic: Add-on therapy for partial and tonic-clonic seizures, atypical absences, Lennox-Gastaut syndrome and juvenile myoclonic epilepsy.

(Zonisep caps 25 mg, 50 mg; zonegram tabs 25 mg, 100 mg; zonit, zonimid, zonicare tabs 50 mg, 100 mg).

Chapter

9

Antiemetics

Chlorpromazine hydrochloride 0.5 mg/kg/dose q 4–6 hr oral or IM. Avoid in children below 1 yr. Maximum dose 1– 5 yr: 40 mg/day, >5 yr: 75 mg/day.

Adult dose: 25–50 mg 3–4 times/day.

Indic: Intractable hiccups, agitation, and chorea.

Caution: Coma, bone marrow suppression, pheochromocytoma. (Chlorpromazine liquid 25 mg and 100 mg/5 ml; largactil megatil, clozine, quietal, thorazine tabs 10 mg, 25 mg, 50 mg, 100 mg, 200 mg; Inj 25 mg/ml in 2 ml ampoule).

Dimenhydrinate 5 mg/kg/day q 6 hr oral, IM or IV. Avoid in children below 2 yr. Maximum dose 2–6 yr: 75 mg/day, 6–12 yr: 150 mg/day.

Adult dose: 50–100 mg q 8–12 hr, injectable 50–100 mg IM q 4–6 hr.

Indic: Motion sickness, vertigo, radiation or cancer chemotherapy induced nausea.
(Dramamine, draminate, gravol tab 50 mg; dramamine liquid 15.625 mg per 5 ml; inj 50 mg per ml).

Often combined with cinnarizine in a fixed dose combination for motion sickness (cinnarizine 20mg + dimenhydrinate 40 mg. Vertizae, Spinfree, Dizitac, Stugeron Plus, Gemvert, Cinez-D tablets).

Domperidone 0.2–0.5 mg/kg/dose every 4 to 8 hr.
Adult dose: 10–20 mg 3–4 times a day before meals. Maximum dose 80 mg daily.

Indic: Acute nausea and vomiting due to any cause.

C/I: Prolactinuria, GI hemorrhage, epilepsy, hepatic impairment.

SE: Gynecomastia in males and galactorrhea in females.

(Domstal, domperon, domi, emitin, gastractiv,gastrium, motinorm, nautigo, nausidome, normodil tab 10 mg; dom-DT, domperi DT, domperon tabs 5 mg, 10 mg; domstal, dom, domperon, gastrium, motinorm, nausidome susp 5 mg/5 ml; domperon, motinorm drops 10 mg per ml. Domstal-CZ and vertigil contain domperidone 15 mg + cinnarizine 20 mg for vertigo and motion sickness).

Granisetron It is a stronger 5-HT3 binding anti-serotonin, which is 10–15 times more potent than ondansetron. Children >2 yr and adults: 10–20 µg/kg/dose IV over 15–60 min before chemotherapy, the same dose may be repeated 2–3 times following chemotherapy. Alternatively, a single dose of 40 µg/kg/dose 15–60 min before chemotherapy has been used.

Adult dose: 1 mg twice daily or 2 mg once daily p.o., initial dose is administered 1 hr prior to cytotoxic therapy.

Caution: Subacute intestinal obstruction or ileus, congenital long QT syndrome or other risk factors for QT prolongation.

(Granicip, grandem, graniset, grantis, granitero cadigran tabs 1 mg, 2 mg; syrup grandem, graniforce, granisol, granny, granday, granilet, granirex 1 mg/5 ml, injection 1 mg per ml).

Itopride hydrochloride It is a prokinetic which is a derivative of benzamide. It has anticholinesterase activity as well as dopamine D2 receptor antagonist. It is available in combination with several proton pump inhibitors. The usual dose is 0.1–0.2 mg/kg (maximum 10 mg/dose) q 6 to 8 hrly. There is limited clinical experience in children.

Adult dose: 50–150 mg t.d.s.

Indic: Dyspepsia, gastroesophageal reflux disease, GI motility disorder.

(Ganton, itoflux, retride 50 mg and 150 mg tabs).

Metoclopramide hydrochloride Gastroesophageal reflux or GI dysmotility or galactagogue 0.1–0.2 mg/kg/dose q 6 to 8 hr oral, IM, IV up to a maximum of 0.8 mg/kg/day. For chemotherapy induced emesis, 2–3 mg/kg/dose before and after chemotherapy.

Adult dose: Parenteral dose 10 mg IV over 1–2 min period, oral dose 10 mg 30 min before each meal.

SE: Use with caution due to risk of extrapyramidal side effects. Avoid below 18 yr.

C/I: Epilepsy, pheochromocytoma.
(Perinorm, maxeron, emenil, metotid, reglan, sigmet, tomid tab 10 mg; metocontin CR-tab 15 mg, perinorm CD cap 15 mg; perinorm, reglan, metotid syrup 5 mg per 5 ml; inj 5 mg per ml as 2 ml ampoule.

Ondansetron hydrochloride Selective 5-HT3 receptor antagonist. Oral dose <4 yr: 2 mg q 4 hr, 4–11 yr: 4 mg q 4 hr, >12 yr: 8 mg q 4 hr. IV dose for >3 yr old 0.15–0.45 mg/kg/dose 30 min before and 4 and 8 hr after emetogenic drugs.

Adult dose: 8 mg orally or slow IV q 4 hr. IV injection can be given after the age of 4 yr.

Indic: Chemotherapy and radiotherapy induced emesis, postoperative nausea and vomiting (prophylaxis).

C/I: Children <3 yr age, liver dysfunction, suspected or proven prolonged QT syndrome, hypersensitivity.
(Ondem MD, ondace, emeset, periset, vomis, ondet, zofer tabs 4 mg, 8 mg; ondem, ondace syrup 2 mg/5 ml, zofram rectal suppository 16 mg; antemiss, emeset, domi up, ondamac, vomif, vomiz, zonda inj 2 mg per ml in 2 ml and 4 ml ampoule).

Palonosetron Nausea and vomiting associated with cancer chemotherapy. Children 1 mon to 17 yr: 20 µg/kg (maximum 1,500 µg) by infusion over 15 min to be given approx 30 min before chemotherapy.

Adult dose: 500 µg single dose oral 1 hr prior to chemotherapy. Intravenous 250 µg single dose, to be given over 30 sec, 30 min before chemotherapy. Do not repeat in next 7 days. Prophylaxis of postoperative nausea and vomiting: 75 µg single dose immediately before induction of anesthesia.

C/I: Intestinal obstruction or ileus, rapid injection may cause transient visual changes. May cause QT prolongation.

(Eme OD tab 0.5 mg; inj. chepatron, emecad, pasetron, plaonget, palonew palnox, palzen, emecad, instantine

Prochlorperazine For children >2 yr of age or >10 kg: 0.4 mg/kg/day q 6–8 hr oral. IM dose is half.

SE: Extrapyramidal symptoms and orthostatic hypotension can occur.

Adult dose: 5–10 mg 8–12 hrly oral.

(Stemetil, emidoxyn, zemetil, ingametil, protil tabs 5 mg, 25 mg; inj 12.5 mg per ml as 1 ml ampoule and 10 ml vial).

Promethazine hydrochloride *See* Antihistamines.

Promethazine theoclate 0.5 mg/kg/dose q 8–12 hr oral. Administer first dose 1–2 hr before travel.

Adult dose: 125 mg night before travel or 2 hr before journey; for nausea 25 mg stat followed by 25 mg in the evening and then daily at bedtime.

Indic: Motion sickness.

C/I: Children <2 yr; asthma, sleep apnea.

(Avomine tab 25 mg, avomine syrup 6.25 mg/5 ml).

Trifluoperazine hydrochloride It is used for treatment of nausea and vomiting.

Child: 3–5 yr maximum dose 1 mg in divided doses; 6–12 yr maximum 4 mg in divided doses.

Adult dose: 1–2 mg 12 hrly, maximum dose 6 mg.

SE: Extrapyramidal side effects, CNS depression, somnolence, agitation, restlessness.

Indic: Nausea and vomiting due to radiation sickness and chemotherapy.

C/I: Comatose state, hepatic damage, children below 3 yr of age, bone marrow depression.

(Stelazine, neocalm tab 10 mg; psycalm tabs 1 mg, 5 mg).

Chapter

10

Antifungal Agents

Conventional Amphotericin B

Neonatal dose 1.0–1.5 mg/kg/day IV once daily, infuse over 2–6 hr. Initiate therapy at target dose.

Pediatric dose Test dose: 0.1 mg/kg IV over 20–60 min (not to exceed 1 mg). Initial dose: 0.25 mg/kg/day OD, gradually increase by 0.25 mg/kg/day to 1.0–1.5 mg/kg/day as IV infusion in 5% dextrose over 4 to 6 hr.

Adult dose: Test dose 1 mg IV over 20–30 min. Maintenance dose: 0.3–1.0 mg/kg/d (maximum 1.5 mg/kg/d) as IV infusion in 5% dextrose over 4–6 hr.

Indic: Candidemia, aspergillosis, blastomycosis, talaromycosis coccidioidomycosis, sporotrichosis cryptococcosis, histoplasmosis, leishmaniasis and fungal endocarditis.

Precautions: Prevent exposure of medicine to light during administration. Monitor serum potassium during therapy and frequently change IV site to prevent phlebitis. Monitor for hepatic and renal toxicity.

SE: During intravenous administration, it may cause chills, fever, vomiting and headache (may premedicate with NSAID ± diphenhydramine or hydrocortisone). Hypokalemia, hypomagnesemia, hypotension, thrombophlebitis, anemia, arthralgia, myalgia, nephrolithiasis, hyposthenuria and deranged renal functions are recognized adverse effects.

(Inj fungizone, fungisome, amfocan, amfotex, AmBisome, fungicin, amphonex, amphotret, phosome 50 mg/vial.)

Liposomal amphotericin B This formulation has been developed to reduce the toxicity of amphotericin B while retaining its therapeutic efficacy. The usual dose is 3–5 mg/kg/day IV once daily as infusion over 2 hr in 5% dextrose.

Adult dose: 3–6 mg/kg/day once daily as infusion over 2 hr in 5% dextrose.

Indic: Candidemia, aspergillosis, blastomycosis, coccidioidomycosis, cryptococcosis, histoplasmosis, leishmaniasis, invasive mucormycosis, sporotricosis and fungal endocarditis.

SE: Lyophilized liposomal amphotericin B provides targeted drug delivery with reduced renal and hepatotoxicity and minimal infusion-related complications.
(Inj fungisome provides liposomal amphotericin B in 10 mg, 25 mg and 50 mg vials for IV use, inj amphoject, amphonex, sporotar, ambisome 50 mg single dose vials).

Capsofungin 70 mg/m^2/day on day 1 followed by 50 mg/m^2/day with a maximum dose of 70 mg/day once daily as IV infusion in normal saline slowly over 1 hr.

Adult dose: 70 mg on day 1 followed by 50 mg/day once daily as IV infusion over 1 hr.

Indic: Invasive candidiasis, aspergillosis resistant or intolerant to amphotericin B, empirical therapy for presumed fungal infection in febrile neutropenic patients.

SE: Thrombophlebitis, fever, diarrhea, rash, hypotension, increased liver enzymes, hypokalemia, anemia, increased creatinine. Concomitant use of caspofungin and ciclosporin lead to a more frequent increase of liver enzymes.
(Casporan, cancidas, canducid, kabifungin 50 mg, 70 mg vials).

Clotrimazole Topical use for oral and vaginal candidiasis, and tinea infections. Significant drug interactions exist, requiring frequent dose adjustments.
(Candid, canesten, decand, lotril, surfaz lotion and gel 1% and 2%, candid, canfem, lotril and surfaz 100 mg vaginal pessaries in a pack of 6).

Fluconazole For mucosal candidiasis, 6 mg/kg on day 1, then 3–6 mg/kg/day once daily for at least 2 wk. Invasive systemic candidiasis 6–12 mg/kg/day once daily (not to exceed 600 mg/day) for 2 wk after clearance from blood and resolution of symptoms. Dosing same for oral and IV routes, IV infusion is given over 1–2 hr.

Adult dose: Mucosal candidiasis 200 mg on day 1, then 100–200 mg once daily for at least 14 days. Systemic candidiasis: 800 mg on day 1 followed by 400 mg/day once daily for 2 wk after clearance from blood and resolution of symptoms.

SE: Headache, rash, nausea, abdominal pain, torsades de pointes and hepatic dysfunction.

Indic: Candidiasis, cryptococcal meningitis, and as a prophylactic agent for prevention of fungal infections in an immunocompromised host, onychomycosis, tinea infection, treatment and prophylaxis of coccidioidomycosis and histoplamosis.
(Flucos, zocon, syscan, flumed, fluzon, flucan, flubit, flucon, fluzole tabs 50 mg, 150 mg, 200 mg; conflu, cancap, fungicon tabs 50 mg, 150 mg; injection 2 mg per ml in a bottle of 100 ml physiological saline).

Flucytosine Neonates: 75 mg/kg/d p.o. q 6–8 hr. Children and adults: 50–150 mg/kg/day p.o. q 6 hr. Maximum daily dose 2 g. It should not be used as a monotherapy for treatment of fungal sepsis.

Indic: Systemic yeast infections (Aspergillosis, Candida, Cryptococcus).

SE: Bone marrow depression, neutropenia, thrombocytopenia, alopecia, GI disturbances, hepatic and renal dysfunction. It is usually administered in combination with amphotericin B with a greater risk of side effects.
(Ancobon caps 250 mg, 500 mg, cytoflu tab 500 mg).

Griseofulvin Use in onychomycosis and tinea infections. Microsize 10–20 mg/kg/day in single or 2 divided doses, maximum dose 1000 mg/day; Ultramicrosize 5–15 mg/kg/day in single or 2 divided doses, maximum dose 750 mg/day;

duration depends on site of infection: 2–4 wk for tinea corporis, 4–6 wk for tinea capitis, 4–8 wk for tinea pedis and 4–6 mon for tinea unguium.

Adult dose: Microsize 500–1000 mg in single or two divided doses; ultramicrosize 375–750 mg in single or 2 divided doses with meals.

C/I: Porphyria, monilial infection.

SE: Rash, urticaria, headache, confusion, diarrhea, dizziness, fatigue and GI disturbances.
(Grisovin, idifulvin tab 125 mg; idifulvin, fluvin, grisactin forte, walavin tab 250 mg; dermonorm, grisovin-FP tabs 250 mg, 500 mg).

Hamycin Local application after each feed for oral thrush. (Hamycin 2,00,000 units per ml susp).

Itraconazole 5–10 mg/kg/day in 2 divided doses, maximum dose: 200 mg/day.

Adults: 200–400 mg/day in a single or two divided doses orally for 12 wk.

Indic: Allergic bronchopulmonary aspergillosis, blastomycosis, candidiasis coccidioidomycosis, cryptococcal meningitis histoplasmosis, microsporidiosis, sporotrichosis, talaromycosis and tinea capitis.

SE: Nausea, vomiting, rash, raised liver enzymes, edema, hypokalemia, peripheral neuropathy and headache.

Caution: Do not use in patients with ventricular dysfunction and congestive heart failure.
(Itrole, itaspor, canditral, candistat, candiforce, sporanox cap 100 mg).

Ketoconazole ≥2 yr 3.3–6.6 mg/kg/day, p.o. once daily. Maximum dose 400 mg/day.

Adult dose: 200–400 mg/day once or twice daily after meals.

Topical: Use shampoo every 3–4 days for up to 8 wk for control of dandruff.

Indic: Blastomycosis, coccidioidomycosis, histoplasmosis, paracoccidioidomycosis, chromomycosis.

C/I: Children below 2 yr and patients with hepatic dysfunction.

Caution: Do not use as first line treatment for systemic infections and avoid using for cutaneous infections because of serious adverse effects (hepatotoxicity) and significant drug interactions.

SE: Suppression of testosterone synthesis and glucocorticoid secretion which can be harnessed for clinical use.
(Funazole, ketozole, ketsan, ketnix, kenazol, sebizole, fungicide, nizral tab 200 mg; nizral susp 100 mg per 5 ml, also available as 2% cream, foam, shampoo and soap).

Micafungin 1.5–3.0 mg/kg/day IV once daily, titrate to a higher dose up to 4–8 mg/kg/day as IV infusion over 1 hr depending on clinical response.

Adult dose: 100–150 mg once daily as IV infusion over 1 hr.

Indic: Invasive candidiasis, aspergillosis resistant or intolerant to amphotericin B, and prophylaxis against invasive fungal infections.

SE: Bone marrow suppression, phlebitis, fever, diarrhea, rash, increased liver enzymes, anemia, renal dysfunction.
(Micafung plus, mycamine 50 mg vial).

Miconazole ≥2 yr: Apply topical cream or powder BD for up to 1 mon.

Adult dose: ≥16 yr: Apply 50 mg buccal tablet over the gum region OD for 14 days.

Indic: Local treatment of candidiasis, tinea infections.

SE: Pruritus, skin rash, contact dermatitis (topical cream/ powder), nausea, diarrhea, and headache.
(Daktarin tab 50 mg used for oral application, candizole, agrozole, decanazole cream 2% for topical skin application and as vaginal pessaries).

Nystatin Use in candidiasis and prevention of secondary fungal infection in peritoneal dialysis. Neonates/infants: 2,00,000– 10

4,00,000 units/dose 4 times a day; pediatric: 4,00,000–6,00,000 units/dose 4 times a day, administer half of the dose to each side of mouth, swish in the mouth and retain for several min before swallowing for oral candidiasis, 0.5 to 1 million units/dose q 8 hr orally for diarrhea due to *Candida albicans*.

Adult dose: Same as pediatric dose.

SE: Nausea, vomiting, diarrhea, stomach pain.

(Mycostatin, nystan, nystatin tab 5,00,000 units; nystatin susp 1,00,000 units per ml).

Sertaconazole Topical long-acting antifungal agent single or two applications per day. Use for cutaneous candidiasis, seborrheic dermatitis and tinea infections (corporis, pedis).

SE: Burning sensation of skin, contact dermatitis, skin tenderness and xeroderma.

(Sertaconazole nitrate cream available as serta, ertaczo, gyno-dermofix cream).

Terbinafine hydrochloride Tinea capitis in children ≥4 yr: <25 kg: 125 mg p.o. once daily, 25–35 kg: 187.5 mg p.o. once a day, >35 kg: 250 mg p.o. once daily for 6 wk; for onychomycosis 10–20 kg: 62.5 mg oral p.o. once daily, 20–40 kg: 125 mg p.o. once daily, >40 kg: 250 mg single dose per day for 6–12 wk.

Adult dose: 250 mg single dose daily for 6–12 wk.

Indic: Fungal infections of skin, nails and hair and sporotrichosis.

SE: Headache, diarrhea, nausea, rash, pruritus and leukopenia, increased serum transaminases, thrombotic microangiopathy, taste and smell disturbances.

(Tebina, exifine, zimig, fungotek, finlin, sebifin tab 250 mg; tebina, exifine 125 mg DT, sebifin, dermafine, tebif, tebina, zimig, terbinaforce 1% skin cream and lotion).

Voriconazole 2–12 yr loading dose 9 mg/kg q 12 hr for 2 doses followed by 8 mg/kg/dose IV q 12 hr; >12 yr loading dose 6 mg/kg q 12 hr for 2 doses followed by 4 mg/kg/dose IV q 12 hr. Oral dose: 9 mg/kg/dose q 12 hrly.

Adult dose: 200 mg (maximum 600 mg/d) p.o. q 12 hr above 40 kg; 100 mg (maximum 300 mg/d) p.o. q 12 hr below 40 kg body weight. IV loading dose 6 mg/kg q 12 hr for first 24 hr followed by maintenance dose of 4 mg/kg q 12 hr.

Indic: Invasive aspergillosis, candidemia in non-neutropenic patients, fluconazole-resistant Candida infections and scedosporiosis.

SE: Visual changes, hypotension, vasodilation, edema, fever, chills, skin rash, hepatotoxicity, torsades de pointes, acute kidney injury.

(Verz, fungivor, voritek, voritop, voraze tabs 50 mg, 200 mg; inj 200 mg ampoule).

Chapter

11

Antihistaminics

Azatadine maleate 6–12 yr: 0.5–1 mg twice a day. >12 yr: 1 mg twice a day.
(Zadine tab 1 mg; syrup 0.5 mg/5 ml).

Bilastine It is a second generation H1-receptor antagonist which is non-sedating and has a prolonged duration of effect up to 24 hr. It is useful against atopic dermatitis, urticaria and allergic rhinitis. It is best given on empty stomach in children above 6 yr. The usual dose is 10–20 mg/day.

Adult dose: 20–40 mg once daily on empty stomach.

C/I: Kidney damage, urinary retention, fructose intolerance breastfeeding.

Caution: The risk and severity of QT_c prolongation is increased when cetirizine is combined with bilastine. It can be combined with leukotriens to enhance anti-allergic effect in patients with hyperactive airway disease.
(Bilasure, bilazap, bilagra, bilazest, bilacip, bilafav tab 20 mg; syrup bilastine 10 mg/5 ml. Combo formulations are available with montelukast as bilasure-M, bilagra-M, bilazap-M, bilazest-M tablets containing bilastine 20 mg + montelukast 10 mg, syrup for children is available with bilastine 10 mg and montelukast 4 mg).

Cetirizine dihydrochloride 6 mo–2 yr: 2.5 mg OD; 2–6 yr: 2.5 mg BD or 5 mg OD, >6 yr: 5–10 mg oral OD or BD.

Adult dose: 10–20 mg daily q 12–24 hr.

Caution: Avoid in children below 6 mon.

(Cetzine, alerid, allerzine, cetcip, cetrine, cetiriz, citrazan, CZ3, zyncef, zyncet, zyrtec tab 10 mg; cetrizet, sizon tab 5 mg; syrup 5 mg per 5 ml).

Chlorpheniramine maleate Children 0.35 mg/kg/day q 4–6 hr. According to age: 1–6 yr: 1 mg, 6–12 yr: 2 mg, >12 yr: 4 mg q 4 to 6 hr. 0.2 mg/kg IV for drug induced dystonic reaction.

Adult dose: 4 mg q 4–6 hr or sustained release 12 mg at bedtime.

Parenteral: 0.2 mg/kg IV for drug-induced dystonic reaction. Adjunct in the emergency treatment of anaphylactic shock. 1 mg/kg SC, IM or slow IV over 1–2 min; up to 4 times/day.

Adult dose: 10–20 mg/dose (maximum 40 mg/day).

(Cadistin, piriton tab 4 mg; polaramine tabs 2 mg, 6 mg; syrup 0.5 mg per 5 ml; inj chlorpheniramine maleate 10 mg/ml ampoule; piriton expectorant 2.5 mg per 5 ml, corex contains chlorpheniramine maleate 4 mg, codeine phosph 10 mg per 5 ml; febrex plus syrup contains chlorpheniramine maleate 1.0 mg, phenylpropanolamine hydrochloride 12.5 mg, paracetamol 125 mg per 5 ml, cosome syrup contains chlorpheniramine maleate 4 mg, dextromethorphan hydrobromide 10 mg, phenylpropanolamine hydrochloride 25 mg per 10 ml).

Cinnarizine 5 to 12 yr: 7.5 to 15 mg q 8 hr oral; >12 yr: 25 to 75 mg q 8 hr.

Adult dose: 25 to 75 mg q 8 hr. Maximum dose: 225 mg/day.

Indic: Vertigo, tinnitus, nystagmus, nausea, and vomiting; prophylaxis of motion sickness.

(Stugeron, Vertigon, Cinzan, Cintigo 25 and 50 mg tab).

Clemastine fumarate 1 to 3 yr: 0.25–0.5 mg BD, 3–6 yr: 0.5 mg BD, 6–12 yr: 0.5–1 mg BD; >12 yr: 1 mg BD Avoid below 1 yr of age.

Adult dose: 1 mg twice a day.

Indic: Allergic rhinitis, skin allergy, and conjunctivitis.

C/I: Narrow angle glaucoma.
(Tavegyl, clamist, tavist tab 1 mg; syrup 0.5 mg/5 ml).

Cyproheptadine hydrochloride 0.25–0.5 mg/kg/day q 8–12 hr oral. Maximum dose 2–6 yr: 12 mg/day, 7–14 yr: 16 mg/day.

Adult dose: 4 mg 3–4 times a day, usually 4–20 mg daily, maximum dose 32 mg daily.

Indic: Appetite stimulant, skin allergy, prophylaxis of migraine.

C/I: Glaucoma, urinary retention, asthma, therapy with MAO inhibitors, hypersensitivity, neonates.
(Ciplactin, peritol, practin tab 4 mg; cypon cap 2 mg; cypon, peritol, ciplactin, cyp-L, practin-EN syrup 2 mg per 5 ml).

Desloratidine Children 1–5 yr: 1 mg; 6–11 yr: 2.5 mg; >12 yr: 5 mg single daily dose.

Adult dose: 5 mg single daily dose.
(D-Loratin, deslor; loreta tab 5 mg).

Dimenhydrinate is a histamine H1 antagonist associated with sedation and anti-emetic effects. It is a theoclate salt composed of diphenhydramine and 8-chlorotheophylline is a 1:1 ratio. It is used to prevent or treat nausea, vomiting and diziness associated with motion sickness (land, air, sea). Dosage schedule in children: <2 yr not recommended, 2–6 yr 12.5–25 mg (maximum 75 mg/d), 6–11 yr 25–50 mg (maximum 150 mg/d) start medication ½–1 hr before travel, may repeat every 4–6 hr in a case of long journey.

Adult dose: 50–100 mg starting ½–1 hr before travel (maximum 400 mg/d). It can be repeated every 4–6 hr during the course of travel.

C/I: Chronic obstructive pulmonary disease, glaucoma, arrhythmias, urinary obstruction, pregnant and nursing mothers.

SE: Drowsiness, hyperactivity, headache, diziness, blurred vision, ringing in the ears, dry mouth and frainting.
(Dramamine, gravol, draminate and Wal-Dram 50 mg, chewable tablets are available).

Dimethindene maleate Children >12 yr: 1–2 mg q 8 hr or 2.5 mg SR twice a day.

Adult dose: 1 mg q 8 hr or 2.5 mg q 12 hr.

Indic: Urticaria, angioedema, and rhinitis.

C/I: Epilepsy, urinary retention.
(Foristal tab 1 mg; foristal lontabs 2.5 mg).

Diphenhydramine hydrochloride 5 mg/kg/day q 6 hr oral, maximum dose 300 mg/24 hr. For anaphylaxis or phenothiazine overdose, 1–2 mg/kg IV slowly.

Adult dose: 10–50 mg per dose up to maximum of 400 mg/day.

C/I: Co-administration with monoamine oxidase inhibitors (MAOIs); bronchial asthma, narrow angle glaucoma, urinary retention.
(Dimiril tab 25 mg; benadryl caps 25 mg, 50 mg; syrup benadryl, dimiril 12.5 mg per 5 ml, inj benadryl 50 mg/ml ampoule and 10 mg/ml vial).

Ebastine Children >6 yr: 5 mg OD; Adults: 10–20 mg OD

SE: Prolonged QT interval.

C/I: Cardiac arrhythmias.
(Ebast DT-tab 5 mg; tabs 10 mg, 20 mg).

Fexofenadine hydrochloride It is an active metabolite of terfenadine. 15 mg BD for 6 mon–2 yr, 30 mg BD for children 2–12 yr and 60 mg BD or 120 mg OD for children >12 yr.

Adult dose: 120–180 mg daily q 12–24 hr.

Indic: Allergic rhinitis, allergic skin conditions (chronic idiopathic urticaria).

SE: Flu-like symptoms, dizziness, drowsiness, dry mouth, sleep disorder and menstrual cramps.

C/I: Phenylketonuria because fexofenadine tablet contains 5.3 mg phenylalanine.
(Allegra tabs 30 mg, 120 mg, 180 mg; fegra, histafree, fexofast, fexo, fexy, fexofen tabs 120 mg,180 mg, allegra, histafree, fexy susp 30 mg/5 ml).

Hydroxyzine hydrochloride 2 mg/kg/day q 6 hr oral; 0.5–1.0 mg/kg/dose q 4–6 hr IM.

Adult dose: 25 mg at night increased up to 25 mg q 3–4 hr orally; 50–200 mg per day in divided doses.

C/I: Not recommended in infants below 6 mon, acute porphyria, ECG changes.
(Atarax, hicope tabs 10 mg, 25 mg; syrup 10 mg per 5 ml; drops 6 mg per ml; injection 25 mg per ml).

Ketotifen Start at a low dose and increase to maximum of 1 mg twice daily for children.

Adult dose: 1–2 mg twice daily with food.

Indic: Prophylaxis of bronchial asthma, symptomatic treatment of allergic rhinitis and conjunctivitis.
(Airyfen, asthafen, ketasma, ketovent, tritofen tab 1 mg; syrup tritofen, asthafen, airyfen 1 mg per 5 ml).

Levocetirizine It is the levoform of racemic mixture of cetirizine with minimal effects on CNS. 2–6 yr: 0.125 mg/kg/d single dose. Children above 6 yr: 2.5 mg in a single or two doses. Avoid below 2 yr of age.

Adult dose: 5 mg in a single or two doses.
(Levocet, airitis, lezyncet, L-cet, leset, levorid, laveta, levora, levozet, zipcet tab 5 mg, susp 2.5 mg/5 ml).

Loratadine It is a long-acting selective peripheral H_1 antagonist with minimal sedation. Above 2 yr up to 30 kg weight: 5 mg oral per day; above12 yr: 10 mg once a day oral.

Adult dose: 10 mg daily single dose.

C/I: Below 2 yr.
(Loridin, alaspan, lorfast, lormeg, claridin tab 10 mg; loridin, lormeg, lorin susp 5 mg per 5 ml).

Meclizine hydrochloride is a non-selective first generation H1 antagonist. It is an antihistamine that is used to prevent and treat nausea, vomiting and diziness due to motion sickness and vertigo. It causes drowsiness and its effects last up to 24 hr. The drug is not approved for use in children less than 12 yr, pregnant and nursing mothers.

Adult dose: 25–50 mg 1 hr before start of journey.
(Antivert, medivert, univert, bonine, meni-D, verticalm tab 16 mg, 25 mg, combo formulations with pyridoxine are preferred. In otogesic vertigo fixed drug combinations of cinnarazine 20 mg + dimenhydrinate 40 mg are available as arlevert (ARL) and cizinate).

Methdilazine hydrochloride Above 3 yr: 4 mg q 12 hr.

Adult dose: 8–16 mg q 12 hr.

C/I: Coma, jaundice with levodopa, and bone marrow depression.

Indic: Pruritus, neurodermatitis.
(Dilosyn tab 8 mg; syrup 4 mg/5 ml).

Mizolastine Children >12 yr: 10 mg OD

Adult dose: 10 mg OD

C/I: Hypokalemia, long QT syndrome, significant bradycardia.
(Elina tab 10 mg).

Pheniramine maleate 0.5 mg/kg/day q 8 hr oral, IM or IV.

Adult dose: 25 mg 8–12 hrly or 50 mg every 12 hrly orally; Inj 22.75–45.5 mg IM 12 hrly.

C/I: Epilepsy, asthma, neonates.
(Avil tabs 25 mg, 50 mg; cosavil tab contains pheniramine maleate 12.5 mg and paracetamol 500 mg, avil syrup 15 mg per 5 ml; inj 22.75 mg per ml as 2 ml ampoule).

Promethazine hydrochloride 0.1 mg/kg/day q 6 to 8 hr and 0.5 mg/kg/dose at night p.o. when needed. Nausea and vomiting or sedation: 0.25–1.0 mg/kg/dose q 4–6 hr oral, IM, IV or PR.

Motion sickness: 0.5 mg/kg/dose q 12 hr oral, 30 min before start of the journey.

Adult dose: 25–75 mg at bedtime, or 10–20 mg q 8–12 hr.

(Phenergan, phena, promet, promethazine tabs 10 mg, 25 mg; syp 5 mg per 5 ml; inj 25 mg per ml, 2 ml ampoule; phensedyl expectorant 5.65 mg per 5 ml, tixylix syrup promethazine hydrochloride 1.5 mg, pholcodine citrate 1.5 mg, phenyl propanolamine hydrochloride 5 mg per 5 ml).

Pseudoephedrine Children <12 yr: 4 mg/kg/day q 6 to 8 hr oral, >12 yr: 30–60 mg/dose q 6–8 hr.

Adult dose: 60 mg/dose oral q 4–6 hr up to maximum dose of 240 mg/day.

(Sudafed tab 60 mg; syrup 30 mg per 5 ml).

Trimeprazine tartrate is also known as alimemazine is an antihistamine useful for treatment of cough and itching. It is not recommended in children less than 2 yr. The usual dose is 2.2–4.4 mg/kg/d.

Adult dose: 2.5 mg 4 times/day.

SE: Allergic reactions, blistering, wheezing, hoarseness, drowsiness, blurred vision.

(Redeltran, panectyl, repeltin, theralene, theraligene, vanectyl, temaril tabs 2.5 mg and 5.0 mg).

Triprolidine hydrochloride Children 6 mon–2 yr: 0.3 mg/dose q 4–6 hr (maximum 1.25 mg/day); 2–4 yr: 0.6 mg/dose q 4–6 hr (2.5 mg/day); 4–6 yr: 0.9 mg/dose q 4–6 hr (maximum 3.75 mg/day); 6–12 yr: 1.25 mg/dose q 4–6 hr (maximum 10 mg/day).

Adult dose: 2.5 mg/dose q 4–6 hr (maximum 10 mg/day).

(Available only in combinations. Actifed plus tab 2.5 mg triprolidine hydrochloride, paracetamol 500 mg and phenylpropanolamine hydrochloride 25 mg; actifed plus pediatric susp 0.625 mg tripolidine hydrochloride, paracetamol 125 mg and phenylpropanolamine hydrochloride 0.625 mg/5 ml).

Chapter

12

Antihypertensives

Amiloride Potassium sparing diuretics. Used as antihypertensive and heart failure. 0.4–0.625 mg/kg/day q 12–24 hr. Available in combination with thiazide or loop diuretic.

Adult dose: 5–10 mg OD or BD (up to maximum of 20 mg).

Indic: Hypertension, edema, nephrogenic diabetes insipidus and loop diuretic associated hypokalemia.

SE: Hyperkalemia, nausea, anorexia, abdominal pain, flatulence, diarrhea, headache dehydration, gynecomastia, hyperchloremic metabolic acidosis, hyponatremia.

C/I: Hyperkalemia, impaired renal function, concomitant use with potassium sparing diuretic or potassium supplementation. (Biduret-L tab: hydrochlorthiazide 25 mg + amiloride 2.5 mg; biduret tab: hydrochlorthiazide 50 mg + amiloride 5 mg; amifru, amf, frumide, frumil, amimide, Exna-K, lasiride tab: furosemide 40 mg + amiloride 5 mg), tab midamor (amiloride 5 mg).

Amlodipine 0.05–0.5 mg/kg/day q 12 to 24 hr. It belongs to the group of calcium channel blocker (CCB) and their names end with "pine" like amlodipine, nifedipine, benedipine, clinidipine, nicardipine. Used in hypertension, angina (chronic stable and vasospastic), and Raynaud phenomenon.

Adult dose: 5 to 10 mg once a day.

SE: Peripheral edema, pulmonary edema, headache, dizziness, fatigue, flushing, palpitations, pruritus, skin rash, abdominal pain and constipation.

(Amlopres, amcard, amlocor, amlosun, stamlo, vamlo, myodura, amlopin tabs 2.5 mg, 5 mg and 10 mg).

Atenolol It is a cardioselective beta blocker. 0.5–2 mg/kg/day single dose oral.

Indic: Chronic hypertension, supraventricular tachycardia, thyrotoxicosis, aortic root dilatation and hemangioma.

Adult dose: 50–100 mg daily.

C/I: Bradycardia, heart block, congestive cardiac failure, bronchial asthma, and peripheral arterial disease.

SE: AV block, bronchospasm, fatigue, insomnia, vivid dreams, memory impairment can mask symptoms of hypoglycemia. (Ziblok, tenomactabs 12.5 mg, 25 mg, 50 mg; aten, altol, catenol, betacard, tenormin, tenolol tabs 50 mg, 100 mg).

Captopril It is angiotensin-converting enzyme (ACE) inhibitor. 0.5–6 mg/kg/day q 8–12 hr should be administered 1 hr prior to meals. It is often used in combination with a diuretic and/or beta blocker. Monitor total leukocyte count and renal functions.

Adult dose: Initially 12.5 mg q 12 hr, maintenance 25 mg q 12 hr; maximum 50 mg 8–12 hrly.

Indic: High renin hypertension, congestive heart failure, acute coronary syndrome, proteinuria in CKD, primary aldosteronism.

SE: Angioedema, cough, hyperkalemia, AKI, skin rash, neutropenia, agranulocytosis, thrombocytopenia, hemolytic anemia, or pancytopenia.

C/I: Aortic stenosis, renal failure, porphyria, and bilateral renal artery stenosis.
(Aceten, capotril tabs 12.5 mg, 25 mg; angiopril tabs 25 mg, 50 mg).

Carvedilol Non-selective beta-adrenergic blocker with alpha-blocking activity. The dose is not established in children. Off label use in hypertension 0.08 mg/kg/dose 12 hrly, maximum 0.75 mg/kg/dose every 12 hrly.

Adult dose: 6.25 mg BD, increase, if required, to 12.5 mg BD; up to maximum of 50 mg per day.

Indic: Hypertension, left ventricular dysfunction, heart failure, angina, atrial fibrillation/flutter, myocardial infarction, ventricular tachycardia, variceal bleed.

SE: Bradycardia, bronchospasm, dizziness, insomnia, diarrhea, fatigue, hypotension, hyperglycemia, masking symptoms of hypoglycemia.

C/I: Asthma, sinus bradycardia, heart block, sick-sinus syndrome, bradycardia, severe liver disease, and congestive cardiac failure. (Caditone, caslot, cardivas, carvas, carvil, carvedil tabs 3.125 mg, 6.25 mg, 12.5 mg, 25 mg).

Clonidine hydrochloride 5–25 µg/kg/day q 6 or 8 hr oral. Taper therapy gradually over 1 wk as rebound hypertension can occur.

Adult dose: 50–100 µg 8 hrly initially, increasing every 2–3 days as required; maximum dose 2400 µg per day.

Indic: Hypertension, attention deficit hyperactivity disorder, prophylaxis of migraine, Tourette syndrome, growth hormone deficiency test and narcotic withdrawal.

SE: Dry mouth, bradycardia, hypotension, dizziness, drowsiness, constipation, fatigue, rebound hypertension.
(Arkamin, catapres, clodict, clonid tab 100 µg; inj catapres, arkamin, cloneon 150 µg/ml).

Diazoxide 8–15 mg/kg/dose q 8–12 hr oral. IV: 3–5 mg/kg/dose; repeat in 20 min if no effect. For hypertensive crisis: 1–3 mg/kg IV up to 150 mg; repeat q 5–15 min until blood pressure is controlled, then q 4–24 hr.

Indic: Hypertensive crisis, and intractable neonatal hyperinsulinemic hypoglycemia.

SE: Hypotension, palpitations, tachycardia, cutaneous candidiasis, loss of scalp hair, pruritus, skin rash, transaminitis.
(Eudemine tab 15 mg; inj hyperstat, eudemine 15 mg per ml in 20 ml ampoule).

Enalapril maleate It is an orally active ACE inhibitor. 0.08–0.6 mg/kg/d q 12–24 hr oral.

Adult dose: Initially 5 mg daily; usual dose 10–20 mg with a maximum dose of 40 mg daily.

Indic: Acute coronary syndrome, heart failure, chronic hypertension, proteinuria in CKD and nephrotic syndrome.

SE: Fatigue, hypotension, cough, hyperkalemia, dizziness, headache, angioedema, AKI, skin rash, neutropenia, agranulocytosis, thrombocytopenia, or pancytopenia.

C/I: Aortic stenosis, bilateral renal artery stenosis, out-flow obstruction, glomerular filtration rate <30 ml/min/m^2.

(Enalapril tabs 2.5 mg, 5 mg, 10 mg, 20 mg; enace, envas, enam, tenam, enaten, minipril, nuril, newace tabs 2.5 mg, 5 mg, 10 mg; ena tabs 5 mg, 10 mg).

Epleronone It is an aldosterone receptor blocker. Pediatric dose is not established.

Adult dose: Start at 25 mg OD, increase up to 50 mg BD.

Indic: Hypertension, heart failure and primary aldosteronism.

SE: Hyperkalemia, increased serum creatinine, hypertriglyceridemia, gynecomastia, atrial fibrillation and postural hypotension.

(Eplerenone, eplecard, epleran, eptus tabs 25 mg, 50 mg; planep tab 25 mg).

Hydralazine hydrochloride It is a directly acting vasodilator and is useful in acute and chronic hypertension, hypertensive emergency and periperative hypertension and heart failure. 0.5–7.5 mg/kg/day q 6 to 8 hr oral, increase gradually over 3–4 wk. For hypertensive crisis: 0.1–0.2 mg/kg/dose q 6 hr IV or IM (maximum 2 mg/kg/dose).

Adult dose: Initial 10 mg q 6 hr up to maximum of 100 mg q 6 hr.

SE: lupus-like syndrome, cardiac toxicity, skin rash, hepatitis, and agranulocytosis.

C/I: Porphyria, SLE, coronary artery disease and rheumatic mitral valve disease.

(Nepresol, apresoline tab 25 mg; inj apresoline 20 mg per ml ampoule; Corbetasine: hydralazine 25 mg + propranolol 40 mg).

12

Labetalol Beta-blocker with alpha-blocking activity. 10–40 mg/kg/day q 12 hr oral after meals. For hypertensive crisis:

0.25 to 1 mg/kg IV over 2 min, repeat after 5–10 min. May be administered by continuous infusion @ 0.4–3.0 mg/kg/hr.

Adult dose: Start with 100 mg twice a day, increase gradually every 2 wk up to 200–400 mg twice a day.

Indic: Hypertensive, emergency, acute and chronic hypertension, aortic dissection.

Caution: Avoid in asthmatics, heart failure, hypoglycemic states, severe bradycardia and 2nd degree/3rd degree heart block.
(Normadate caps 50 mg, 100 mg, 200 mg; labeta cap 50 mg, trandate tabs 100 mg, 200 mg, 400 mg; lobet, labil, gravidol tab 100 mg; inj gravidol 5 mg per ml, inj lobet, labeta 20 mg per ml, inj lobesol 20 mg, 100 mg, 200 mg, inj labit 20 mg, 100 mg).

Losartan It belongs to the group of angiotensin II receptor blockers (ARBs) and their names end with "sartan", like losartan, eprosartan, valsartan, telmisartan, candesartan. They are useful for treatment of hypertension, proteinuria in CKD, aortic root dilation, heart failure. Children >6 yr of age: 0.7–1.4 mg/kg (maximum 100 mg) once a day.

SE: Hypotension, AKI and hyperkalemia.

Adult dose: 50 mg OD or b.i.d.
(Losacar, tozaar, asart, alsartan, losakind, losar, zaart, convance 25 mg, 50 mg tabs).

Lisinopril Children >6 yr of age: 0.07 mg/kg/day. Slowly titrate upwards till 0.61 mg/kg/day, maximum single dose 5 mg.

Adult dose: 5–40 mg OD

Indic: Hypertension and proteinuria in CKD.

Caution: Aortic and renal artery stenosis, renal dysfunction, collagen vascular disease and hyperkalemia.
(Linvas, listril, lisoral, zestril, cipril 2.5 mg, 5 mg, 10 mg tabs; lisonil 2.5 mg, 5 mg, 10 mg, 20 mg tabs).

Methyldopa 5–60 mg/kg/day q 6 to 8 hr oral. Maximum daily dose 3 g/day.

Adult dose: 0.5–2 g/day in 2–3 divided doses.

C/I: Liver disease, pheochromocytoma, depression, use of MAO inhibitors.

(Emdopa, alphadopa, dopagyt, methyldopa, sembrina, aldopam, gynapres tabs 250 mg).

Metoprolol Selective β1 receptor blocker. 1–2 mg/kg/day q 12 hr oral up to maximum 6 mg/kg or ≤200 mg/day. For cyanotic spells: 0.1 mg/kg over 1–2 min, repeated q 5–10 min.

Adult dose: 100 mg OD or 50 mg BD, increase as required; maximum dose 450 mg daily.

Indic: Angina, acute myocardial infarction, supraventricular tachycardia, ventricular tachycardia, congestive heart failure, hyperthyroidism and prevention of migraine headaches.

SE: Tiredness, dizziness, depression, confusion, bradycardia, headache, diarrhea and bronchospasm.

C/I: Sinus bradycardia, heart block, sick-sinus syndrome, pheochromocytoma, and congestive cardiac failure.

(Betaloc, cardibeta-XR, met-XL 12.5 mg, metolar, lopresor, embeta-XR, metapro tabs 25 mg, 50 mg, mepol 50 mg; inj betaloc, metolar 1.0 mg/ml in 5 ml ampoule).

Minoxidil Initial dose 0.2 mg/kg/24 hr as a single dose, thereafter dosage may be increased stepwise to 0.25–1.0 mg/kg every 24 hr under careful titration.

Adult dose: 5 mg OD or 2.5 mg BD, increase gradually to 10 mg, 20 mg and 40 mg; maximum of 100 mg daily.

SE: Hypertrichosis, pericarditis, pericardial effusion, angina pectoris, cardiac failure, tachycardia, skin rash, sodium and water retention, weight gain.

C/I: Pheochromocytoma.

(Loniten tabs 2.5 mg, 10 mg; dilminox, lonit, lonitab tab 5 mg).

Olmesartan medoxomil It is an angiotensin II receptor antagonist with elimination half life of 13 hr. It can be used alone or in combination with a diuretic (hydrochlorothiazide) or another antihypertensive. Children 6–16 yr, 10 mg once a day, may be increased to 20 mg after 2 wk.

Adult dose: 20 mg once daily. May be increased up to 40 mg per day after 2 wk.

C/I: Biliary obstruction and pregnancy because of risk of fetal malformations.

SE: Gastrointestinal disturbances, dizziness, weight loss, electrolyte abnormalities and elevation of blood glucose.
(Benitec, benicar, culmi, olmezest, olmefast, olmesar tabs 10 mg, 20 mg, 40 mg. It is available in combination formulations with 12.5 mg hydrochlorothiazide).

Prazosin Alpha 1 blocker. 0.05–0.1 mg/kg/d oral q 8 hr (maximum 20 mg).

Adult dose: 1 mg oral q 8 to 12 hr.

Indic: Chronic hypertension, Reynaud's phenomenon, post-traumatic stress disorder and scorpion envenomation.

SE: Orthostatic hypotension ("first dose"), floppy iris syndrome, palpitations, dizziness, drowsiness, fatigue, headache.

(Minipress-XL, prazopil-XL, prazopress-XL tabs 2.5 mg, 5 mg; prazopress, unipraz tabs 1 mg, 2 mg).

Phentolamine Alpha 1 blocker is used for pheochromocytoma (diagnosis, prevention and management of hypertension episodes), extravasation of sympathomimetic vasopressors (e.g. dopamine, epinephrine, norepinephrine, phenylephrine), reversal of oral soft tissue (lip, tongue) anesthesia. 0.05–0.1 mg/kg/dose IV or IM for treatment of hypertensive crisis during pheochromocytoma surgery (maximum dose 5 mg).

SE: Bradycardia, cerebrovascular occlusion, hypotension, myocardial infarction, post-injection pain.
(Fentosol, phentosol, fentanar inj 10 mg per ml).

Propranolol hydrochloride For hypertension: 0.5–1 mg/kg/day q 6–12 hr oral (maximum dose 4 mg/kg/day). For arrhythmia/cyanotic spells: 2–6 mg/kg/day q 6–8 hr oral. Migraine prophylaxis: <35 kg: 10–20 mg t.d.s., >35 kg: 20–40 mg t.d.s.

Adult dose: 40–160 mg daily in divided doses. For migraine prophylaxis: 40 mg in a single or two doses in a day.

Indic: Hypertension, tachyarrhythmias, essential tremors, anxiety, thyrotoxicosis, during surgery of pheochromocytoma, portal hypertension, capillary hemangioma, migraine prophylaxis, cyclic vomiting syndrome, tetralogy spells, angina, atrial fibrillation/flutter, supraventricular tachycardia, moderate to severe burns, performance anxiety disorder, variceal hemorrhage.

C/I: Bronchial asthma, COPD, congestive heart failure, diabetes mellitus, bradycardia and high degree AV block.

SE: Lethargy, cold and clammy skin, bradycardia, hypotension, hypoglycemia and bronchospasm.
(Inderal, ciplar, betapro tabs 10 mg, 40 mg, 80 mg; norten, peeler, pronol tabs 10 mg, 20 mg, 40 mg, 60 mg, 80 mg; inj ciplar, pranosol, properol 1 mg per ml as 5 ml ampoule).

Ramipril Safety not established in children.

Adult dose: 2.5 mg OD, increase up to maximum of 20 mg daily as OD or BD

SE: Headache, cough, hypotension, dizziness, fatigue, and angioedema.

C/I: Hypersensitivity with any ACE inhibitor.
(Cardace, cardiopril, hopace, ramipres tabs, 1.25 mg, 2.5 mg, 5 mg, 10 mg; hoperam tabs 1.25 mg, 2.5 mg; ramihart, ramicard tabs 2.5 mg, 5 mg; ramcor, ramicard, corpril caps 1.25 mg, 2.5 mg, 5 mg).

Reserpine 0.02 mg/kg/day q 8 to 12 hr oral, not to exceed 0.25 mg/day. For hypertensive encephalopathy: 0.07 mg/kg/dose IM.

Adult dose: 0.1 mg 1–3 times a day, up to maximum of 1.0 mg daily.

C/I: Depression, active peptic ulcer, patients receiving electroconvulsive therapy and ulcerative colitis.
(Serpasil tab 0.25 mg; inj 1 mg per ml ampoule).

Sodium nitroprusside US Boxed warning for hypotension and cyanide toxicity. 0.3 to 10 μg/kg/min intravenous infusion.

50 mg is dissolved in one liter of 5% dextrose to provide concentration of 50 μg/ml.

SE: Cyanide toxicity, bradycardia, flushing, palpitations, substernal pain, arrhythmias, severe hypotension, restlessness, headache, sweating, nausea, vomiting, hypothyroidism, skin rash, decreased platelet aggregation and methemoglobinemia.

Caution: Wrap bottle and infusion tubing in aluminium foil to prevent exposure of drug to light. The solution may appear brownish but if it is discolored blue, green, orange or red, it should be discarded.

C/I: Increased intracranial pressure, hypertension secondary to arteriovenous shunts or coarctation of aorta, acute congestive cardiac failure, and severe hepatic impairment.
(Sonide, niside, nipress, pruside, nitroplus 50 mg ampoule).

Timolol maleate It is a non-selective beta-adrenergic blocking agent. It is available as oral formulation and ophthalmic drops for treatment of glaucoma. It is 8 times more potent than propranolol. The usual dose is 0.1 to 0.2 mg/kg/day in a single or two divided doses.

Adult dose: 10 to 20 mg twice a day up to maximum oral dose of 30 mg BD.

Indic: Hypertension, migraine prophylaxis, glaucoma, infantile hemangioma.

C/I: Cardiac failure, bronchial asthma, severe COPD, bradycardia, greater than 1st degree AV block.
(Timol, blocadren tabs 5 mg, 10 mg, 20 mg; timoptic, timolol, istalol 0.25%, 0.5% eye drops, glucomol gel and ocupress eye gel is available which can be applied over infantile hemangioma).

Verapamil 4–8 mg/kg/day q 8 hr oral, 0.1–0.3 mg/kg IV over 2 min under continuous ECG and BP monitoring. Maximum 5 mg/dose.

Indic: Supraventricular tachycardia, ventricular arrhythmias, chronic stable angina, chest pain associated with cocaine ingestion, prevention of cluster headache and migraine.

Adult dose: 80–480 mg in 2–3 divided doses daily.

SE: Headache, gingival hyperplasia, constipation, dizziness, acute decompensated heart failure, bradyarrhythmia and transaminases.

C/I: Cardiogenic shock, AV block, LV dysfunction, sick sinus syndrome, hypotension.
(Veramil, calaptin, vasopten, verpitos tabs 40 mg, 80 mg; inj VPL 5 mg per 2 ml ampoule).

Chapter

13

Antileprosy Drugs

Clofazimine 1 mg/kg/day and 4–6 mg/kg once a month. For *Lepra reaction*, 100 mg twice or thrice a day for a month with dose reduction once adequate response is achieved.

Adult dose: 50 mg daily or 100 mg on alternate days.

Caution: May cause skin pigmentation which usually resolves after stopping the drug.
(Lamprene, clofozine, hansepran caps 50 mg, 100 mg).

Diaminodiphenyl sulfone (DDS) 1–2 mg/kg/day (maximum dose 100 mg). To begin with, use the minimum dose and increase wkly so that at the end of 7th wk patient is receiving the maximum dose.

Adult dose: 50 mg twice in a wk.

Indic: Leprosy, dermatitis herpetiformis, prophylaxis and treatment of *Pneumocystis jirovecii* pneumonia (PJP) infection.

C/I: G6PD deficiency may cause dose-related hemolysis.

SE: Hemolytic anemia, methemoglobinemia, agranulocytosis, nephrotic syndrome, lupus erythematosus, and peripheral neuropathy.
(Dapsone tabs 5 mg, 10 mg, 25 mg, 50 mg, 100 mg)

Rifampicin 10–20 mg/kg/day single dose empty stomach.

Adult dose: <50 kg: 450 mg daily as a single dose; >50 kg: 600 mg daily.

SE: Hepatic damage, hypersensitivity.

(R-cin, rifacilin, coxid, macox, monocin, ticin, rimactane, rifamycin, rifampin caps 150 mg, 300 mg, 450 mg, 600 mg, suspension R-cin 100 mg per 5 ml).

Multiple Drug Therapy Regime

(WHO, National Leprosy Eradication Program)

The revised classification and treatment of leprosy are summarized in Table 13.1.

Multibacillary leprosy: Initial intensive therapy for 2 wk with daily dose of dapsone, clofazimine and rifampicin followed by continuation phase consisting of rifampicin 10 mg/kg once monthly given under supervision, DDS 2 mg/kg daily self-administered, clofazimine 6 mg/kg once monthly supervised and 1 mg/kg daily self-administered. WHO recommends treatment for at least 2 yr and whenever possible till smear is negative.

Paucibacillary leprosy: Rifampicin 10 mg/kg once a month supervised for 6 mon, DDS 2 mg/kg daily for 6 mon. Therapy may be extended up to 12 mon.

Single skin lesion paucibacillary leprosy: For adults, the standard regimen is a single daily dose of rifampicin 600 mg, ofloxacin 400 mg and minocycline 100 mg.

TABLE 13.1: Revised classification and treatment of leprosy in India*

Any one or more of the cardinal signs and/or laboratory test results as mentioned below:

S. No.	*Type*	*Skin lesions*	*Nerve(s) involvement*	*Bacilli in laboratory-based test (Slit-Skin Smear)*
1.	Pauci-Bacillary (PB)	1–5	None (0)	Absent (Negative)
2.	Multi-Bacillary (MB)	More than 5 (>5)	One or more nerves involved (≥1)	Present (Positive)

Revised treatment regimens of leprosy in India*

S. No.	*Types*		*Duration of treatment*	*Dapsone*	*Clofazimine*	*Rifampicin*
1.	Pauci-Bacillary (PB)	Adult	6 mon	100 mg daily	300 mg once a mon and 50 mg daily	600 mg once a mon
		Child (9–14 yr)	6 mon	50 mg daily	150 mg once a mon and 50 mg alternate day	450 mg once a mon
2.	Multi-Bacillary (MB)	Adult	12 mon	100 mg daily	300 mg once a mon and 50 mg daily	600 mg once a mon
		Child (9–14 yr)	12 mon	50 mg daily	150 mg once a mon and 50 mg alternate day	450 mg once a mon

**DGHS, GOI D.O. No Z-14020/80/2023-Lep dt 17th Jan 2024.*

Chapter

14

Antimalarials

Artemether For severe falciparum malaria (used if other alternatives are not available because its absorption is erratic): 3.2 mg/kg IM on first day followed by 1.6 mg/kg daily subsequently for a total of 5 days (total dose of 9.6 mg/kg). Shift to oral medicines as soon as feasible.

Adult dose: 80 mg q 12 hrly IM first day then 80 mg daily for next 4 days; total dose 480 mg.

C/I: G-6-PD deficiency, immunocompromised patients.
(Inj paluther, larither, rezart-M 80 mg/ml, 1 ml ampoule; larither cap 40 mg tab lumerax-20 DT, fixed-dose combinations: Combither, ARH-L, Actizo, lumerax-20 DT (artemether 20 mg + lumefantrine 120 mg), lumerax-40 (artemether 40 mg + lumefantrine 240 mg), lumerax-80 (artemether 80 mg + lumefantrine 480 mg). 5–14 kg (<3 yr): 1 tab (artemether 20 mg + lumefantrine 120 mg) BD for 3 d; 15–24 kg (3–8 yr): 2 tab BD for 3 d; 25–34 kg (9–14 yr): 3 tab BD for 3 d; >34 kg (>14 yr): 4 tab BD for 3 days. Tab lumerax-80, artivil plus, alither forte, arte plus, rezatrin forte, combither forte (artemether 80 mg and lumefantrine 480 mg), syrup lumerax, combither, ARH-L (artemether 20 mg + lumefantrine 120 mg/5 ml), lumether, artivil plus, epither, anther (artemether 40 mg + lumefantrine 240 mg/5 ml). Give after food and with milk. Prime with ondansetron to prevent vomiting. If vomiting occurs within one hr, repeat the dose. Avoid in patients with severe cardiac disease and arrhythmia.

Artesunate Severe falciparum malaria: 2.4 mg/kg/dose IV or IM at 0, 12, 24 hr, then once a day until patient is able to take orally followed by oral ACT therapy for 3 days (duration is not specified). As per the recent WHO recommendations, children weighing <20 kg should receive a higher dose of artesunate (3 mg/kg per dose) than larger children and adults (2.4 mg/kg per dose) to ensure equivalent exposure to the drug.

Uncomplicated falciparum malaria: Artemisinin-based combination therapy is the recommended treatment and it is shown in Table 14.1.

Tab Falcigo plus kit contains artesunate 50 mg, mefloquine 250 mg, Larinate-200 kit: artesunate 200 mg + sulphadoxine 500 mg + pyrimethamine 25 mg, larinate-100 kit: artesunate 100 mg + SD-PM as above, larinate-50 kit: artesunate 50 mg + SD-PM as above, larinate-MF: artesunate 200 mg + mefloquine 250 mg).

C/I: G-6-PD deficiency, immunocompromised patients.

(Arnet, falcigo, ARH, dunate, falcimax, falciquin tab 50 mg; inj larinate, falcigo, rezart-S, arnet, asunate, falcimax, falcinil 60 mg vial which is reconstituted in 1 ml of 5% sodium bicarbonate. It is further diluted with 2 ml normal saline or 5% glucose for IM use and 5 ml normal saline or 5% glucose for IV use.)

Areas with Chloroquine Sensitive *P. vivax*

Chloroquine phosphate Total dose should be 25 mg base/kg. It is given in a dose of 10 mg/kg on day 1, 10 mg/kg on day 2, and 5 mg/kg on D3 (WHO 2022 recommendations) *250 mg of chloroquine phosphate provides 150 mg of chloroquine base*. For prophylaxis of malaria: 5 mg base/kg once a wk. In chikungunya acute stage, 5 mg/kg/d can be given for 7 days. In juvenile chronic arthritis (JCA), chloroquine base 250 mg daily can be given for 3 mon without any side effects.

Adult dose: 600 mg of base orally first dose followed by 300 mg base after 6 hr, 300 mg daily for 2 days.

(Lariago, cloquin, ciplaquin, malaquin, cadiquin, emquin, melubrin, nivaquine, resochin, stadmed, la quin tabs 250 mg equivalent to 150 mg of chloroquine base; lariago DS tab 300 mg base, syrup lariago, cloquin, nivaquin, emquin 50 mg of chloroquine base per 5 ml, inj lariago 40 mg/ml as 2 ml, 5 ml and 30 ml vials).

Hydroxychloroquine sulfate It is useful for treatment of chloroquine sensitive malaria and a variety of autoimmune disorders. Hydroxy chloroquine sulfate 200 mg provides 155 mg base.

Malaria treatment: 10 mg base/kg followed by 5 mg/kg after 6 hr, 18 hr and 24 hr. PO with food or milk.

Prophylaxis: 5 mg base/kg wkly, starting 2 wk before exposure and continued for 4 wk after departure from an endemic area.

Adult dose

Malaria: Acute treatment 800 mg stat followed by 400 mg 6–8 hr later, then 400 mg at 24 and 48 hr PO.

Prophylaxis: 400 mg wkly PO starting 2 wk before exposure and continued for 4 wk after departure from endemic area.

Rheumatoid arthritis: 400–600 mg daily for 4–12 wk, followed by maintenance dose of 200–400 mg daily.

Systemic lupus erythematosis: 400 mg once or twice daily followed by maintenance dose of 200–400 mg daily.

Porphyria cutanea tarda (off-label) 100–200 mg 2–3 times/wk.

COVID-19 (off-label) 200 mg 3 times/day for 10 days along with azithromycin 500 mg once daily for 10 days.
(Hydroquin, arthroquin, bioquin, orthokind, hqtor, hcqs, oxcq, rutor tabs 200 mg (155 mg base) and 400 mg (310 mg base)).

Lumefantrine It is used in combination with artemether. See dosages and combination formulations under artemether.

Mefloquine hydrochloride Treatment of drug-resistant uncomplicated *P. falciparum* malaria (in combination with artesunate): 25 mg/kg split over 2 days as 15 mg/kg and 10 mg/kg or 8.3 mg/kg/day once a day for 3 days. Prophylaxis of chloroquine-resistant malaria: 3.5 mg/kg of base wkly. 250 mg of mefloquine hydrochloride contains 228 mg of mefloquine base.

Adult dose: 1250 mg as a single oral dose. Malaria prophylaxis: mefloquine 5 mg/kg (up to 250 mg) wkly single dose 2 wk before, during stay and 4 wk after leaving the malarious region.

C/I: Seizures, neuropsychiatric disorder, cardiac dysfunction. (Mefque, mefax, mefliam, mefloc, meflotas, lariam, altimef, confal, larimef tab 250 mg).

Primaquine In view of the concern about safety of the previously recommended dose of 0.75 mg/kg in individuals with G6PD deficiency, a WHO panel reviewed the safety of primaquine as a *P. falciparum* gametocytocide and concluded that a single dose of 0.25 mg/kg of primaquine base is unlikely to cause serious toxicity, even in individuals with G6PD deficiency. Thus, where indicated a single dose of 0.25 mg/kg of primaquine base should be given on the first day of treatment, to all patients with parasitologically confirmed *P. falciparum* malaria except for pregnant women, infants <6 mon of age and women breastfeeding infants <6 mon of age, because there is insufficient data on the safety of its use in these groups.

Adult dose: 15 mg daily for 14 days for radical cure of *P. falciparum* or single dose of 15 mg can be given.

Caution: G-6-PD deficiency. A single dose of 0.25 mg/kg is safe in G-6-PD deficient individuals.

C/I: SLE, rheumatoid arthritis.
(Malirid, Pmq Inga, evaquin, malquine, pimaquin, primacip tabs 2.5 mg DT, 7.5 mg, 15 mg of base).

Pyrimethamine Treatment of toxoplasmosis: 1 mg/kg/day (maximum 25 mg/day) oral q 12 hr for 3 to 6 wk with sulfadiazine 85 to 100 mg/kg per day in four divided doses (maximum 8 g/day). If signs of folic acid or folinic acid deficiency develop, reduce the dosage or discontinue the drug according to response of the patient. Leucovorin (folinic acid) should be administered until normal hematopoiesis is restored. For symptomatic and asymptomatic congenital infection,

duration of therapy is prolonged up to one yr. It is not used alone either for prophylaxis or treatment of malaria.
(Daraprim tab 25 mg).

Pyrimethamine and sulfadoxine It is given for treatment of chloroquine-resistant uncomplicated *P. falciparum* infections known to be sensitive to pyrimethamine. It is given in combination with artesunate: Artesunate 4 mg/kg/day OD along with a single administration of 20 mg/1.0 mg/kg sulfadoxine-pyrimethamine.

Adult dose: 2 tablets (500/25) single dose.

Caution: Not recommended for long-term prophylaxis because of potential toxicity.

C/I: Infants less than 2 mon of age and history of allergic reactions to sulphonamides.
(Reziz, croydoxin FM, laridox, malocide, pyralfin, rimodar tabs contain pyrimethamine 25 mg and sulfadoxine 500 mg; syrup reziz, pyralfin containing 12.5 mg pyrimethamine and 250 mg sulfadoxine/5 ml).

Quinine dihydrochloride 20 mg/kg of salt given in a concentration of 1 mg/ml of normal saline or 5% dextrose infused over a period of 4 hr as a loading dose followed by 10 mg/kg 8 hrly as a 4-hr infusion for 7–10 days. Infusion rate should not exceed 5 mg base/kg/hr.

Quinine dihydrochloride 12 mg of salt is equivalent to 10 mg base. Shift to oral therapy as soon as possible. If the patient is critically ill for more than 48 hr or develops acute renal failure and requires continuation of IV quinine, the dose should be reduced by 1/2 to 1/3 to avoid quinine toxicity. Total duration of therapy is 7–10 days. Intramuscular route is as efficacious as IV and can be given in a loading dose of 20 mg/kg (diluted to 60 mg/ml divided and injected into both anterior and lateral aspects of thighs and buttocks) followed by 10 mg/kg q 8 hr. The patient is shifted to oral therapy as soon as possible. A single course of primaquine 0.75 mg/kg is given on completion of quinine therapy to eradicate gametocytes and prevent transmisson.

Indic: Severe falciparum malaria.

C/I: Optic neuritis, myasthenia gravis, prolonged QT interval, G-6-PD deficiency, and tinnitus.

Caution: Lethal hypotension, if injected rapidly, cinchonism and hypoglycemia may occur. The loading dose should be avoided, if there is reliable evidence that patient received quinine, halofantrine or mefloquine in the past 24 hr.

Adverse effects: Cardiac arrhythmias with long QT syndrome including torsades de pointes, thrombocytopenia due to hemolytic uremic syndrome and thrombotic thrombocytopenic purpura, leukopenia, disseminated intravascular coagulation, kidney failure, skin rashes like urticaria, angioedema, Stevens-Johnson syndrome and toxic epidermal necrolysis. Cinchonism may occur which is characterized by headache, vasodilation and sweating, nausea, tinnitus, hearing impairment, vertigo, or dizziness, blurred vision and disturbances in color perception. (Inj qinarsol-300, quininga, Rez-Q, quinine dihydrochloride 2 ml ampoule 300 mg per ml).

Quinine sulfate For uncomplicated chloroquine-resistant *P. falciparum* infections: 30 mg/kg/day of quinine base q 8 hr oral for 7 days. It is preferably used in combination with either tetracycline (40 mg/kg/day q 6 hr for 10 days) or clindamycin (20–40 mg/kg/day q 8 hr for 3 days) or pyrimethamine (0.75 mg/kg/day q 12 hr for 3 days) or sulfadiazine (150 mg/kg/day q 8 hr for 6 days) to prevent emergence of drug resistance.

Adult dose: 300–600 mg q 8 hr for 7 days, maximum 2 g daily (Cinkona, falciquin, Rez-Q tabs 100 mg, 300 mg, 600 mg; quininga tabs 100 mg, 300 mg. Inj cinkona 300 mg/ml).

For uncomplicated malaria in children and adults:

- Artemether + lumefantrine
- Artesunate + amodiaquine
- Artesunate + mefloquine
- Dihydroartemisinin + piperaquine
- Artesunate + sulfadoxine–pyrimethamine (SP)
- Artesunate + pyronaridine.

The revised WHO guidelines for treatment of malaria are summarized in Table 14.1.

TABLE 14.1: Revised WHO guidelines for treatment of malaria

Body weight in kg	*Dose (mg) of artemether + lumefantrine given twice daily for 3 days*
5 to <15	20 + 120
15 to <25	40 + 240
25 to <35	60 + 360
≥35	80 + 480
	Artesunate + amodiaquine dose (mg) given daily for 3 days
5 to <9	25 + 67.5
9 to <18	50 + 135
18 to <36	100 + 270
≥36	200 + 540
	Artesunate + mefloquine dose (mg) given daily for 3 days
5 to <9	25 + 55
9 to <18	50 + 110
18 to <30	100 + 220
≥30	200 + 440
	Dihydroartemisinin + piperaquine dose (mg) given daily for 3 days
5 to <8	20 + 160
8 to <11	30 + 240
11 to <17	40 + 320
17 to <25	60 + 480
25 to <36	80 + 640
36 to <60	120 + 960
60 <80	160 + 1280
>80	200 + 1600

(Contd.)

(Contd.)

	Artesunate dose given daily for 3 days (mg)	*Sulfadoxine/pyrimethamine dose (mg) given as a single dose on day 1*
5 to <10	25	250/12.5
10 to <25	50	500/25
25 to <50	100	1000/50
≥50	200	1500/75

As per WHO 2022 guidelines, revised dose recommendation for dihydroartemisinin + piperaquine in young children: Children weighing <25 kg treated with dihydroartemisinin + piperaquine should receive a minimum of 2.5 mg/kg body weight per day of dihydroartemisinin and 20 mg/kg body weight per day of piperaquine daily for 3 days.

Chapter

15

Antimyasthenic and Antimyotonic Agents

Edrophonium chloride Initial dose: 0.04 mg/kg/dose (maximum 1 mg for <30 kg) IV or IM. If no response after 1 min, may repeat 0.16 mg/kg/dose for a total of 0.2 mg/kg (maximum total dose is 5 mg for <30 kg).

Adult dose: 2 mg/min up to maximum of 8 mg.

Caution: Keep atropine available in a syringe and have resuscitation equipment ready. It may precipitate cholinergic crisis, arrhythmia, and bronchospasm. Hypersensitivity to a test dose (fasciculations or intestinal cramps) is an indication to stop the medication. It is contraindicated in patients with GI or genitourinary obstruction and arrhythmias.

Indic: Diagnosis of myasthenia gravis, reversal of non-depolarizing neuromuscular blockage, differentiation of cholinergic crisis from myasthenic crisis.
(Inj tensilon 10 mg per ml ampoule).

Ephedrine 3 mg/kg/day in 3–4 divided doses.

Indic: Congenital myasthenia syndrome due to DOK-7 mutation.

Adverse effects: Nervousness, insomnia, palpitation and hypertension.

Flouxetine hydrochloride It is an antidepressant of the selective serotonin reuptake inhibitor class. Starting at 12.5–25 mg, can be hiked slowly up to 80–100 mg/day depending on response.

Indic: Congenital myasthenia syndrome due to slow channel mutation; depression, obsessive–compulsive disorder, anxiety, panic disorder, bulimia nervosa, premenstrual dysphoric disorder (PMDD) and mood stabilizer.

Adult dose: 20–60 mg single daily dose.

Adverse effect: Nausea, nervousness, insomnia, hyponatremia.

SE: Increases the risk of suicide-related behavior in depressed children and adolescents.
(Prodep, prozac, flunil, platin caps 10 mg, 20 mg; fluxal, depzac, oxedep cap 20 mg; fludep-20 tab and fludac, exiten, flutine, prodep suspension 20 mg per 5 ml).

Neostigmine 0.025–0.04 mg/kg IM for diagnosis of myasthenia gravis. Repeat in 4 hr if equivocal or no response. Ensure atropine and IV fluids available bedside. For treatment neonatal dose: 0.05–0.1 mg, 10–20 min before feedings; use parenteral (IM, SC) route first, then change to 1 mg 30 min before feeds p.o. Children: 2 mg/kg/24 hr or 60 mg/m^2/day q 3–4 hr p.o., 0.01–0.04 mg/kg/dose q 2–3 hr IM, SC, IV.

Adult dose: 15–30 mg at suitable intervals throughout the day up to a total dose between 75 and 300 mg/day.

C/I: Intestinal and urinary obstruction.
(Prostigmine-neostigmine bromide, tilstigmin tab 15 mg; inj neostigmine methyl sulfate 0.5 mg and 2.5 mg per ml).

Pyridostigmine bromide Infants of myasthenic mothers: 0.05–0.15 mg/kg/dose. Titrate the dose to elicit the desired response. Children with myasthenia gravis; 7 mg/kg/24 hr divided into 5–6 doses, use atropine to counteract muscarinic side effects.

Adult dose: 60 mg 2–3 times/day up to maximum daily dose of 120–180 mg.
(Mestinon, distinon, mustone tab 60 mg).

3, 4-Diaminopyridine 1 mg/kg/day in 2–3 divided doses.

Adult dose: 20 mg 4 times in a day.

Adverse effects: Peripheral and perioral paresthesias, adrenergic side effects (palpitations, sleeplessness, ventricular extrasystoles) and cholinergic side effects (increased bronchial secretions, cough, and diarrhea).

Indic: Lambert-Eaton myasthenic syndrome with incremental response on repetitive stimulation. End plate AChR deficiency shows additional benefit after adding 3, 4-DAP to pyridostigmine.

C/I: History of seizures because high doses may lower seizure threshold.

Quinidine sulfate 15–60 mg/kg/day in 3–4 divided doses (maximum adult dose 200 mg q 8 hrly) to maintain serum drug level between 1.0 and 2.5 μg/ml.

Indic: Congenital myasthenia syndrome due to slow channel mutation.

Adverse effects: Gastrointestinal side effects, diarrhea and cinchonism, hypersensitivity reaction, abnormal liver function tests, hemolytic anemia, agranulocytosis, thrombocytopenic purpura, and drug rash. Quinidine worsens atrioventricular conduction defects, and can aggravate a prolonged QT interval which predisposes to ventricular arrhythmias. Quinidine also inhibits cytochrome P450 and thereby impairs the metabolism of codeine, tricyclic antidepressants, antiarrhythmic drugs, warfarin and digoxin.

Antimyotonic Agents

Carbamazepine Starting dose 5 mg/kg/day in 2–3 divided doses. Maintenance dose: 5–25 mg/kg/day.

Adult dose: 100–200 mg once or twice daily initially, increased gradually to 400 mg q 8–12 hr.

Adverse effects: Refer to section on Anticonvulsants.

Mexiletine 1–8 mg/kg in 2–3 divided doses.

Adult dose: 300–1200 mg/day in three divided doses.

Indic: Myotonia congenita, myotonic dystrophy, ventricular arrhythmias.

 C/I: Cardiac arrhythmia, cardiomyopathy, patients on intravenous lignocaine, hepatic impairment.

Adverse effects: Nausea, vomiting, tremors, blurred vision, confusion, incordination, acute hepatic injury, leukopenia.
Monitor baseline ECG, complete blood counts and liver function tests.
(Mexitil caps 50 mg, 150 mg and 200 mg).

Phenytoin sodium 4–8 mg/kg in two divided doses.

Adult dose: 150–300 mg daily in a single or two divided doses. For adverse effects and formulations, refer to section on Anticonvulsants.

Indic: Congenital myotonia, myotonic dystrophy.

Salbutamol 0.1–0.4 mg/kg/dose q 8 hr orally

Adult dose: 2–4 mg/dose 3–4 times/day up to maximum of 32 mg/day

Indication: Congenital myasthenia syndrome due to DOK-7 mutation.

Adverse effects: Irritability, tremors, tachycardia, nervousness, dizziness and hypokalemia
(Asthalin, ventorlin tabs 2 mg, 4 mg; asthalin syrup 2 mg/5 ml).

Chapter

16

Antiprotozoal Agents

Amphotericin B 1.0 mg/kg/day single daily dose or on alternate days IV up to a total dose of 20 mg/kg. Liposomal amphotericin B: 1–3 mg/kg IV daily for 5 days and a 6th dose is given on day 10.

Adult dose: Liposomal amphotericin B (L-AmB) 3–5 mg/kg daily by infusion for 3–5 days up to total dose of 15 mg/kg or alternatively 10 mg/kg as a single dose by intravenous infusion.

Indic: Systemic leishmaniasis resistant to other drugs.

SE: Monitor renal, hepatic, electrolytes and hematologic status. (Inj Fungizone, amfocan, amfocare, amphotex, amphotin 50 mg vial; Inj ambisome, fungisome, phozone (liposomal AmBisome, amphomul, amphocil, abelcet, kalsome) 10 mg, 25 mg and 50 mg vial; Inj lambin-10 provides 10 mg liposomal amphotericin B for intravenous use.

Chloroquine phosphate 10 mg/kg/day of base once a day for the first two days followed by 5 mg/kg once a day for 14–21 days for both intestinal and extraintestinal amebiasis. For malaria, *see* Antimalarials.

Adult dose: 1 gm chloroquine phosphate (600 mg base) orally OD for 2 days followed by 500 mg chloroquine phosphate (300 mg base) orally OD for 21 days.

Indic: Extraintestinal amebiasis, malaria.

C/I: Retinal or visual field changes of any etiology, hypersensitivity to chloroquine, 4-aminoquinoline compounds.

(Lariago, lariago DT, malaquine, melubrin, resochin tab 250 mg equivalent to 150 mg of chloroquine base, lariago susp 50 mg/ 5 ml, betaquine drops 50 mg/10 ml).

Dehydroemetine dihydrochloride 1 mg/kg/day IM for 6–10 days. If necessary, the course may be prolonged till the 15th day. 1–3 mg/kg/day PO q 8 hr for 10 days.

Adult dose: 60–100 mg SC/IM OD for not more than 10 days.

Indications: Acute amebic dysentery, amebic liver abscess, liver fluke infestation.

C/I: Renal and cardiac toxicity can occur.
(Inj dehydroemetine, inj tilemetin 30 mg/ml, 1 ml and 2 ml ampoules; dehydroemetine tab 10 mg).

Di-iodohydroxyquin 30–40 mg/kg/day q 8 hr oral for 3 wk.

Adult dose: 650 mg TDS (not to exceed 2.0 gm/day for 14 days)

Indications: Asymptomatic intestinal amebiasis.

C/I: Hypersensitivity to iodine, hepatic damage.
(Diodoquin tab 650 mg; susp 210 mg per 5 ml).

Diloxanide furoate 20 mg/kg per day in three divided doses for 10 days.

Adult dose: 500 mg TDS for 5–10 days.

Indications: Amebiasis.

C/I: Known hypersensitivity to diloxanide furoate.
(Amcline, furamide 500 mg tab).

Fluconazole 6 mg/kg as a loading dose followed by 3 mg/kg/ day. Cryptococcal infection: postneonatal age: 6–12 mg/kg/ day (maximum of 400 mg daily); in neonates, the same dose is given every 72 hr up to 2 wk and subsequently every 48 hr during 2–4 wk of age.

Adult dose: For mucosal infections: 50–100 mg daily for 14–30 days; For systemic infections: 400 mg on day 1 followed by 200–400 mg/day for a minimum of 28 days; prophylaxis in high-risk patients: 50–100 mg once daily.

Indic: Candidiasis, cryptococcal meningitis, and as a prophylactic agent for prevention of fungal infections in immunocompromised host.

C/I: Co-administration of cisapride or terfenadine, may cause QTc prolongation.
(Zocon, forcan, ultican, flucos, onecan, nuforce, flucon, flucom, flutas, fluzole, flumed, flutrox, nipcan tabs 50 mg, 150 mg, 200 mg, 300 mg, 400 mg; forcan, syscan caps 50 mg, 100 mg, 150 mg, 200 mg).

Metronidazole 15–20 mg/kg/day q 8 hr orally for 5–7 days for giardiasis, 35–50 mg/kg/day q 8 hr orally for 10 days for intestinal and extraintestinal amebiasis (in order to destroy cysts, add diloxanide furoate 20 mg/kg/day q 8 hr for 3 days), 20 mg/kg/day q 6 hr orally or IV for anaerobic infections, 20 mg/kg/dose (maximum 400 mg/d) q 8 hr oral for 7–10 days for antibiotic associated diarrhea.

Adult dose: 200–400 mg q 8 hr.

Indic: Amebiasis, giardiasis, trichomoniasis, *Balantidium coli* infection, *H. Pylori* infection, duodenal ulcer, propionic acidemia, methylmalonic acidemia.

C/I: Avoid in first trimester pregnancy, use with caution in CNS disease, blood dyscrasias, severe liver or renal disease.
(Flagyl, aristogyl, metrogyl rogyl tabs 200 mg, 400 mg; susp 200 mg per 5 ml; aristogyl susp 100 mg per 5 ml; inj metron, metrogyl 500 mg/100 ml).

Miltefosine It is an oral drug for treatment of visceral and cutaneous leishmaniasis, the usual dose is 2.5 mg/kg/day for 28 days.

Adult dose: 100–200 mg per day for 28 days.

Indic: Visceral and cutaneous leishmaniasis.

C/I: Nausea, vomiting pregnancy and teratogenicity.
(Impavido, miltex,mitepran caps 10 mg and 50 mg).

Nitazoxanide 1–3 yr: 100 mg every 12 hr; 4–11 yr: 200 mg every 12 hr; >12 yr: 500 mg every 12 hr. All doses to be taken for 3 days. Not recommended in infants below one year.

Adult dose: 500 mg q 12 hr for 3 days.

Indic: Giardiasis, cryptosporidiosis, *E. histolytica, Blastocystishominis* and *Clostridium difficile.*

C/I: Caution in hepatic or renal impairment, diabetes mellitus, HIV or other immunodeficiency disorders.

(Nitcol, nitacure, netazox, nitarid, nitazet, nizonide, nitzix, zoxakind syp 100 mg per 5 ml, zoxakind DT, netazox DT 200 mg, nitacure, nitcol, nitarid, nitacure tabs 200 mg, 500 mg, nitzix tab 200 mg).

Ornidazole 40 mg/kg OD for 3 days for intestinal amebiasis and 40 mg/kg OD for 2 days for giardiasis.

Adult dose: Amebiasis: 500 mg q 12 hr for 5–7 days. Amebic dysentery: 1.5 gm once a day for 3 days. Giardiasis: 1.0–1.5 gm once a day for 1–2 days.

Indic: Amebiasis, trichomoniasis, giardiasis, anaerobic infections, *Trichomonas vaginalis* infections.

C/I: Avoid in patients with CNS disorder.

(Oniz,dazolic, intrazole, lumigard, ornizen, ornida, onidaz, orni, ornimax, zil tab 500 mg).

Paromomycin 25–35 mg/kg/day in 3 divided doses. 5–7 days for intestinal amebiasis, 14–21 days for cryptosporidiosis associated diarrhea in HIV infected patients and 7 days for *Dientamoeba fragilis*.

Adult dose: 500 mg TDS

Indic: Intestinal amebiasis, adjunctive management of hepatic coma, cryptosporidiosis associated diarrhea in HIV infected patient, *Dientamoeba fragilis* infection.

C/I: Intestinal obstruction.

(Humantin, gabbroral tab 250 mg, 500 mg)

Pentamidine isethionate For systemic leishmaniasis: 4 mg/kg deep IM injections on alternate days for 14 to 21 injections. For *Pneumocystis jirovecii* pneumonia: 4 mg/kg/day in IV dextrose over 1 hr for at least 14 days.

Adult dose: 500 mg IM or IV daily for 14–21 days.

Indic: Antimony-resistant leishmaniasis, *Pneumocystis jirovecii* infection.

C/I: Hypotension, renal damage, hypoglycemia and risk of development of diabetes mellitus, torsades de pointes.
(Inj pentacarinate, pentam 300 mg vial)

Quinacrine hydrochloride Also known as mepacrine. 2 mg/kg/d q 8 hr oral for 5–7 days for giardiasis. The course may be repeated after 15 days.

Adult dose: The recommended dose is 100 mg TID for 5–7 days.

Indic: Giardiasis, malaria, certain types of lupus erythematosus.

C/I: Caution should is advocated in children under 5 yr of age, and severe liver disease.
(Atabrine, maladin tab 100 mg).

Secnidazole 30 mg/kg single dose for intestinal amebiasis and giardiasis. In case of severe invasive disease, administer it for 5 days.

Adult dose: 2 gm as a single dose.

Indic: Intestinal amebiasis, giardiasis, trichomonal vaginitis, bacterial vaginosis.

C/I: Nausea, metallic taste, urticaria, and cholestatic hepatitis.
(Seczol, secnil, snida, entosec, sectop, ambiform, secnitor, ami tabs 500 mg and 1 g).

Sodium stibogluconate 20 mg/kg/day IV or IM for 20 days, preferably up to 28 days and even up to 40 days for systemic leishmaniasis in areas with high incidence of resistance like Bihar. In stibogluconate-sensitive patients who develop a relapse, therapy is given for 60 days. For cutaneous leishmaniasis, 10 days of therapy is adequate.

Adult dose: 20 mg/kg once a day (maximum 850 mg) deep IM or IV for 20–30 days.

Indic: Cutaneous, mucosal and visceral leishmaniasis

16 *C/I:* Slow IV injection, stop in case of cough and substernal pain. Monitor QT interval on EKG.

(Inj sodium stibogluconate, pentostam, stibati, solustibosan containing pentavalent antimony 100 mg/ml, 100 ml bottle).

Tetracycline 25–50 mg/kg/day orally divided every 6 hrly, maximum 3 g/day.

Adult dose: 250–500 mg q 6–12 hr

Indic: Luminal entameba

C/I: In children less than 8 yr, avoid in complete renal failure and use with caution in hepatic dysfunction.
(Resteclin, hostacycline, tetra care tab 250 mg, 500 mg).

Tinidazole 50 mg/kg single dose oral for giardiasis and 60 mg/kg/day as single dose oral for 3 days for amebiasis.

Adult dose: 2 g once daily for 2–3 days for amebiasis; 2 g single dose for treatment of giardiasis.

Indic: Amebiasis, giardiasis, *Trichomonas vaginalis*.

C/I: Hypersensitivity to tinidazole, nitroimidazole derivatives, or any component of the formulation, use with caution in severe liver disease.
(Tiniba, enidazol, tini, tinitas, zil, tinizox, fasigyn, dazolic, tridazole tabs 150 mg, 300 mg, 500 mg; tinidafyl tab 1000 mg; tini susp 150 mg, 300 mg per 5 ml).

Chapter

17

Antispasmodics

Dicyclomine hydrochloride 6 mon to 2 yr: 5–10 mg three to four times a day (maximum dose 20 mg a day), above 2 yr: 10 mg three to four times a day (maximum dose 40 mg). Avoid below 6 mon.

Adult dose: Initial dose 20 mg three to four times a day. Maintenance doses 40 mg up to 4 times a day after 1 wk of initial dose.

Indic: Intestinal colic, GI spasm, irritable colon, renal colic. (Coligon, Cyclominol, declor 20, merbentyl tab 20 mg; actipas plus, antica, baralgan, cyclopam, colimex, colirid, griponil, temifix spas, spasmoflexon tab contains dicyclomine hydrochloride 20 mg and paracetamol 500 mg, arispas coliza, cycklac-MF, cyclomef, cyclosym, dimef spas, paraspas, spaswin antspas contains dicyclomine hydrochloride 10 mg and mefenamic acid 250 mg, colispas, meftal spas tab contains dicyclomine hydrochloride 20 mg and mefenamic acid 250 mg, meftal spas DS tab contains dicyclomine hydrochloride 20 mg and mefenamic acid 500 mg, cyclopam plus tab contains dicyclomine 20 mg, paracetamol 500 mg and mefenamic acid 250 mg, spasmoproxyvon cap contains dicyclomine hydrochloride 10, dextropropoxyphene 65 mg and acetaminophen 400 mg, meftal spas, cyclospas D, and cyclopam susp contains dicyclomine hydrochloride 10 mg and dimethylsiloxane 40 mg per 5 ml; nops syrup contains dicyclomine hydrochloride 5 mg and simethicone 50 mg per 5 ml, biospas, cloact, colimex, colispas, cyclopam, griponil, meftal spas, respas, spasmindon, spasrindrops contain 10 mg dicyclomine hydrochloride and 40 mg activated dimethicone per ml; merbentyl syrup 10 mg/5 ml. Colicaid, colicare, coligo drops contain simethicone 40 mg, dil oil 0.005 ml and fennel oil 0.0007 ml per ml. They are safe in infants below 6 mon, inj cyclopam, and meftal spas contains 10 mg/ml dicyclomine hydrochloride, inj spasmoproxyvon forte contains dicyclomine hydrochloride 20 mg and diclofenac 50 mg as 2 ml ampoule).

Drotaverine hydrochloride 1–6 yr: 20 mg 3 times/day, >6 yr: 40 mg 3 times/day.

Adult dose: 40–80 mg 3 times a day.
(Baralgan D, colicare, drotin, dotarin, drotikind, doverin, drovera, spasmoter, verin, tabs 40 mg and 80 mg, drotin DS, drotaflex tab 80 mg, drotin susp 10 mg/5 ml, arikspas, asdot MF, drorrit, drotin-M, and dorin-M tab contain drotaverine 80 mg plus mefenamic acid 250 mg, drotin plus contains drotaverine 80 mg plus paracetamol 500 mg, inj baralgan-D, dotra, drotin, 20 mg/ml inj spasmoter 40 mg/ml ampoules).

Hyoscine butylbromide not recommended under 6 yr. 6–12 yr: 10 mg q 8 hr oral, 10–20 mg IV or IM bolus.

Adult dose: 10–20 mg q.i.d., inj 20 mg IV, IM prn.

Indic: Intestinal and biliary colic.

C/I: Glaucoma.
(Buscopan, buscogast, biscotas, hyocimaximum tab 10 mg; inj 20 mg/ml; suppository 7.5 mg, 10 mg; buscogast hyoscine tab 10 mg and paracetamol 500 mg).

Oxyphenonium bromide 2.5 to 7.5 mg/day q 6–8 hr oral.

Adult dose: 5–10 mg q.i.d. oral.

SE: Dry mouth, blurred vision, retention of urine, dizziness, and tremors.
(Antrenyl tabs 5 mg, 10 mg; drops 10 mg per ml).

Pipenzolate methyl bromide 2.5–5 mg every 8 hr oral. Below 6 mon: 4 drops, 6 mon to 1 yr: 8–10 drops, 1–3 yr: 16 drops before feeds.

(Pipcol drops, pipen drops contain pipenzolate methyl bromide 4 mg and dimethyl polysiloxane 4 mg per ml).

Propantheline bromide 15 mg every 8 hr, one hr before meals, 30 mg h.s., maximum 75 mg/day.

SE: Dry mouth, blurred vision, urinary hesitancy and retention, loss of taste sensation, and dizziness.
(Probanthine, spastheline tab 15 mg).

Simethicone It is a useful antiflatulent. Children <2 yr: 20 mg q.i.d., 2–12 yr: 40 mg q.i.d.

Adult dose: 40–125 mg q.i.d.
(Diegicure, Epumisan, flatbust cap 80 mg; epumisan drops 40 mg/ml. It is mostly available in combo formulations as drops and syrup. antica DF, colicaid, cymbi, colimex DF, coliwin NF, carmicide gastica drops contain simethicone 40 mg, dill oil 0.025 ml and fennel oil 0.0007 ml per ml, colicaid EZ drops contain in addition pepsin 5 mg, fungal diastase 33.3 mg; colicaid syrup contains simethicone 40 mg, dill oil 0.005 ml, fennel oil 0.0007 ml per 5 ml, spazof, spaztus drops and suspension contain simethicone 40 mg, and dicyclomine 10 mg per 1 ml and 5 ml, respectively.)

Chapter

18

Antitoxins and Immunoglobulins

Anti-Rh D immune globulins It is given for prevention of rhesus sensitization of Rh negative mother. The baby or abortus should be Rh-positive and indirect Coombs' test during pregnancy should be negative. For antenatal prophylaxis, give 300 µg IM at 28 wk and 34 wk of gestation or a single dose within 72 hr of delivery. In case of abortion, evacuation, procedures (chorionic villus sampling, amniocentesis, cordocentesis, antepartum hemorrhage, external cephalic version) and trauma during pregnancy give 150 µg IM, if procedure is done before 12 wk of gestation (1 microgram = 5 international units).

Anti-D immunoglobulins have also been used with some success in treating chronic idiopathic thrombocytopenic purpura in Rh-positive patients who have not been splenectomized. In case of transfusion of Rh(D) positive blood to Rh(D) negative recipient; administer 20 µg per ml of transfused red blood cells. (Inj mastergam-P by zydus, rhogam by Johnson and Johnson, imogam by Ranbaxy 300 µg, 350 µg 1.5 ml vial, rhoclone (monoclonal anti-D) Bharat Serum and Vaccines Ltd 100 µg, 150 µg and 300 µg for IM).

Anti-snake venom It contains a mixture of four enzyme-refined lyophilized polyvalent antisnake venom serum against Krait, Cobra, Russell's viper and Saw-scaled viper. The total dose of antivenin serum is around 5 vials (50 ml) for mild, 5–15 vials for moderate manifestations (50–150 ml) and 15–20 vials (150–200 ml) for severe cases. *Smaller children may require one and half times* *of this dose because they receive larger dose of venom per unit body weight*. The antivenin is given IV diluted in 250 ml of one-fifth normal saline. It is safe to maintain an infusion rate of 20 ml/kg/hr. Use steroids and antihistamines along with antivenin. Exclude horse serum allergy by injecting intradermal 0.02 ml of 1:10 diluted antivenin. In subjects with hypersensitivity, careful desensitization is undertaken.

C/I: Sensitivity to equine antiserum.

(Lyophilized polyvalent equine antitoxin 1 ml neutralizes 0.5 mg cobra, 0.45 mg krait, 0.6 mg Russell's viper and 0.45 mg Saw-scaled viper venoms, Inj polyvalent snake anti-venin 10 ml vials by Haffkine and SII, ASVS by Serum Institute, anti- snake venom serum by Congruent Parmachem Private Limited 20 ml vial).

Diphtheria antitoxin (Equine)

For Schick test positive contacts: One dose of diphtheria toxoid should be given in one arm and 500–2000 units of diphtheria antitoxin IM in the other arm. Six weeks later, give 3 doses of diphtheria toxoid or Td at monthly interval in order to complete the course of active immunization.

Treatment of diphtheria: The dose is not related to the age and weight of the patient.

- Pharyngeal or laryngeal diphtheria of 48 hr duration: 20,000–40,000 units IV.
- Nasopharyngeal diphtheria: 40,000–60,000 units IV.
- Extensive disease of 3 days or more with neck swelling: 80,000–1,20,000 units IV.

The antitoxin should be diluted in 1:20 isotonic sodium chloride solution and administered at a rate not exceeding 1 ml/min. The antitoxin may be given IM in mild to moderate cases. The dose should be administered intravenously over 60 min in order to inactivate toxin rapidly.

(Diphtheria antitoxin 10,000 IU, per 5 ml/10 ml ampoule by Haffkine).

18 **Equine rabies specific immunoglobulins (ERIG)** 40 IU/kg is the usual dose. Infiltrate maximum possible or total dose around

the wounds and any left over dose can be given at gluteal region by deep IM injection. Equine rabies immunoglobulins (ERIG) should be used as second choice only when human rabies specific immunoglobulin is not available. Intradermal skin sensitivity is not needed but epinephrine should be kept handy.

SE: Anaphylaxis and serum sickness.
(Equirab SII 1500 i.u./5 ml, ERIG 1000 i.u./5 ml, Imorab 1000 i.u./5 ml).

Human immunoglobulins They are used for prophylaxis in primary immunodeficiency disorders and treatment of various immune mediated inflammatory disorders.

Primary immunodeficiency disorders: 300–400 mg/kg IVIG once every 3–4 wk. Subcutaneous infusion can be administered in a of dose 80–100 mg/kg/wk (cumulative monthly dose of 0.4–0.8 g/kg).

Attenuation of disease among close contacts:

- Measles: 0.5 ml/kg IM or 400 mg/kg IV, most effective within 72 hr but can be given up to 6 days of exposure; considered for immunocompromised individuals, infants less than 9 mon and non-immune pregnant women.
- Hepatitis A: 0.1 ml/kg IM within 14 days of possible exposure or close contacts who have chronic liver disease or immunocompromised state.

The doses refer to 10% solution of immunoglobulins. There is no role of immunoglobulins for attenuation of chickenpox, poliomyelitis and mumps. The protective role of HIG against rubella during pregnancy is controversial.
(Bharglob and gamma IV by Bharat Serum, gammaren and globucel by Intas, Ivnex safe by Biozon Bioproducts, Sandoglobulin by Novartis, Immunorel 3 gm, 5 gm, 6 gm, 10 g in 5% and 10% vials, subcutaneous Globucel, 16.5% as 1 ml, 10 ml and 20 ml injections.

Human hepatitis B immunoglobulins 0.06–0.1 ml/kg or 40 units/kg IM at the time of exposure to infected blood or its products. For neonates of mothers who are HBsAg positive (especially if e-antigen positive) use 0.5–1 ml or 100–200 i.u. preferably within 12 hr of birth (up to 72 hr). Active immunization is started simultaneously by administration of (Biovac B by Merind, Revac B by Bharat Biotech 1 ml contains 160 mg of human antihepatitis B immunoglobulins in ampoules of 0.5 ml, 1.0 ml, 3.0 ml and 5.0 ml, Hepabig (VHB Life Sciences) and Hepaglob (Sun Pharmaceuticals) 100 i.u./0.5 ml, 200 i.u./1 ml. Human hepatitis B immunoglobulin 100 i.u./1 ml by Savyt Life Care).

Human high dose intravenous immunoglobulins (IVIG) They are administered IV for treatment of Kawasaki disease, and other immune mediated inflammatory disorders such as ITP, Guillain-Barré syndrome, juvenile dermatomyositis.

For Kawasaki disease; 2 gm/kg over a 10–12 hr duration of the infusion can be given slowly in cases with increased risk of cardiac failure/fluid overload.

Precautions/adverse events: Severe systemic symptoms (hemodynamic changes, respiratory failure and anaphylaxis), headache, aseptic meningitis, acute renal failure (increased risk with sucrose containing IVIG and pre-existing renal compromise) acute venous thrombosis (increased risk with sucrose containing IVIG).

Intraglobin is available in ampoules of 5 ml (250 mg), 10 ml (500 mg), 20 ml (1 g) and infusion bottles of 50 ml (2.5 g), 100 ml (5.0 g) and 200 ml (10 g).

Pentaglobin is available in ampoules of 5 ml, 10 ml, 20 ml and infusion bottles of 50 ml, 100 ml. Each 5 g (100 ml bottles) contains IgG 3.8 g, IgM 0.6 g, IgA 0.6 g, glucose 2.5 g, sodium chloride 0.45 g. It has higher concentration of IgM immunoglobulins to offer protection against Gram-negative infections. The therapeutic utility is controversial and needs further evaluation.

Sandoglobulins They are available in 3 g and 6 g vials. For life-threatening infection: 400 mg/kg daily IV for 5 days or 1.0 g/kg daily IV for 2 days.

(Gamma IV, IV globulin, isiven IV, venimunn, globomin IV, ZY-IVGG 0.5 g, 1.0 g, 2.5 g, 5.0 g vials).

Human rabies-specific immunoglobulins (HRIG) The usual dose is 20 units/kg. Use maximal possible or total dose for infiltration around the site of bites and give the rest IM over gluteal region or lateral thigh, if patient presents within 24 hr. If the wound is large, dilute with saline (twofold or threefold) and infiltrate over large areas around the bite. The total dose is given IM if patient presents between 1 and 7 days. The rabies vaccine should also be administered simultaneously at a separate site. *The immunoglobulins are now recommended for all subjects with animal bite who are at risk for development of rabies except those who are previously immunized with rabies vaccine.*
(KamRab 150 i.u./ml in 2 ml vial, Rabglob 300 i.u./ml, Berirab-P 150 i.u./ml in 2 ml and 5 ml vials).

Human tetanus-specific immunoglobulins
Prophylactic: 250 units IM, increase to 500 units IM in case 24 hr have elapsed or when there is a heavily contaminated wound.

Therapeutic: 3000 to 6000 units/kg IM.
(Inj tetraglobulin, tetagam-P 250 units per 2 ml vial; tetanus immunoglobulin, tetglob, immunotetan 250 units, 500 units for IM, IV).

Recombinant rabies human monoclonal antibodies (R-Mab) 3.33 i.u./kg is infiltrated into and around the wound as early as possible but within 7 days of bite. In multiple wounds, it can be diluted with 0.9% sodium chloride solution. Keep epinephrine handy during administration. The left over antibodies can be administered IM. *Rabishield should never he given in the same syringe or at the same site as rabies vaccine.*

SE: Headache, myalgias, fatigue, chills and fever, local pain, swelling and redness.
(Rabishield® SII 100 i.u./2.5 ml and 250 i.u./2.5 ml vials).

Respiratory syncytial virus immunoglobulins (RSV-IGIV) 750 mg/kg IV every 30 days in infants with a history of prematurity (<35 wk) and/or bronchopulmonary dysplasia for prophylaxis against respiratory syncytial virus infection.

RSV-IVIG 750 mg/kg is administered in accordance with the following schedule: Start RSV-IGIV at 1.5 ml/kg/hr for 15 min, increase the rate to 3 ml/kg/hr for 15 min. If clinical condition does not contraindicate, higher dose with a maximum rate of 6 ml/kg/hr is infused. In critically ill children, particularly those with BPD, slower rates of infusion are recommended. In infants and children receiving RSV-IVIG prophylaxis (750 mg/kg dose), immunization with measles-mumps-rubella and varicella vaccines should be deferred for 9 mon after the last dose of IVIG. (Respi Gam 50 mg/ml).

Tetanus antitoxin (Equine)

Antitetanus serum is recommended only when tetanus immunoglobulin is not available. It can be administered as a single dose 50,000–1,00,000 units (half IM and half IV after skin test).

Caution: Horse serum reaction.

(Inj tetanus antitoxin Bengal Immunity 750 i.u., 5000 i.u., 10,000 i.u., 20,000 iu, 50,000 i.u., Biological Evans 750 i.u., 1500 i.u., 10,000 i.u., Haffkine 1500 i.u./1 ml, 10,000 iu, 3.4 ml ampoule; 20,000 i.u. 5 ml ampoule).

Varicella zoster immunoglobulin (VZIG) 125 units for neonates and 125 U for every 10 kg increment in weight, maximum 1 g (IM route). To be administered as soon as possible, not later than 10 days of exposure.

Indic: Neonates of mothers who develop chickenpox 5 days before or 48 hr after delivery, postnatally exposed preterm infants of susceptible mothers, immunocompromised children and pregnant women. VZIG is not indicated if mother has herpes zoster (shingles).

(VZIG 125 units per vial, Varitect CP 25 i.u./ml in 5 ml ampoules).

Chapter

19

Antitubercular Drugs

In pediatric population, only daily doses of antitubercular drugs are recommended; thrice weekly regimen is no longer recommended.

Amikacin sulfate 15–20 mg/kg/day single dose up to maximum of 1.0 g IM or IV. Effective against *Mycobacterium tuberculosis* and some atypical mycobacteria. It is infrequently used in current regimens.

Adult dose: 1.0 gm single daily dose IM.

SE: Nephrotoxicity, ototoxicity.
(Inj amicin, ivimicin, pakacin, xenocin 100 mg, 250 mg and 500 mg in 2 ml vials).

Bedaquiline Recommended only for patients >5 yr (15 kg or more) for a maximum period of 6 mon in combination with other drugs. Weight 15–30 kg, 200 mg OD for 2 wk followed by 100 mg thrice a wk. Children >30 kg 400 mg OD for 2 wk f/b 200 mg thrice a wk.

SE: Headache, pain abdomen, palpitations, QTc prolongation, tremors, anxiety, depression (Sirturo tab 100 mg, 20 mg DT).

Capreomycin 15–30 mg/kg/day up to maximum of 1.0 g IM. It is used in multidrug resistant (MDR) tuberculosis.

SE: Nephrotoxicity, ototoxicity (Inj capreo 500 mg vial).

Clarithromycin 15 mg/kg/day q 12 hr oral (do not exceed 500 mg/dose). Used in *Mycobacterium avium* infections.

Adult dose: 500 mg q 12 hr.

(Claribid, crixan, clarithro-250, clamycin tab DT 125 mg, 250 mg; clarimac, clarbact tabs 250 mg, 500 mg; syrup claribid, crixan, synclar 125 mg and 250 mg/5 ml).

Clofazimine 2–5 mg/kg/day single dose (maximum dose 100 mg/day). May be used on alternate days in children below 15 kg. Used in leprosy and drug-resistant tuberculosis.

SE: It may cause transient blackish discoloration of the body. icthyosis and dry skin.

(Cap or tab clofozine, hansepran 50 mg, 100 mg).

Cycloserine 15–20 mg/kg/day q 12 hr oral (maximum dose 1000 mg/day). It is a second line bacteriostatic drug, used in MDR tuberculosis.

Adult dose: 250 mg q 12 hr for 2 wk and then increase to 500 mg q 12 hr.

SE: Neurological toxicity, depression, suicidal tendency.

C/I: Epilepsy, renal failure.

(Cyclorin, myser, coxerin, pamserine cap 250 mg).

Delamanid WHO approved 3 yr onwards, 6–11 yr-50 mg BD for 24 wk; 12–17 yr-100 mg BD for 24 wk. Used in multidrug resistant TB.

SE: headache, nausea, QT-prolongation, neurological toxicity like tremors, paresthesia, depression.

(Deltyba tab 50 mg)

Ethambutol 15–25 (average 20) mg/kg/day single dose oral. Maximum daily dose is 2 g/day.

Maximum adult dose: 2 g/day.

SE: Retrobulbar neuritis, red and green color blindness.

(Albutol, combutol, tibitol, themibutol, mycobutol, myambutol tabs 200 mg, 400 mg, 600 mg and 800 mg).

Ethionamide 15–20 mg/kg/day q 12 hr oral. Maximum dose 1000 mg per day. It is second line drug, to be used when first line drugs fail.

Adult dose: 500–1000 mg q 8–12 hr, maximum 1 g/day.

SE: Hallucinations, hypothyroidism, menstrual disturbances, gynecomastia, neuropathy. Monitor thyroid function tests every 3 months.
(Ethide, myobid, mycotuf, ethiocid tab 250 mg).

Isoniazid 7–15 (average 10) mg/kg/day single daily dose on empty stomach up to maximum of 300 mg. High dose INH for drug resistant TB-15–20 mg/kg/day.

Adult dose: 300 mg/day.

SE: Hepatic damage, peripheral neuropathy, coadminister with pyrodoxine.
(Isonex, solonex DT 100 mg, isonex forte, solonex; isokin tab 300 mg; syrup isokin, ipcazide, siozide 100 mg per 5 ml).

Kanamycin sulfate 15–20 mg/kg/d in single or two divided doses IM. Maximum dose 1000 mg. It is a second line anti-tubercular agent.

Adult dose: 1 g/day single dose IM.

SE: Deafness, nephrotoxicity.
(Inj kancin, efficin, kanamac 500 mg, 1000 mg vial).

Levofloxacin <5 yr—15–20 mg/kg in two divided doses >5 yr—10–15 mg/kg OD. Classified as group A drug for drug resistant TB.

SE: Diarrhea, nausea, arthralgia.
(Levoflox, leon, levoday, zilee tabs 250 mg, 500 mg, 750 mg; syrup 125 mg/5 ml).

Linezolid 15 mg/kg OD in 1–15 kg, 10 mg/kg OD in >15 kg child, maximum 600 mg/day. Classified as group A drug for drug resistant TB.

Adult dose: 300 mg once/twice daily (maximum 600 mg/day for MDR tuberculosis).

SE: Diarrhea, bone marrow suppression, neuropathy, visual disturbances. Monitor complete blood count every visit.
(Tab alzolid, cadlizo, linospan, lizbid, lizolid, walibur 600 mg, syrup lizomed 100 mg/5 ml).

Moxifloxacin 10–15 mg/kg OD. Classified as group A drug for drug resistant TB.

SE: Tendinopathy, GI disturbances, headache, and prolonged QTc interval.

(Tab 400 mg, 100 mg dt)

Para-aminosalicylic acid (PAS) 150 mg/kg/day q 8–12 hr oral after food, maximum 12 g/day. PAS (including PAS sodium) is administered in acidic medium (e.g. yoghurt or orange juice) for improved absorption.

Adult dose: 12–16 gm/day q 6–8 hr.

SE: GI symptoms, crystalluria, hypothyroidism. Monitor thyroid function tests.

(Tab monopas 1 g, PAS sachet 4 g each, Q-PAS granules contain 800 mg PAS per gram of granules; each leveled scoop provides 3.5 g).

Prothionamide It is a thioamide derivative useful in multidrug-resistant (MDR) tuberculosis. The usual dose is 15–20 mg/kg/day in 2–3 divided doses. Maximum dose 1000 mg/day.

Adult dose: 250 mg 3 times a day, up to maximum of 1.0 g/day.

Caution: Avoid in patients with hepatic dysfunction, porphyria and psychiatric disorder.

(Pethide, prothiocid, protomid, and mycotuf-P tab 250 mg).

Pyrazinamide 30–40 (average 35) mg/kg/day single daily dose up to maximum of 2 g.

Adult dose: 30–40 mg/kg once a day (maximum 2 g/d) or 50 mg/kg on alternate days or 75 mg/kg twice weekly.

SE: Hepatotoxicity, hyperuricemia, arthralgia, rash.

(Pyzid tab 300 mg; PZA-Ciba, P-zide, pyzina, piraldina, copyrazin tabs 500 mg, 750 mg and 1000 mg, pyzin kid tab 300 mg; PZA-Ciba tab 250 mg, syrup PZA-Ciba 250 mg/5 ml).

Rifampicin 10–20 (average 15) mg/kg/day single dose empty stomach. Maximum dose 600 mg/day. Effective for CNS and genitourinary tuberculosis, as it readily penetrates into all tissues and body secretions including urine which is stained orange. For *H. influenzae* type b prophylaxis to the close contacts of index child: 20 mg/kg/day once a day (maximum 600 mg/day) oral for 4 days (below 1 mon of age 10 mg/kg/day). For *N. meningitidis* prophylaxis: 10 mg/kg, maximum 600 mg (5 mg/kg for infants <1 mon of age) every 12 hr for 4 doses. It is also useful in cat-scratch disease.

SE: Orange discoloration of secretions, cholestatic jaundice, hepatitis, flu-like syndrome (fever, chills, myalgia, thrombocytopenia, anemia, etc.), hemolysis.

C/I: Hepatic damage.
(R-cin, rifacilin, rifamycin, rimactane, rimpin, rifampin caps 150 mg, 300 mg, 450 mg, 600 mg; syrup R-cin, rimactane, ticin 100 mg per 5 ml).

For better compliance: Fixed dose combinations (FDCs) may be used, provided bioavailability data is available for the formulations and doses are appropriate.

Rifampicin + isoniazid: The usual dose should be rifampicin 15 mg/kg and INH 10 mg/kg per day.
Tab rimactazid kid, ticinex, R-cinex, AKT-2, coxter-2, coxinex, mycocox, tab contain rifampicin 450 mg + INH 300 mg

Rifampicin + isoniazid + pyrazinamide: The usual dose should be rifampicin 15 mg/kg, INH 10 mg/kg and pyrazinamide 30–35 mg/kg daily. Pediatric FDC under National Tuberculosis Eradication Program (NTEP). Rifampicin 75 mg + Isoniazid 50 mg + Pyrazinamide 150 mg: One tab for each 5 kg body weight; Cavirip 1000: rifampicin 450 mg + isoniazid 300 mg + pyrazinamide 1000 mg (1 tab appropriate for 30 kg child); Tab caviter, rifater: rifampicin 120 mg + isoniazid 80 mg + pyrazinamide 250 mg (1 tab appropriate for 8 kg child); Tab rinizide, R-cinex Z kid, akurit-3: rifampicin 150 mg + isoniazid 100 mg + pyrazinamide 375 mg (1 tab for 10 kg child).

Rifampicin + isoniazid + ethambutol + pyrazinamide: Mycocox-4, zucox-4 contains rifampicin 450 mg, isoniazid 300 mg, ethambutol 800 mg and pyrazinamide 750 mg.

Streptomycin sulfate 15–20 mg/kg/day IM daily. For drug resistant TB 20–40 mg/kg/day IM daily. Maximum daily dose 1 g.

Adult dose: 15 mg/kg/day (maximum 1.0 g) single dose IM can be given up to 3 mon.

SE: Hypersensitivity, vestibular damage, local pain, nephrotoxicity.

(Inj streptomycin sulfate 1 g vial; inj ambistryn-S, cipstryn, isos 0.75 g, 1 g vials).

Thioacetazone (amithiozone) 3–4 mg/kg/day, maximum 150 mg once daily. Used as third line agent for MDR tuberculosis.

Adult dose: 150 mg OD.

SE: Rash, GI symptoms, giddiness, leukopenia.

(Isokin-T forte tab contains isoniazid 300 mg + thioacetazone 150 mg, unithiben tab provides isoniazid 75 mg + thioacetazone 37.5 mg + pyridoxine 0.75 mg).

Chapter

20

Antiviral Agents

Aciclovir Neonatal HSV: Skin, eye, oral and CNS manifestations: 20 mg/kg q 8 hr IV for 14 days; Disseminated and CNS disease: 20 mg/kg q 8 hr IV for 21 days. HSV encephalitis: Age >28 days to <12 yr: 20 mg/kg q 8 hr IV for 21 days; ≥12 yr: 10 mg/kg q 8 hr IV for 21 days. Varicella in immunocompetent host: 20 mg/kg q 6 hr (maximum 800 mg/dose) for 5 days (beneficial only when given within first 24 hr of onset of rash). Recommended only in individuals at increased risk of moderate to severe varicella: Non-pregnant individuals >12 yr, individuals >12 mon with chronic cutaneous and pulmonary manifestations, short-term steroid, long-term salicylate therapy and secondary cases of household contacts. Varicella-zoster in immunocompromised children: 10 mg/kg q 8 hr or 500 mg/m^2/dose IV q 8 hr for 7–10 days. Herpes zoster or chickenpox in adolescents and adults 800 mg q 6 hr for 5 days. Herpes simplex 200 mg q 4 hr for 5 days.

Caution: The recommended final concentration for IV administration is ≤7 mg/ml. Administer over at least one hr to prevent renal tubular damage.

(Zovirax, zovir, acivir, civir, intravir, ocuvir, axovir, acyclor, herperex, herpikind, herpex tabs 200 mg, 400 mg, 800 mg; zovirax susp 400 mg/5 ml in 100 ml bottle, inj acivir, noherp, zovirax 250 mg, 500 mg; ophthalmic ointment 3% and herpex, ocuvir skin ointment 5%).

Adefovir dipivoxil Lamivudine-resistant HBV infection. However, it has been widely replaced by tenofovir. Oral 10 mg/day can be administered up to the age of 5 yr.

(Adesera, adfovir, adheb tab 10 mg).

Adenine arabinoside (Vidarabine) Neonatal HSV: 15–30 mg/kg/d given in single dose IV as a slow infusion during 12–24 hr for 10–21 days.

Indic: Herpes simplex infections.

(Vira A injection 200 mg per ml, vira A ophthalmic ointment 3%).

Amantadine hydrochloride 4–8 mg/kg/day in 2 divided doses. Maximum dose of 150 mg/day up to 10 yr of age and 200 mg/day after 10 yr. Duration of treatment until 24–48 hr after resolution of symptoms (usually up to 7 days).

Adult dose: 200 mg OD or 100 mg BD up to maximum of 300 mg/day.

Indic: Antiviral agent for prophylaxis and treatment of influenza A, drug-induced extrapyramidal reactions and parkinsonism.

C/I: Epilepsy.

(Amantrel, comantrel, neaman, parkitidin, flublast, symmetrel cap 100 mg, syrup 50 mg per 5 ml).

Famciclovir It is recommended above 18 yr of age. Herpes zoster: 500 mg q 8 hr for 7 days. Genital herpes simplex: 250 mg q 8 hr for 7–10 days. Recurrent herpes labialis: 1.5 g single dose. Recurrent genital herpes: 250 mg BD for one year.

(Famtrex, microvir, penvir, virovir, famicimac tabs 250 mg, 500 mg).

Foscarnet CMV retinitis in patients with AIDS: 180 mg/kg/d q 8 hr IV slow infusion over 1 hr for 21 days (induction), then 90–120 mg/kg once daily as maintenance dose. Aciclovir- resistant HSV and herpes zoster in an immunocompromised host: 120 mg/kg/d q 8 hr IV till resolution of infection or duration of 3 wk.

SE: Dizziness, hypertension, seizures, and dyselectrolytemia.
(Inj foscavir 500 mg, 1 g vials).

Ganciclovir Acquired CMV retinitis, pneumonitis and GI infections in an immunocompromised host: 5 mg/kg/dose q 12 hr IV for 14–21 days (induction), then 5 mg/kg single daily dose for maintenance. Prophylaxis of CMV in high-risk host (e.g. transplant patients): 5 mg/kg/dose q 12 hr IV for 7 days then 5 mg/kg/d PO for 100 days. Oral drug has poor bioavailability of 5–6%.

Indic: Acquired CMV retinitis in immunocompromised patients (including AIDS), congenital CMV pneumonia, prevention of CMV disease in transplant recepients at risk of CMV disease.

Caution: Monitor blood counts, platelet count and serum creatinine level; administer at a final concentration of 10 mg/ml over 1–2 hr as a slow infusion.
(Cymevene, ganguard cap 250 mg, 500 mg; natclovir, neoclovir tabs 250 mg, 500 mg; inj cytogan, gavir 500 mg per vial; galtevir eye gel 0.15%).

Idoxuridine Topical instilation in the eyes for herpetic keratitis. (Ridinox, idwin, toxil, xurin ophthalmic drops 0.1%, toxil eye ointment 0.5%).

Isoprinosine 50–100 mg/kg/day q 12 hr oral. Indic: Subacute sclerosing panencephalitis (Isoprinosine tab 500 mg).

Oseltamivir Treatment of influenza A and B including H1N1: Infants <3 mon: 12 mg q 12 hr, 3–5 mon: 20 mg q 12 hr, 6–11 mon: 25 mg q 12 hr for 5 days. According to body weight: <15 kg 30 mg q 12 hr, 15–23 kg 45 mg q 12 hr, 23–40 kg 60 mg q 12 hr, >40 kg 75 mg q 12 hr oral for 5 days; Prophylaxis: same dose as above but once daily for 7–10 days after the last known exposure.

Adult dose: 75 mg q 12 hr for 5 days.

SE: Nausea, vomiting, abdominal pain, epistaxis, skin rash.
(Fluvir, tamiflu, natflu, antiflu caps 30 mg, 45 mg and 75 mg, suspension 12 mg/ml).

Ribavirin Dilute 6 g of ribavirin in 300 ml of sterile water and nebulize for 12–18 hr/d or 2 g over 2 hr 3 times daily for 3–7 days. Oral dose 15–20 mg/kg/day q 6–8 hr for 7–10 days up to maximum dose of 1800 mg/day.

Adult dose: Herpes simplex 200 mg q.i.d. for 7–10 days; influenza 200 mg q.i.d. for 3–5 days; chronic hepatitis C 1000 mg daily (400 mg morning, 600 mg evening) for 48 wk (genotype 1) and for 24 wk (genotype 2 and 3).

Indic: RSV infection (bronchiolitis, pneumonia) and chronic hepatitis C (along with IFN-α2b).
(Ribavin cap, rebetol, virazide tabs 100 mg, 200 mg, syrup virazide, ribavin 50 mg/5 ml).

Trifluridine Topical use for herpes simplex conjunctivitis and keratitis q 12 hr (with IV aciclovir or vidarabine) 1 drop in each eye every 2 hr (maximum 9 drops) for 7 days. Following re-epithelialization, 1 drop every 4 hr (minimum 5 drops/day). Do not exceed treatment beyond 21 days.
(Viroptic ophthalmic drops 1%).

Valganciclovir It is a prodrug of ganciclovir. Treatment: 16 mg/kg/dose (maximum 900 mg) 12 hrly. CMV prophylaxis in post-transplant patients (start within 10 days of transplant): 16 mg/kg/dose (maximum 900 mg) once daily oral for 100 days.

CMV retinitis in adults: 900 mg/dose 12 hrly for 21 days (induction), then 900 mg/dose once daily (maintenance). 250 mg/m^2/d for 3 wk, then 125 mg/m^2/d oral for another 3 wk for CMV hepatitis and biliary atresia due to CMV.
(Valcept, valgan, valcyte, vagacyte, valgaids, valniche, valstead tab 450 mg).

Zanamivir It is recommended for prophylaxis and treatment of H1N1 infection in children above 7 yr of age. It is available in powder form with an inhalation device. For treatment, give inhalation of 10 mg twice a day for 5 days within 48 hr of onset of symptoms. For prophylaxis, inhalation should be started within 36 hr of exposure with a daily single dose of 10 mg for 7 days.

SE: Inhalation may cause severe bronchospasm in patients with reactive airway disease. Common adverse effects include dizziness, behavior disturbances and severe allergic reactions including angioedema.

(Relenza, virenza and Z Flu DPI are available to provide 5 mg zanamivir per actuation along with a delivery device for inhalation).

ANTI COVID-19 MEDICATIONS

Remdesivir Nucleotide analog prodrug, inhibits ribonucleic acid. ≥3 to <40 kg: 5 mg/kg IV loading dose on day 1, followed by 2.5 mg/kg IV OD and ≥40 kg: 200 mg IV loading dose on day 1, followed by 100 mg IV OD for up to 5 days in severe disease and up to 10 days in critical disease.

SE: Nausea, vomiting, anemia and elevated transaminases. remdesivir not recommended if eGFR <30 ml/min/m^2; AST/ALT >5 times UNL.

(Inj remdac, remwin, redyx, cipremi, jubi-r, remivir and covifor 100 mg/vial).

Favipiravir Prodrug, inhibits RNA-dependent RNA polymerase. 3.6 g on day 0 followed by 1.6 g daily to complete 7 days course.

SE: Liver dysfunction, diarrhea, nausea, abdominal pain and thrombocytopenia.

(Avigan, avifavir, avipiravir, areplivir, fabiflu, favipira, reeqonus, and qifenda tab 100 mg, 200 mg).

Molnupiravir Nucleoside analogue, 800 mg PO twice daily for 5 days in patients ≥18 yr.

SE: Diarrhea, nausea and dizziness.

(Esplevir, lagevrio, molulife, molena, marck, cap 200 mg).

Lopinavir–Ritonavir Fixed dose combination of lopinavir/ritonavir (400 mg and 100 mg, respectively) twice a day for 14 days in adults.

SE: Diarrhea, nausea, abdominal pain, asthenia, headache, vomiting, rash and hyperlipidemia.

Caution: Lopinavir-ritonavir induces the hepatic activity CYP3A subsets.

(Alltera, emletra, hivus-LR, lopimune, lopinovir R, luprareg, ritocom, ritoford, prolavir LR, tab 200/50 mg).

Nirmatrelvir–Ritonavir Nirmatrelvir 300 mg and ritonavir PO co-administered twice daily for 5 days.

SE: Taste change, diarrhea, vomiting, rise in blood pressure, muscle pain.
(Paxzen, paxlovid, pimovir and paxista tab 100 mg, 150 mg).

Bebtelovimab Neutralizing human IgG1 monoclonal antibody. Approved only for emergency (EUA) use. Age ≥12 yr and weighing ≥40 kg: IV: 175 mg as a single dose.

SE: Infusion related reactions, rash, nausea, vomiting.
(Bebtelovimab 175 mg/2 ml injection).

Tocilizumab Humanized monoclonal antibody against the IL-6 receptor, approved for emergency use (EUA). 8 mg/kg IV once (maximum dose: 800 mg), a second dose may be considered ≥8 hr after the first dose.

Caution: US boxed warning for developing serious infections.

SE: Increase in cholesterol, derangement of liver functions, hypersensitivity, leukopenia.
(inj. actemra, roactemra, actpen 400 mg/20 ml).

ANTIRETROVIRAL AGENTS (HIV DRUGS)

Abacavir 8 mg/kg q 12 hr for children >3 mon of age with maximum dose of 300 mg.

Adult dose: 300 mg BD or 600 mg OD.

SE: Abdomen discomfort, numbness/tingling of hands and feet, sores in mouth, cough.
(Abamune, abavir, virol, synabac, ulcom, abec, ziagen tab 300 mg; susp 20 mg/ml).

Didanosine Neonatal dose up to 90 days: 50 mg/m^2 q 12 hr. ≥3–8 mon: 100 mg/m^2 q 12 hr. Pediatric dose (>8 mon): 120 mg/m^2 q 12 hr (range 90–150 mg/m^2); maximum 200 mg/dose.

20 *Adolescent dose:* <60 kg 250 mg OD and >60 kg 400 mg OD, give 30 min before or 2 hr after meals.

SE: Headache, pancreatitis, peripheral neuropathy, optic neuritis, and liver dysfunction.
(Videx EC, DDI, Ddretro, virosine, dinex tabs 25 mg, 50 mg, 100 mg, 150 mg, 200 mg; dinex EC caps 250 mg, 400 mg, oral susp 10 mg/ml).

Dolutegravir (DTG) Used as 1st line therapy for children above 6 yr (>20 kg). Usual dose is 50 mg BD (often used as FDC with other ART).

SE: Hepatotoxicity, skin rashes, weight gain, sleep disturbance.

Efavirenz (EFV) Pediatric dose for 10 to 15 kg: 200 mg OD, 15 to 20 kg: 250 mg OD, 20 to 25 kg: 300 mg OD, 25 to 32.5 kg: 350 mg OD, 32.5 to 40 kg: 400 mg OD, >40 kg 600 mg OD In case of oral suspension, use a 30% higher dose.

Caution: Severe CNS and psychiatric symptoms can occur.
(Sustiva caps 50 mg, 100 mg and 200 mg; efirenz, efavir, estiva, evirenz caps 200 mg and 600 mg; eferven, efcure tabs 200 mg, 600 mg; oral suspension 30 mg/ml).

Lamivudine (3TC) Reverse transcriptase inhibitor used in combination with zidovudine and/or other anti-HIV drugs. Neonates: 4 mg/kg/day p.o. q 12 hr; Children: 4 mg/kg/dose p.o. q 12 hr. Maximum daily dose is 150 mg.

Adult dose: 300 mg OD
(Lamidac, hepavud, hepitec, lamivir, virolam tab 100 mg; ladiwin, lamda, cytocom, lamivir, retrolam, virolam tab 150 mg; susp 10 mg/ml).

Lopinavir plus Ritonavir 14 days to 12 months: 16 mg/kg lopinavir + 4 mg/kg ritonavir q 12 hr with food; >12 mon–18 yr: <15 kg: 12 mg/kg lopinavir + 3 mg/kg ritonavir q 12 hr with food; 15–40 kg: 10 mg/kg lopinavir + 2.5 mg/kg ritonavir q 12 hr with food. Administer with food to enhance bioavailability.

Indic: Alternative first line ART regime for children <3 yr age or <10 kg not tolerating nevirapine or in infants with prior exposure to NNRTI. Protease inhibitor often effective against saquinavir and zidovudine-resistant strains of HIV virus. Ritonavir-resistant strains are often cross-resistant with other agents. (Lopimune, ritocom, ritomax-L, V-L etra cap contains lopinavir 133.3 mg and ritonavir 33.3 mg).

Nelfinavir Children over 2 yr: 45–55 mg/kg twice daily up to maximum dose of 2 g.

Adult dose: 1250 mg q 12 hr with food.

Indic: No longer recommended in children due to inferior potency compared to other regimes.
(Nelvir, retronel, nelfin, nel tab 250 mg).

Nevirapine (NVP) Used for prevention of mother to child transmission either alone or in combination of syrup zidovudine as per NACO 2021.

Birth to 6 wk

- <2 kg: 2 mg/kg or 0.2 ml/kg of suspension
- 2–2.5 kg: 10 mg OD or 1 ml OD of suspension
- >2.5 kg: 15 mg OD or 1.5 ml OD of suspension.
- < 6wk to 6 mon: 20 mg or 2 ml OD of suspension
- >6 mon to 9 mon: 30 mg or 3 ml OD of suspension
- >9 mon till breastfeeding ends: 40 mg or 4 ml OD of suspension.

The duration of nevirapine prophylaxis is minimum for 6 wk which can be extended up to 12 wk, if mother has not received ART triple prophylaxis from 24 wk of gestation.

Children: 200 mg/m^2/dose oral q 12 hr (maximum dose 200 mg). Induction dose: Once daily for first 14 days; maintenance dose: Increase to q 12 hr, if no risk/untoward effect. It is a non-nucleoside reverse transcriptase inhibitor and is specific for HIV-1 transcriptase (not HIV-2) or human polymerase.

Adult dose: 200 mg OD for 2 wk; increase the dose to 200 mg BD, if no rash occurs.

SE: Skin rash, Stevens-Johnson syndrome, liver dysfunction.
(Nevimune, neve, nevipan, neviretro tab 200 mg; susp 10 mg/ml).

Stavudine (d4T) ≥14 days and <30 kg: 1 mg/kg/dose q 12 hr p.o.

Adolescents and adult dose: 30 mg BD

SE: Nausea, headache, peripheral neuropathy, pancreatitis. (Zerit caps 15 mg, 20 mg, 30 mg, 40 mg; stavir, stag, virostav, stadine caps 30 mg, 40 mg; susp 1 mg/ml).

Tenofovir First line ART for adults and pregnant women and children >10 yr. Not recommended below 2 yr of age. 2 yr–<12 yr: 8 mg/kg/dose OD; Adolescents (>35 kg): 300 mg OD

Adult dose: 300 mg OD

SE: Nephrotoxicity, hypophosphatemia.
(Tenvir, tenof, tentide, tenohep, tavin tab 300 mg).

Zalicitabine (DDC) Pediatric dose <13yr: 0.01 mg/kg q 8 hr. Adolescents >13 yr: 0.75 mg q 8 hr, one hr before or two hr after meals.

Adult dose: 1 mg q 12 hr.
(Hivid, DDC tabs 0.375 mg, 0.75 mg).

Zidovudine (ZDV, AZT) IV dose (term): 1.5 mg/kg q 6 hr; IV (preterm): 1.5 mg/kg q 12 hr; For prevention of mother to child transmission; First 6 wk: <2 kg: 4 mg/kg/dose q 12 hr; 2–2.5 kg: 10 mg q 12 hr; ≥2.5 kg: 15 mg q 12 hr; >6–12 wk: 60 mg q 12 hr.

Pediatric dose: <4 wk: 4 mg/kg q 12 hr; ≥4 wk: 4 to <9 kg: 12 mg/kg q 12 hr; 9–<30 kg: 9 mg/kg q 12 hr; ≥30 kg: 300 mg q 12 hr.

Adult dose: 300 mg q 12 hr.
(Retrovir, zidovir cap 100 mg, zido-H tab 100 mg; zidovir-300, zillion tab 300 mg; syrup 50 mg/5 ml).

According to NACO 2021 recommendations, the first line regimen for ART for retropositive children:
Age <6 yr (<20 kg): Abacavir+ lamivudine (3TC) + lopinavir/ritonavir;
Age 6–10 yr (20–30 kg): Abacavir + lamivudine (3 TC) + dolutegravir (DTG)
Age >10 yr (wt >30 kg): Tenofovir (TDF) + lamivudine (3 TC) + dolutegravir (DTG).

Chapter

21

Bronchodilators and Other Drugs for Asthma

Adrenaline (epinephrine) 0.01 ml/kg per dose (maximum 0.5 ml per dose) of 1:1000 solution IM. Repeat the dose after 15–20 min. For cardiac arrest, intravenous 0.1 ml/kg per dose of 1:10,000 solution, and endotracheal: 0.1 ml/kg per dose of 1:1000 solution. *Do not use 1:1000 solution IV unless ten times diluted.* For laryngeal edema due to anaphylaxis and croup, give 0.5 ml/kg (maximum 5 ml) of 1:1000 solution by nebuliser.

Adult dose: 0.5–1.0 ml of 1:1000 solution IM.
(Inj adrenaline 1 mg per ml; ampoule 1:1000 solution).

Aminophylline 15 to 20 mg/kg/day q 8 hr oral. For status asthmaticus: 5 mg/kg loading dose IV followed by continuous infusion at the following rate: 6 mon – 1 yr: 0.6–0.7 mg/kg/hr; 1–9 yr: 1.0–1.2 mg/kg/hr; 9–12 yr: 0.9 mg/kg/hr; >12 yr: 0.7 mg/kg/hr.

The loading dose should be diluted and given slowly. If patient is already receiving oral aminophylline derivatives, do not use the loading dose. For apneic attacks in preterm infants: 5 mg/kg loading dose IV slowly followed by 2 mg/kg q 8 hr orally or IV as maintenance.

SE: Nausea, vomiting, irritability, restlessness, palpitations and convulsions.
(Aminophylline tab 100 mg; inj aminophylline 250 mg/2 ml in 10 ml ampoule).

Bambuterol hydrochloride It is an oral prodrug of terbutaline. Children between 2 and 5 yr: 5 mg, 6 and 12 yr: 10 mg single dose at night. Presently recommended for use in children above 2 yr of age.

Adult dose: 10–20 mg/day single dose.
(Bambudil, bemlo, roburol, betaday, asthafree, abel tabs 10 mg, 20 mg; syrup 5 mg and 10 mg per ml).

Beclomethasone dipropionate Inhalation of 50–1000 µg per day in 2 or 4 divided doses. (Low dose: 6–11 yr: 50–100 µg/d, 12 yr and older: 100–200 µg/d; medium dose: 6–11 yr: >100–200 µg/d, 12 yr and older: >200–400 µg/d; high dose: 6–11 yr: >200 µg/d, 12 yr and older: >400 µg/d). Chronic asthma patients require regular and prolonged treatment.

Beclomethasone nasal spray 50 µg metered dose aerosol once or twice a day for allergic rhinitis, vasomotor rhinitis, symptomatic relief of nasal polyposis.

SE: Hoarseness, candidiasis of mouth and throat. Rinse mouth after using inhaled steroid preparations.
(Beclate metered dose inhaler (MDI) provides 50 µg, 100 µg, 200 µg per puff/actuation; becoride MDI 100 µg; becoride forte 250 µg per puff, aerocort inhaler provides 100 µg salbutamol and 50 µg beclomethasone, aerocort rotacap provides 200 µg salbutamol and 100 µg beclomethasone; beclate rotacaps 100 µg, 200 µg, and 400 µg beclomethasone).

Budesonide Inhalation steroid for long-term asthma control at dose 100–800 µg per day q 12 hr. (Low dose: 6–11 yr: 100–200 µg/d, 12 yr and older: 200–400 µg/d; medium dose: 6–11 yr: >200–400 µg/d, 12 yr and older: >400–800 µg/d; high dose 6–11 yr: >400 µg/d, 12 yr and older: >800 µg/d). Once daily dosing may be considered in patients where asthma is controlled with 100–200 µg. For croup nebulize: 2 mg in 2.5 ml of normal saline single dose, if there is poor response it may be repeated q 12 hr for 48 hr.
(Pulmicort MDI provides 100 µg per dose/actuation; budecort, derinide, budez 100 µg and 200 µg per dose/actuation; budecort 100 µg, 200 µg and 400 µg rotacaps; budecort, bunase, pulmicort respules 0.5 mg and 1.0 mg in 2 ml ampoules for nebulization).

Budesonide plus formoterol fumarate Starting dose 400 µg for moderate and 800 µg for severe asthma per day q 12 hr as per budesonide component. Doses need to be increased or decreased on follow-up as per quality of asthma control. At present, formoterol is not recommended for children below 4 yr of age.

(Foracort, budamate, budetrol inhaler and rotacaps contain 6 µg formoterol fumarate and 100 µg, 200 µg and 400 µg budesonide per dose).

Ciclesonide Long-acting steroid for chronic asthma control 80–640 µg day. (Low dose 6–11 yr: 80 µg/d, 12 yr and older: 80–160 µg/d; medium dose 6–11 yr: 80–160 µg/d, 12 yr and older: >160–320 µg/d; high dose 6–11 yr: >160 µg/d, 12 yr and older: >320 µg/d).

Ciclesonide nasal spray for allergic rhinitis. 2–11 yr: 50 µg spray 1–2 puffs daily, maximum 200 µg/d, 12 yr and older: 2 puffs once daily, maximum 200 µg/d.

(MDI ciclohale 80 µg, 160 µg; ciclohale rotacap 200 µg, 400 µg/cap, nasal spray ciclospray, cinase, osonase 50 µg/puff, combination inhaler simplyone has ciclesonide 80 µg/160 µg and formeterol 4.5 µg per puff).

Doxofylline It is a new generation long-acting oral methyl xanthine derivative. It is given to children above 6 yr in a dose of 6 mg/kg q 12 hr.

Adult dose: 400 mg single dose at night or twice a day.

(Doxiflo, synasma, befree, asmadox, freefil, theobed-D tab 400 mg, doxiba, synasma, doxiflo, amidox, fyline, freefil syr 100 mg/5 ml).

Fluticasone propionate Inhaled steroid for long-term asthma control is administered in a dose of 100–500 µg/d in two divided doses. Low dose: 6–11 yr: 100–200 µg/d, 12 yr and older: 100–250 µg/d; medium dose: 6–11 yr: 200–500 µg/d, 12 yr and older: 250–500 µg/d; high dose: 6–11 yr: >500 µg/d, 12 yr and older: 500 µg/d.

Adult dose: 100–1000 µg/day.

(Flohale MDI 25 µg, 50 µg, 125 µg per dose/actuation; flohale rotacaps 100 µg, 250 µg per dose).

Fluticasone propionate plus salmeterol Starting dose 250 µg for moderate and 500 µg for severe asthma per day q 12 hr as per fluticasone component. Dose is adjusted as per level of asthma control. At present, salmeterol is not recommended for children below 4 yr of age.

(Seroflo inhaler provides fluticasone 50 µg, 125 µg and 250 µg with salmeterol 25 µg) and seroflo rotacaps (fluticasone 100 µg, 250 µg and 500 µg with salmeterol 50 µg.); respules 0.5 mg and 1 mg/ml. Seretide accuhaler provides 50 µg salmeterol and fluticasone 50 µg, 250 µg, 500 µg; Forair, serobid, seroflo rotacaps 50 µg salmeterol per cap along with fluticasone 100 µg, 250 µg, 500 µg).

Formoterol fumarate It is a long-acting selective beta-2 adrenergic agonist. Always used in combination with inhaled corticosteroids.

(Foracort inhaler and rotacaps contain 6 µg formoterol fumarate and 100 µg, 200 µg and 400 µg budesonide per dose).

Ipratropium bromide For acute asthma, nebulization 125 µg for below 1 yr, 250 µg for 1–12 yr, 500 µg for more than 12 yr, diluted in 3–4 ml of normal saline and given over 10 min. Alternatively, 2 puffs are given with an MDI-spacer every 20 min for 3 doses followed by every 4–6 hr up to 4 doses. It can be used in combination with salbutamol.

(Ipravent respirator solution 250 µg per ml, ipravent respule 500 µg/2.5 ml, ipravent MDI provides one metered dose of 20 µg. Duolin inhaler delivers levosalbutamol 50 µg and ipratropium bromide 20 µg per actuation, duolin rotacap provides levosalbutamol 100 µg and ipratropium bromide 40 µg, duolin respule contains levosalbutamol 1.25 mg, ipratropium bromide 500 µg per 2.5 ml).

Levosalbutamol Rescue therapy for asthma exacerbation 2 puffs of 50 µg MDI q 4–6 hr. Nebulization: 0.075 mg/kg (minimum 1.25 mg, maximum 5 mg) for 3 doses every 1–4 hrly or 0.25 mg/kg/hr continuous nebulization. The efficacy and side effects are similar to salbutamol. In emergency, it may be nebulized in combination with ipratropium; the dose is adjusted on the basis of ipratropium content.

(Levolin tabs 1 mg, 2 mg; syrup 0.5 and 1.0 mg/5 ml; levolin MDI 50 µg/puff; duolin MDI provides levosalbutamol 50 µg + ipratropium 20 µg per puff. Rotacaps provide levosalbutamol 100 µg and ipratropium bromide 40 µg; respules 0.31 mg, 0.63 mg and 1.25 mg. Duolin respules provide levosalbutamol 1.25 mg + ipratropium bromide 500 µg per 2.5 ml).

Mometasone furoate It is a corticosteroid used topically to reduce inflammation of the airways. It is recommended for children >2 yr with allergic rhinitis and nasal polyps and obstructive sleep apnea. Dose is one spray of 50 µg/dose into each nostril once daily for children between 2 and 11 yr. In children ≥12 yr, two sprays into each nostril once a day.

SE: Hypersensitivity reactions, rarely glaucoma, and cataracts. (Furomet, momeflo, avamys, momate, evocort, formost, metaspray, metatop, metasafe, nasonex nasal spray 50 µg/spray).

Montelukast sodium 6 mon –5 yr: 4 mg once a day, 6–14 yr: 5 mg once daily, >14 yr: 10 mg once daily in the evening.

Adult dose: 10 mg once daily in the evening.

Indic: Prophylaxis and treatment of chronic asthma, and allergic rhinitis.

(Montair, singulair, ventair, emlucast, romilast, telekast tabs 4 mg, 5 mg and 10 mg, syp montelukast 4 mg/5 ml).

Omalizumab (anti-IgE) In refractory allergic asthma, subcutaneous injection of 150–375 mg every 2–4 wk according to total serum IgE levels and body weight of the child.

(Inj xolair, bolstran 150 mg vial).

Salbutamol 0.1–0.4 mg/kg/dose every 8 hr oral. For acute exacerbation, up to 3 treatment protocols of 2–4 puffs (100 µg per puff) by MDI at 20 min intervals followed by 2 puffs every 4–6 hr. A spacer and mask is used in preschool children. For nebulization: 0.15 mg/kg/dose (minimum single dose is 2.5 mg and maximum single dose is 5 mg) is given every 20 min for

3 doses through a nebulizer using airflow of 6 L/min delivering 2–5 micron particle size. This can be continued till patient improves, thereafter nebulization is given every 2–6 hr. Use of oral salbutamol is not recommended for management of acute asthma. Dose for continuous nebulization for very severe exacerbation is 0.5 mg/kg/hr. Injection salbutamol 4–6 µg/kg/dose SC, IM or IV q 6–8 hr.

Adult dose: 2–4 mg/dose 3–4 times/day up to maximum of 32 mg/day.

SE: Irritability, tremors, tachycardia, nervousness, dizziness, and hypokalemia.

(Asthalin, ventorlin, asmanil, bronkotab, salbetol tabs 2 mg, 4 mg; ventorlin CR 4 mg cap, bronkotus, mucolinc tabs contain salbutamol 2 mg and bromhexine 8 mg, forte tabs contain salbutamol 4 mg, bromhexine 8 mg. Syrup SAAM BR contain salbutamol 2 mg, bromhexine 4 mg per 5 ml, syrup ventryl expectorant contains salbutamol 2 mg and bromhexine 8 mg per 5 ml, salmucolite contains salbutamol 2 mg + ambroxol 30 mg per 5 ml, syrup asthalin, ventorlin, bronkosyrup 2 mg (with guaiphenesin 100 mg) per 5 ml; bronkoplus syrup contains salbutamol 2 mg and theophyllin 100 mg per 5 ml. Asthalin, derihaler, ventorlin MDI 100 µg per metered dose; asthalin rotacaps contain 200 µg/cap; salsol nebuliser 3 ml solution contains 2.5 mg; asthalin repirator sol 1.0 ml contains 5 mg, respules 2.5 ml contains 2.5 mg, budesal respule contains salbutamol 2.5 mg + budesonide 5 mg in 2.5 ml).

Salmeterol xinafoate It is a long-acting naphthoic acid bronchodilator. Not recommended for children below 4 yr of age. Children ≥4 yr and adolescents 50 µg per inhalation twice a day.

Indic: Moderate to severe asthma, not to be used as monotherapy but as add-on to inhaled corticosteroids.

(Seretide accuhaler provides 50 µg salmeterol and fluticasone 50 µg, 250 µg, 500 µg; Esiflo, serobid, seroflo rotacaps 50 µg salmeterol per cap along with fluticasone 100 µg, 250 µg, 500 µg; combitide, esiflo, seroflo MDI contains 25 µg salmeterol and 50, 125, 250 µg fluticasone).

Sodium cromoglycate Initial dose is 1–2 puffs (5 mg per MDI dose) 3–4 times/d or 1 rotacap (20 mg/cap) 3–4 times/d. Maintenance dose: 1 puff 3–4 times/d or 2–3 rotacaps per day.

Adult dose: 2 puffs 4 times daily. Continuous prophylaxis is required, may take 4–6 wk for providing beneficial effect. It is rarely used nowadays.
(Cromal, ifiral 20 mg rotacap for inhalation; fintal inhaler provides 1 mg metered dose; cromal-5 inhaler provides 5 mg per metered dose).

Terbutaline sulfate 0.1–0.15 mg/kg/day q 8 hr oral. 0.005–0.01 mg/kg (0.01–0.02 ml/kg) SC up to 4 times in a day. IV infusion 2–10 µg/kg loading dose, then 0.1–0.4 µg/kg/min, increment every 30 min by 0.1–0.2 µg/kg/min. Inhalation of 1–2 puffs of 250 µg q 6–8 hr. For hyperkalemia: 125–150 µg/kg/dose SC. The nebulizer dose is 2.5 mg in children below 20 kg and 5 mg in children above 20 kg.

Adult dose: 2.5–5.0 mg q 8 hr oral. The parenteral dose is 0.25 mg stat followed by 1–10 µg/kg/hr.
(Bricanyl, asmaterb tabs 2.5 mg, 5 mg; syrup 1.5 mg per 5 ml; bricarex, bromenyl expectorant 1.5 mg per 5 ml; brozedex expectorant 2.5 mg per 10 ml, terphylin, theobiric tabs contain terbutaline sulfate 2.5 mg, etophylline 100 mg, tergil syrup 1.5 mg per 5 ml; tergil tab 2.5 mg; inj bricanyl 0.5 mg per ml; bricanyl MDI 250 µg per metered dose; bricanyl nebulising sol 10 mg per ml).

Theophylline 10–16 mg/kg/day (start with 10 mg/kg/day, then increase) q 8 hr oral (maximum starting dose 300 mg and maximum daily dose 800 mg/day). Toxicity at blood levels >30 µg/ml, useful when inhalation route not possible; and can be used as add-on therapy in severe asthma.

Apnea of prematurity: 5–7 mg/kg loading dose followed by maintenance 3–6 mg/kg/day q 6–8 hrly.

Adult dose: Loading dose 5 mg/kg, maintenance dose 10 mg/kg/day q 8 hr oral. Maximum daily dose 900 mg.

(Broncordil 80 mg per 15 ml; cadiphylate tab 250 mg; elixir 80 mg per 5 ml; deriphyllin tab contains etophylline 77 mg and theophylline 23 mg, deriphyllin retard tabs 150 mg, 300 mg, 450 mg, deriphyllin pediatric syrup contains etophylline 46.5 mg and theophylline 14 mg per 5 ml; inj deriphyllin containing etophylline 169.4 mg and theophylline 50.6 mg per 2 ml ampoule, etophylate elixir 125 mg per 5 ml; theolong tabs 100 mg and 200 mg, long-acting theophylline; unicontin SR tabs 400 mg, 600 mg, theo PA 100 mg, 300 mg controlled release tablets, theo-asthalin tab contains theophylline 100 mg, salbutamol 2 mg, forte tab theophylline 200 mg, salbutamol 4 mg, SR tab theophylline 300 mg, salbutamol 4 mg, theo-asthalin syrup contains theophylline 100 mg, salbutamol 2 mg per 10 ml; theoped syrup provides 100 mg theophylline anhydrous per 10 ml).

Tiotropium A long-acting muscarinic antagonist. Used as add on therapy in difficult to control asthma. Dose 9 µg daily single dose by inhaler. Approved for use in children above 6 yr of age.

SE: Dry mouth, constipation, nasal stuffiness.
(Aerotrop, tiomist, tiova 9 µg and 18 µg per puff MDI combinations include aerotrop-F, airtio-F, combihale-FT, duova contain triotropium 18 µg + formoterol 12 µg MDI).

Zafirlukast 20 mg twice a day for prophylaxis and treatment of asthma in children older than 12 yr. 10 mg twice a day for 7–11 yr of age.

Adult dose: 20–40 mg q 12 hr oral on empty stomach. (Zuvair tabs 10 mg, 20 mg).

Note: *Metered dose inhalers should be used with spacer and mask in children below three yr of age and with spacer in children above three yr. Never use MDI device without a spacer. Rotacaps are administered by using a rotahaler/dry powder inhalers and rotacap dose is double of the inhaler dose. Mouth should be rinsed after using inhaled steroids; the water used for rising should not be swallowed.*

Chapter

22

Cardiotonics

Adrenaline (epinephrine) For intravenous or intraosseous use for cardiac arrest: 0.1 ml/kg per dose of 1:10,000 solution. For endotracheal use: 0.1 ml/kg per dose of 1:1000 solution (to be flushed with 5 ml of normal saline and followed with 5 ventilations). In case of non-response during CPR: 0.1 ml/kg of 1:10,000 solution IV may be repeated every 3–5 min. Anaphylaxis and bronchial asthma: 0.01 ml/kg (1:1000 solution) IM, can be repeated at 5–10 min intervals. For shock: 0.1–1.0 μg/kg/min intravenous infusion, autoinjectors are available in doses of 0.15 mg (weighing 15 to 30 kg) and 0.3 mg (weighing $\geq$30 kg). Laryngeal edema: 0.1 ml/kg (maximum 5 ml) of 1:10,000 solution by nebulization.

Indic: Cardiac arrest, bronchial asthma, laryngeal edema, hypoglycemia, anaphylactic shock and allergic reaction.
(Injection adrenaline, enatrate, vasocon ampoule 1 mg per ml of 1:1000 dilution, epi-pen 0.15 mg and 0.3 mg, auvi-q 0.1 mg).

Amrinone 0.75 mg/kg IV bolus over 2–3 min, then 5–15 μg/kg/min continuous infusion. Inotropic and vasodilatory action. Maximum dose 10 mg/kg/day.

Adult dose: 750 μg/kg slow injection over 2–3 min followed by maintenance dose of 5–10 μg/kg/min by infusion.
(Inj anicor, cardiotone 100 mg/20 ml).

Digoxin Digitalizing dose for premature infants: 20 μg/kg/day, full-term neonates: 30 μg/kg/day, children <2 yr of age: 40–50 μg/kg/day, children 2–10 yr of age: 30–40 μg/kg/day, children >10 yr of age: 0.75–1.5 mg/day PO (parenteral dose is 2/3rd of this amount). One-half of digitalizing dose is given stat followed by 1/4th after 8 hr and remaining 1/4th after 16 hr. The daily maintenance digoxin is about 1/4th of initial digitalizing dose. Currently *digitalization is not practiced routinely*. Maximum dose 200 μg IV; 250 μg oral.

Digoxin immune fab (DigiFab) or digoxin-specific antibody (Digibind) is an antidote for overdose of digoxin.

Adult dose: 0.125–0.25 mg once a day.

Caution: Hypokalemia, hypercalcemia, hypomagnesemia.

SE: Anorexia, nausea, vomiting, diarrhea, abdominal pain, headache, disorientation, confusion, blurred yellow/green vision, skin rash, gynecomastia, extrasystoles, and conduction defects.

C/I: Ventricular fibrillation, sick sinus syndrome, AV block, hypertrophic obstructive cardiomyopathy.

(Lanoxin, cardioxin, dixin, digitran, digox, celoxin tab 0.25 mg; digoxin pediatric elixir 50 μg per ml; inj lanoxin, dixin 0.5 mg per 2 ml ampoule).

Dobutamine hydrochloride Used for inotropic support, and acute decompensated heart failur. 2–20 μg/kg/min IV continuous infusion. Do not mix with sodium bicarbonate.

Indic: Inotropic support in cardiogenic shock, stress imaging for coronary artery disease in adults.

SE: Chest pain, increased heart rate, increased systolic blood pressure, palpitations, premature ventricular contractions, nausea, headache and dyspnea.

Caution: May precipitate ventricular arrhythmia.

(Dobutrex, dobustat, dobucin, dobutam 250 mg vial; cardiject, myocard, cardiforce 50 mg, 250 mg vials).

Dopamine Dopamine infusion 2 μg/kg/min increased slowly to a maximum of 20 μg/kg/min. Lower doses have inotropic effect and doses >10 μg/kg/min have more vasopressin action. Severe constriction of renal vessels may occur at higher concentrations, necessitating renal function monitoring. One ml of dopamine dissolved in 100 ml of 5% dextrose gives a concentration of 400 μg/ml.

$$\text{mg/100 ml of dobutamine or dopamine solution} = \frac{6 \times \text{weight in kg} \times \text{dose } (\mu g/kg/min)}{(\text{Fluid infusion rate (ml/hr)})}$$

Or 15 × body weight (kg) = amount in mg dissolved in 24 ml 5% dextrose and infuse the solution @ 1 ml/hr ~10 μg/kg/min.

Indic: Shock unresponsive to fluid replacement, hemodynamic imbalance associated with trauma, septic shock, cardiac surgery, and congestive cardiac failure.

C/I: Pheochromocytoma, and cardiac arrhythmias.

Caution: Extravasation may lead to necrosis and gangrene.
(Inj dopamine, dopacin, dopar, dopinga, dopacard 5 ml ampoule 40 mg/ml).

Levosimendan Calcium channel sensitizer. Limited data is available in children.

Adult dose: Loading dose: 6–24 μg/kg over 10 min intravenously followed by continuous infusion of 0.05–0.2 μg/kg/min, adjusted according to response.
(Inj simdax, simenda 12.5 mg/5 ml).

Mephentermine sulfate 0.4 mg/kg per dose as bolus or slow IV infusion. Intravenous drip is prepared by adding 2 vials (30 mg each) to 500 ml 5% dextrose solution.

Adult dose: 15–60 mg depending on severity.

Indic: Hypotension following surgery or spinal anesthesia, vasopressor in cyanotic spell.

C/I: Shock which is hypovolemic or due to chlorpromazine.

Caution: Avoid in patients on MAO inhibitors and tricyclic antidepressants.

SE: Drowsiness, hallucinations, convulsions, slow heart rate.

(Mephentine tab 10 mg; inj mephentine, mephentermine sulfate, termin containing 15 mg, 30 mg of base per ml, as 10 ml vial).

Milrinone 50–75 μg/kg loading dose, by IV push over 10–60 min followed by 0.25–0.75 μg/kg/min continuous infusion. Inotropic and vasodilatory action.

Adult dose: 50 μg/kg loading dose over 10 min followed by maintenance dose of 0.375–0.75 μg/kg/min IV continuous infusion.

Indic: Short-term management of cardiac failure in patients unresponsive to digitalis, diuretics and vasodilators.

SE: Ventricular arrhythmia, ectopy, fibrillations, hypokalemia bronchospasm and thrombocytopenia.
(Inj milicor, milron, milzucia 10 mg/ml in 10 ml ampoule; inj primacor 1 mg/ml).

Norepinephrine 0.05–0.1 μg/kg/min. Titrate dose to the desired effect (maximum dose 2 μg/kg/min). Used in vasodilatory and septic shock.

Adult dose: Same as above.

Indic: Cardiogenic shock, septic shock, postcardiac arrest shock.

Caution: Correct hypovolemia before starting norepinephrine. Extravasation can cause tissue necrosis.

SE: Bradycardia, cardiac arrhythmia, peripheral vascular insufficiency, anxiety, transient headache and dyspnea
(Inj adrenor, norad, adronis 1 mg/ml).

Vasopressin Limited data is available in children. 0.17 to 8 mU/kg/min. Used for catecholamine refractory vasodilatory septic shock, bleeding from esophageal varices, pulseless arrest, ventricular fibrillation, ventricular tachycardia and diabetes insipidus. 10–20 units are dissolved in 100–200 ml 5% dextrose solution, infused 0.002–0.005 units/kg/min IV for 12–24 hr to a maximum titrated dose 0.01 units/kg/min, gradually taper off over 24–36 hr.

For cardiac arrest: IV 0.4 units/kg as single dose after at least two doses of adrenaline during CPR.

Adult dose: 0.01–0.04 mU/min via continuous infusion.

SE: Atrial fibrillation, bradycardia, ischemic heart disease, limb ischemia (distal), low cardiac output, right heart failure, hyponatremia, mesenteric ischemia, decreased platelet count.

Caution: Extravasation can cause local tissue damage, may cause water overload.

(Inj petresin, vasopin, c-pressin 20 units/ml).

Chapter

23

Diuretics

Acetazolamide It is carbonic anhydrase inhibitor. 5 mg/kg/day q 12 to 24 hr oral as diuretic and 20–100 mg/kg/day q 8 hr oral for hydrocephalus. Also useful in glaucoma, high altitude sickness and epilepsy (8–30 mg/kg/day).

Adult dose: 250–500 mg per day q 12–24 hr for edema or glaucoma; 8–30 mg/kg/day q 8 hr (maximum 1 g/day) in epilepsy.

Indic: Diuretic, closed angle glaucoma, antiepileptic, brain edema, high altitude sickness and metabolic alkalosis.

C/I: Sodium or potassium depletion, marked hepatic and renal dysfunction.

SE: Flushing, ataxia, confusion, allergic skin reaction, urticaria, fever, hypo- or hyperglycemia, hypokalemia, hyponatremia, metabolic acidosis, crystalluria, agranulocytosis, liver dysfunction, rarely aplastic anemia, growth retardation, metabolic acidosis and paresthesia.

(Diamox, zolamide, avva, acetamide tab 250 mg, avva SR, iopar SR cap 250 mg).

Amiloride Potassium sparing diuretics. Use as antihypertensive and heart failure (as adjunct): 0.4 to 0.625 mg/kg once daily. Adults: 5–10 mg daily in 1–2 divided doses. Maximum up to 20 mg/day.

Indic: Hypertension, edema control, nephrogenic diabetes insipidus and loop diuretic associated hypokalemia.

SE: Hyperkalemia, dizziness, fatigue, headache, constipation/ diarrhea, muscle cramps, cough, dehydration, gynecomastia, hyperchloremic metabolic acidosis, hyponatremia and impotence.

C/I: Elevated serum potassium (>5.5 mEq/l), anuria, acute/ chronic renal insufficiency, hepatic impairment.

[Available as combination tab biduret–L (hydrochlorthiazide 25 mg + amiloride 2.5 mg); tab biduret (hydrochlorthiazide 50 mg + amiloride 5 mg), tab midamor (amiloride 5 mg)].

Bumetanide 0.01–0.02 mg/kg/dose oral, if needed may be repeated at intervals of 12 hr. Patients refractory to furosemide may respond to bumetanide. It is approximately 40 times more potent than furosemide (bumetanide 1 mg = furosemide 40 mg = torsemide 10 to 20 mg).

Adult dose: 0.5–2.0 mg OD or every 12 hr up to maximum of 10 mg/d.

SE: Fluid and electrolyte loss (US box warning), AKI, muscle cramps, gynecomastia, leukopenia, thrombocytopenia and ototoxicity.

C/I: Hepatic coma, anuria.

(Bumet, bumex, burinex tab 1 mg).

Chlorthalidone 1–2 mg/kg/day single dose oral for edema or hypertension

Indic: Hypertension, edema control and prevention of calcium nephrolithiasis.

Adult dose: 25 to 100 mg/day single dose daily or on alternate days.

SE: Electrolyte disturbances (hypokalemia, hypomagnesemia, hypercalcemia and hyponatremia), gout, hypersensitivity reaction and angle-closure glaucoma.

C/I: Anuria.

(Thalizide 12.5 mg, hydrazide 25 mg; hythalton tab 100 mg).

Ethacrynic acid Use for refractory edema especially in children who develop a hypersensitivity reaction to sulfonamide-based loop diuretics, e.g. furosemide, bumetanide, torsemide) 0.5–1.0 mg/kg/dose IV every 12 to 24 hr or 1–3 mg/kg/day q 12 hr oral.

Adult dose: 25–50 mg IV; 50–200 mg oral up to maximum of 400 mg/day.

SE: Thrombophlebitis with intravenous use, fatigue, headache, fever, IgA vasculitis, skin rash, abnormal calcium/phosphate, hyponatremia, abdominal pain, agranulocytosis, abnormal LFT, deafness and tinnitus.
(Edecrin, ethacrin tab 50 mg; inj edecrin 50 mg per vial).

Furosemide Potent loop diuretic (US boxed warning), 2–6 mg/kg/day q 12 hr oral. In emergency situations: 1–2 mg/kg/dose q 6–8 hr may be given. The IV dose is one-half of the oral dose. IV infusion rate 0.1–1.0 mg/kg/hr.

Adult dose: 40–80 mg per day. For oliguria: 250 mg/dose increase every 6 hr up to maximum of 2 g/dose.

SE: Hypovolemia and electrolyte disturbances (e.g. hypocalcemia, hypokalemia, hypomagnesemia), necrotizing angiitis, orthostatic hypotension, headache, vertigo, skin photosensitivity, fever, urticaria, glycosuria, hyperuricemia, increased serum triglycerides, abdominal cramps, increased liver enzymes, blurred vision, deafness, interstitial nephritis. Risk of ototoxicity increases when infusion rate exceeds 4 mg/min.
(Lasix, salinex, frusenex, frusem tab 40 mg; frusenex tab 100 mg lasix tab 500 mg; furoped drops 10 mg/ml; inj lasix, fru, frusim, frusix ampoule 10 mg per ml in 2 ml and 15 ml vials, inj lasix high dose ampoule 250 mg per 25 ml).

Hydrochlorothiazide 1–2 mg/kg/day q 12 hr oral. The dose of hydrochlorthiazide is 1/10th of chlorthiazide. As anti-hypertensive: 12.5 to 25 mg once a day (maximum 50 mg/day). Adult dose: 25–50 mg q 12 hr.

Indic: Hypertension, edema, hypercalciuria, calcium nephrolithiasis, diabetes insipidus (central), and bronchopulmonary dysplasia.

SE: Electrolytes disturbances (hypokalemia, hypomagnesemia, hypercalcemia, and hyponatremia), dermatologic toxicity, gout, hypersensitivity reactions and rarely acute angle-closure glaucoma.

(Esidrex, hydrazide, aquazide tabs 25 mg, 50 mg; hygrotone tab 100 mg; biduret-L tab: hydrochlorthiazide 25 mg + amiloride 2.5 mg; biduret tab: Hydrochlorthiazide 50 mg + amiloride 5 mg).

Metolazone It is thiazide-like diuretic. 0.2–0.4 mg/kg/day q 24 hr. As antihypertensive: 2.5–5.0 mg once daily to achieve the desired therapeutic effect.

Adult dose: 2.5–10 mg OD up to maximum of 10 mg per day.

C/I: Anuria, hepatic comas.

SE: Electrolyte disturbances (hypokalemia and hypomagnesemia), hypersensitivity reactions, hypotension, including orthostatic hypotension.

(Diurem, metolaz, metiz, memtiz, metoral, metinex, zytanix, metevix, zolat tabs 2.5 mg, 5 mg, 10 mg).

Spironolactone It is aldosterone receptor antagonist which is a potassium sparing diuretic. Dose is 2–3 mg/kg/day single dose p.o. It is administered in combination with thiazides. It is also used as an antihypertensive (1.0–3.3 mg/kg/day q 6–12 hr) and for primary hyperaldosteronism (100–400 mg/m^2/day q 12–24 hr). When taken on empty stomach, its bioavailability increases by 90–95%.

Adult dose: 25–200 mg in 1–2 divided doses.

Indic: Edema, hypertension, primary and secondary hyperaldosteronism, ascites due to cirrhosis, heart failure, female pattern hair loss and acne vulgaris.

SE: Hyperkalemia, drowsinss, confusion, and gynecomastia.

C/I: Hyperkalemia, renal failure.

(Aldactone, lactone tabs 25 mg, 50 mg, 100 mg; combination dytor 20 contains torasemide 10–20 mg and spironolactone 50 mg).

Tolvaptan It is selective competitive vasopressin receptor 2 antagonist used to treat hyponatremia associated with congestive heart failure, nephrotic syndrome, cirrhosis and inappropriate antidiuretic hormone (SIADH). It leads to excretion of free water. The usual dose is 0.1–0.8 mg/kg per day.

Adult dose: 15 mg OD up to maximum of 60 mg/d.
(Tab samsca 15 mg).

Torasemide (torsemide) It is a loop diuretic. 10–20 mg once daily (maximum 200 mg/day) for treatment of edema. As antihypertensive: 5 to 10 mg daily.

SE: ECG abnormalities, fluid/electrolyte loss, acute kidney injury, hypersensitivity reaction, ototoxicity, chest pain, constipation, diarrhea, nausea, arthralgia, rhinitis, cough, polyuria.

C/I: Anuria, hepatic coma.
(Aribol, demmator, diurator, dyamide, dytor, edeto, metor tabs 10 mg, 20 mg, 100 mg; inj dytor 10 mg/ml).

Triamterene It is a potassium sparing diuretic. It blocks sodium, potassium and hydrogen exchange in the distal tubules and is used in conjunction with thiazides or furosemide 2–4 mg/kg/day q 12 hr oral.

Adult dose: 100 mg q 12–24 hr, reduce to alternate days after one week.

C/I: Hyperkalemia (US Boxed Warning), renal failure, severe liver disease.
(Ditide tab: triamterene 50 mg + benzthiazide 25 mg; frusemene tab: triamterene 50 mg + furosemide 20 mg or 40 mg).

Chapter

24

Hormones and Drugs for Endocrinal Disorders

ADRENALS

The relative efficacy of different corticosteroid preparations is summarized in Table 24.1.

TABLE 24.1: Relative efficacy of different corticosteroid preparations

Compound	*Tablet*	*Approximate anti-inflammatory effect*	*Potency of mineralocorticoid effect*	*Equivalent dosage for anti-inflammatory effect*
Cortisone	25 mg	0.8	0.8	100 mg
Hydrocortisone	20 mg	1	1	80 mg
Prednisolone	5 mg	4	0.8	20–25 mg
Triamcinolone	4 mg	4	None	16–20 mg
Dexamethasone	0.5 mg	25	Minimal	2–4 mg
Betamethasone	0.5 mg	40	Negligible	2–3 mg

Betamethasone 0.1–0.2 mg/kg daily in divided doses oral. 750 µg is equivalent to 5 mg of prednisolone.

Up to 1 yr: 1 mg, 1–5 yr: 2 mg, 6–12 yr: 4 mg daily.

Adult dose: 0.5–6 mg/day.

Indic: For enhancing fetal lung maturity, when labor starts before 34 wk, administer 12 mg IM to the mother in 2 doses 24 hr apart. Betnesol drops are used in addition to phenobarbitone in neonatal cholestasis to improve sensitivity and diagnostic accuracy of HIDA scan (2 mg/kg/day for 5 days prior to HIDA scan).

Caution: Betnesol drops are often misused and result in exogenous Cushing syndrome.
(Betnesol, betacortil, solubet, celestone, walacort tab 0.5 mg; betnesol, betnelan, betacortril forte tab 1 mg; betnesol, celestone, solubet oral drops 0.5 mg per ml; inj betnesol, betni 4 mg per ml for IM or IV).

Cortisone acetate: 0.7–1 mg/kg/day q 8 hr oral for physiological requirement. Therapeutic dose is 2.5–10 mg/kg/day q 8 hr oral. Half dose is given for IM or IV use.

Adult dose: 25–300 mg/day in 1–2 divided doses.

C/I: Hepatic damage.
(Cortin tabs 5 mg, 25 mg; cortelan, cortisyl tab 25 mg; cortistab tab 5 mg; inj cortone 25 mg, 50 mg per ml).

Deflazacort It is a glucocorticoid with anti-inflammatory and immunosuppressive effects. It is given in a dose of 0.25–1.5 mg/kg/day q 8–12 hr. Deflazacort 6 mg is equivalent to 5 mg of prednisolone. The dose in patients with Duchenne muscular dystrophy is 0.9 mg/kg/day for a protracted period.

Adult dose: 120 mg per day in acute conditions followed by maintenance dose of 6–18 mg/day.
(Defcort, enzocort, deflon, defsure, dfz, defza tabs 1 mg, 6 mg, 18 mg and 30 mg, syrup defcort, dezocort, dezacor, alcoza 6 mg/5 ml).

Dexamethasone 0.05–0.5 mg/kg/day oral. For anti-inflammatory action: 0.08–0.3 mg/kg/day q 6 hrly. For cerebral edema: 0.5 mg/kg/dose q 6 hr IM or IV. Hib meningitis: 0.6 mg/kg/day q 6 hrly for 2 days, should be given prior to administration of antibiotics or along with first dose of antibiotics. For laryngotracheobronchitis (croup): 0.6 mg/kg stat. For high dose pulse dexamethasone therapy for autoimmune disorders affecting skin, joints and kidneys, give 5 mg/kg as a slow infusion (maximum 100 mg).

For severe COVID-19 pneumonia: IV 0.15 mg/kg/day (*Adult dose* IV 6 mg q 24 hr).

(Decadron, decdan, dexasone, wymesone, dexona tabs 0.5 mg, 0.75 mg, 1.0 mg, 1.5 mg, 2 mg, 4 mg, 6 mg. Oral solution 0.5 mg/5 ml and intensol oral solution 1 mg/ml; inj dexamethasone, dexona, celodex 4 mg per ml; dexona-20, 20 mg per ml).

Fludrocortisone acetate Dosage in infancy: 0.01–0.3 mg/day in 2 divided doses. In older children: 0.05–0.1 mg/day as single dose.

Adult dose: 0.1–0.2 mg oral single daily dose.

Indic: Adrenocortical insufficiency, congenital adrenal hyperplasia. (Florinef, floricort tab 0.1 mg).

Hydrocortisone sodium succinate For anti-inflammatory action: 2.5–10 mg/kg/day divided 6 hrly. Status asthmaticus: 4–5 mg/kg/dose stat followed by 10–20 mg/kg/day in four divided doses IV. Acute adrenal insufficiency: 50 mg/m^2/day IV initially followed by 100 mg/m^2/day and for long-term physiological replacement give 8–10 mg/m^2/day in 3 divided doses. In Congenital adrenal hyperplasia, the initial dose is slightly higher than physiological dose to suppress pituitary ACTH and adrenal androgen production (10–15 mg/m^2/day divided in 3 doses).

Caution: Abrupt withdrawal may cause adrenal insufficiency in patients on prolonged steroid therapy.
(Hisone, hydrocortone tabs 5 mg, 10 mg, 20 mg; inj efcorlin, lycortin 100 mg per vial).

Methylprednisolone 0.5–1.7 mg/kg/day IM, IV or oral. In emergency situations, use higher doses of 30 mg/kg IV bolus over 10 to 20 min and repeat after 4 hr, if necessary. For pulse therapy: 30 mg/kg is given daily for 3–5 days.

Adult dose: 24 mg/d q 6 hr, gradually tapered over 21 days. Pulse therapy 1.0 g/d IV for 3–5 days.

Indic: ITP, pulse therapy, used as anti-inflammatory and immunosuppressant glucocorticoid in allergic, neoplastic and inflammatory disorders.

24 *Caution:* Administration of live virus vaccine, suspected tuberculosis or fungal infection.

(Medrol tabs 4 mg, 8 mg, 16 mg; inj solu-medrol 140 mg, 500 mg, 1 g, 2 g; inj unidrol, depo-medrol 40 mg per ml as 1 ml and 2 ml vials).

Prednisolone For anti-inflammatory action: 1–2 mg/kg/day q 6 to 8 hr oral after meals. Predominantly anti-inflammatory effect with minimal sodium retaining activity. For congenital adrenal hyperplasia: 2–4 mg/m^2/day.

For severe COVID-19 pneumonia: 1 mg/kg/day for 5-14 days.

Adult dose: 60 mg/m^2.

Indic: Nephrotic syndrome, rheumatic carditis, systemic-onset rheumatoid arthritis, bronchial asthma, pemphigus, and congenital adrenal hyperplasia after completion of linear growth.

SE: Obesity, hypertension, osteoporosis, diabetes mellitus, hirsutism, and acne.

(Wysolone, nucort tabs 5 mg, 10 mg, 20 mg, 30 mg, 40 mg; delta-cortil, hostacortin 'H', solucort, predcip, predinga tab 5 mg; syr besone, kidpred, predone, omnacortil, nucort 5 mg/5 ml, predone forte 15 mg/5 ml, omnacortil forte 15 mg/5 ml, kidpred forte 15 mg/5 ml).

Triamcinolone Oral up to 24 mg daily in divided doses. Deep IM 40 mg or intra-articular 2.5–15 mg. No sodium retention effect. Avoid in children below 6 yr.

SE: Proximal myopathy, depression, atrophy of tissues at local site.

(Kenacort, ledercort tab 4 mg; inj kenalog 40 mg per ml; inj kenacort 10 mg, 40 mg/ml).

PITUITARY

Adrenocorticotropin (ACTH) Aqueous preparation for IV/IM use.

For dynamic testing of adrenal function: Short ACTH stimulation test <6 mon: 62.5 µg, 6 mon to 2 yr: 125 µg, >2 yr: 250 µg.

Long-acting adrenocorticotropin (ACTH): For anti-inflammatory action: 0.8–1.6 units/kg/IM single dose. For infantile spasms: 20–40 units/kg/day in 2 divided doses IM. Maximum single dose is 100 IU.

Indic: Infantile spasms, West syndrome, testing of adrenal function.
(Acthar gel, acton prolongatum 20 units per ml in 5 ml vial; 40 units per ml in 2 ml, 5 ml vials; 80 units per ml in 5 ml vial; cosyntropin 250 μg/ml, synacthen 250 μg/ml) (1.0 IU of ACTH gel = 10 μg of aqueous ACTH).

Desmopressin Analogue of vasopressin for nasal instillation. It is devoid of pressor activity. 5–40 μg once or twice daily intranasal for central diabetes insipidus. Oral dose: Start with 0.05 mg/dose BD, gradually increase to maximum 0.8 mg/day to achieve the desired effect. For primary nocturnal enuresis: 20 μg intra- nasal at bedtime increased to 40 μg (never use for >28 days period). Give half dose in each nostril. IM or IV dose is 4 mg.

SE: Severe hyponatremia, water intoxication and seizures.

Caution: In patients with central diabetes insipidus, allow few hours of diuresis before the next dose in order to prevent hyponatremia.
(Desmospray, minirin, adiuretin 10 μg/spray; DDAVP: Desmopressin 100 mg/ml; inj 4 mg/ml, adiuretin tabs 100 μg (0.1 mg) and 200 μg (0.2 mg), minirin tabs 0.1, 0.2 mg).

Leuprolide acetate (gonadotropin releasing hormone or GnRH agonist): 3.75 mg (wt < 30 kg) or 7.5 mg (wt > 30 kg) every 4 wk depot/11.25 mg (wt < 30 kg) or 22.5 mg (wt > 30 kg) 3 monthly, deep IM.

Indic: Precocious puberty.
(Inj lupron depot, leuprodex, lupride, lucrin)
Triptorelin acetate (gonadotropin releasing hormone or GnRH agonist). 3.75 mg every 4 wk depot/11.25 mg 3 monly, deep IM. (Inj decapeptyl 3.75 mg, Inj palmorelin 11.25 mg).

Somatropin (human growth hormone) GH deficiency: 0.02–0.03 mg/kg/day. Give GH till accepted height is achieved or epiphyseal fusion occurs. It is advocated in children with Turner syndrome and small-for-gestational age (with failure of catch-up growth).

(SGA) infants: 0.375 mg/kg/wk.
Turner syndrome: 0.45–0.65 mg/kg/day.
Prader-Willi syndrome: 0.33–0.45 mg/kg/day.

Indic: Growth hormone deficiency, Turner syndrome, chronic renal failure, SGA with poor catch up growth, idiopathic short stature, Prader-Willi syndrome, GH neurosecretory dysfunction due to cranial irradiation.

SE: Pseudotumor cerebri (headache/vomiting), peripheral edema, slipped capital femoral epiphysis, gynecomastia and worsening of scoliosis.
(Inj eutropin, inj genotropin 4 units, 12 units and 16 units vials, norditropin 16 units vial; inj saizen 4 units, 10 units ampoules, inj headon 4 units/ml, inj zomactan 12 units/ml).

Stomatostatin (octreotide) 10–40 µg/kg/day in 3–4 divided doses. Long-acting preparation can be given every 2–4 wk.

Indic: Congenital hyperinsulinism, growth hormone excess.

SE: Inhibits gastrointestinal hormone activity leading to nausea and loose stools.
(Sandostatin 50 µg/ml, 100 µg/ml, Sandostatin LAR 10 mg/ml).

Triptorelin (gonadotropin-releasing hormone or GnRH agonist) 3.75 mg every 4 wk depot, deep IM.

Indic: Precocious puberty.

SE: Sterile fluid collection at the injection site.

C/I: Hypersensitivity to GnRH.
(Leuprodex/lupron depot 3.75 mg; 11.25 mg; decapeptyl 3.75 mg).

Vasopressin 2.5–10 units every 6–12 hr SC or IM for diabetes insipidus. For central diabetes insipidus: 0.5–10 mU/kg/hr. For bleeding esophageal varices: 0.33 mU/kg IV over 15 min, followed by 0.2 mU/min or 0.33 mU/kg/hr. For catecholamine refractory vasodilatory septic shock: 0.3–2.0 mU/kg/min.

Indic: Pituitary diabetes insipidus, bleeding esophageal varices, catecholamine refractory septic shock.

C/I: Heart failure, bronchial asthma, and epilepsy.

SE: Water intoxication and hyponatremia (Inj pitressin 20 units per ml).

PANCREAS

Glucagon It is used for treatment of severe hypoglycemia in children with type 1 diabetes mellitus or congenital hyperinsulinism.

<12 yr: 0.5 mg IM/subcutaneous, >12 yr: 1 mg IM/subcutaneous.

Adult dose: 0.5–1.0 mg IM or IV. (Glucagon, glucagen hypokit 1 mg/ml vial, glucagen contains glucagon 1 mg and lactose 107 mg in 1 ml vials.)

Insulin for Diabetic Ketoacidosis (DKA)

Start with 0.05–01 unit/kg/hr continuous infusion of regular insulin in normal saline with the help of an infusion pump till blood sugar comes down to 300 mg/dl. Switch over to N/2 saline in 5% dextrose and give 0.25 units/kg regular insulin every 1–2 hr before stopping infusion and then half an hr before oral meals.

Starting dose for type 1 diabetes mellitus: Toddlers 0.2–0.4 unit/kg/d; prepubertal 0.5–0.8 unit/kg/d; adolescents 0.8–1.5 unit/kg/d. 30–50% of insulin dose is given as a long acting or intermediate acting. Rest of the daily dose is given as short or rapid acting insulin in divided doses before meals.

In case of newer short-acting analogues (Lispro, aspart, glulisine), the onset of action is 5–10 min, and duration 4 hr. In case of long-acting analogues (Glargine, detemir), action lasts for 18–24 hr duration. In case of long-acting analogue degludec, the action lasts up to 36–48 hr.

Regular insulin 40 IU, 80 IU per ml, 10 ml vials; isophane (NPH) insulin 40 IU, 80 IU per ml vials; ultra-long-acting analogues glargine (lantus/basalog), detemir (levemir), degludec (tresiba) 100 IU/ml, 10 ml vials and 3 ml penfills. The short-acting analogues include humalog (lispro), novorapid (aspart), apidra (glulisine) 100 IU/ml penfill cartridges and disposable pen devices).

THYROID

Carbimazole 0.5–1 mg/kg per day q 8 hr oral.

Adult dose: Starting dose 20 mg daily in 3 divided doses up to maximum of 40–45 mg/day followed by 5–10 mg daily as maintenance.

SE: Urticaria, loss of taste, alopecia, pigmentation, and bone marrow suppression.

(Neomercazole, thyrozole, carmazole tabs 5 mg, 10 mg, 20 mg).

Liothyronine sodium 0.5–1.5 mg/kg/day single dose oral. For hypothyroid coma: 5–20 mg IV every 12 hr.

Adult dose: 10 mg; septic shock 100–200 mg/day. (Tetroxin tab 20 μg; inj triiodothyronine 20 mg ampoule.)

Methimazole: Starting dose 0.25–1 mg/kg/day (maximum 30 mg/day). It has a long half-life and is given as a single daily dose.

Maintenance dose: 1/3rd to 1/2 of initial dose, to be administered with food.

(Tapozole tabs 5 mg, 10 mg).

Potassium iodide 0.5–1 ml saturated Lugol's iodine solution per day q 8 hr oral (1 ml = 15 drops) or potassium iodide 50–150 mg/day q 8 hr oral; congenital hyperthyroidism 1 drop 8 hrly.

Indic: Thyrotoxic crisis, preparation for surgery.

(Lugol's iodine 5% with 10% potassium iodide freshly boiled and cooled, contains iodine 130 mg/ml. Collosol liquid provides 8 mg iodine/5 ml).

Propylthiouracil 1–4 mg/kg/day. Under 10 yr: 50–150 mg/day q 8 hr and >10 yr: 150–300 mg/day q 8 hr. Maintenance dose 50 mg twice daily. The use of propylthiouracil is not recommended in the pediatric population (due to risk of acute hepatic failure), except in rare circumstances when methimazole/carbimazole are contraindicated and surgery/radioiodine ablation cannot be done.

Adult dose: 200–400 mg daily q 8–12 hr followed by maintenance dose of 50–150 mg daily.

(Propylthiouracil, PTU tab 50 mg).

Thyroxine sodium (levothyroxine) Neonates: 10–15 µg/kg/day; Infancy: 6–8 µg/kg/day; Children: 1–3 yr, 5–6 µg/kg/day; 5–10 yr, 4–5 µg/kg/day; >10 yr, 2–3 µg/kg/day, in a single oral dose on empty stomach in the morning.

Adult dose: 100–200 µg (2 µg/kg/day) oral single daily dose on empty stomach.

Caution: In patients with panhypopituitarism and concomitant adrenal insufficiency, starting with thyroid replacement therapy may precipitate adrenal insufficiency. In such patients start with steroid replacement prior to replacement therapy for hypothyroidism.

Note: *In newborn babies, TSH monitoring is done every month till 6 mon and then every 2–3 mon till 2 yr of age.*

(Eltroxin tabs 25 µg, 50 µg, 75 µg, 100 µg, 125 µg, 150 µg, 200 µg) thyronorm, lethyrox, thyrofit, thyromed, thyrox tabs 12.5 µg, 25 µg, 50 µg, 75 µg, 100 µg, 125 µg, 150 µg, 200 µg).

Chapter

25

Tranquillizers, Hypnotics, Sedatives and Antidepressants

Amitriptyline hydrochloride For depression and hyperactivity: 1 mg/kg/day q 12 hr, may gradually increase the dose to 1.5 mg/kg/day till optimal effect is produced. For nocturnal enuresis: <12 yr: 10–25 mg and >12 yr: 25–50 mg at bedtime for 8 wk. For migraine prophylaxis 0.1–0.25 mg/kg/dose at bedtime, may increase every 2 wk by 0.25 mg/kg up to maximum of 2 mg/kg/dose.

Adult dose: 10–25 mg q 8 hr, increase every 2–3 days to a maximum of 150–225 mg/day.

(Amit, amitone, amidone, amixide, amline tabs 10 mg, 25 mg, 50 mg, 75 mg; sarotena tabs 10 mg, 25 mg, 50 mg; tridep, tryptomer, eliwel tabs 10 mg, 25 mg, 75 mg).

Aripiprazole Initial dose 5–10 mg per day; gradually increase by 5 to 10 mg every 2 wk; maximum 30 mg/d.

Indic: Irritability, hyperactivity, stereotypes associated with autistic disorders, and schizophrenia.

C/I: Cardiovascular disease, seizure disorder, pregnancy.

Adverse effect: Headache, fatigue, hypotension, gastrointestinal side effects, anorexia, insomnia, somnolence, blurred vision.

(Sarotema, arip, amitone, tadamit, eliwel, amypres tabs 10 mg, 25 mg, 50 mg and 75 mg).

Atomoxetin It is a selective norepinephrine reuptake inhibitor. 0.5 mg/kg/day, gradually increase every wk up to maximum daily dose of 1.2 mg/kg in single or two divided doses (morning and late afternoon). Onset of action is slow but it is sustained.

Indic: Non-stimulant medication for ADHD, mood disorders, agression, autism, OCD.

Caution: Not recommended below 6 yr.

SE: Drowsiness, dizziness, vertigo, fainting, anorexia, weight loss, and liver damage.
(Tomoxetin, axepta tabs 10 mg, 18 mg, 25 mg, 40 mg, 60 mg; Attentrol tabs 10 mg, 18 mg, 25 mg, 40 mg).

Chlordiazepoxide 0.3–0.5 mg/kg/day q 8 to 12 hr oral.

Adult dose: 5 mg q 12 hr may increase to 30–40 mg/day.
(Equilibrium tab 10 mg; librium, poxid, dibrium tabs 10 mg, 25 mg).

Chlorpromazine hydrochloride 2.5–6 mg/kg/day q 6 hr oral. In chorea, start with 50 mg/day oral and increase by 25 mg/day till chorea is controlled or maximum dose of 300 mg/day is achieved. For neonatal tetanus: 1 to 2 mg/kg per dose q 2 to 4 hrly.

Adult dose: Maximum oral dose is 100 mg; IM/IV dose is one-half of oral dose. "Lytic cocktail": Chlorpromazine 1 mg/kg, promethazine 1 mg/kg, pethidine 2 mg/kg. Avoid it due to risk of severe hypotension.

Indic: Sedation, muscle relaxant, chorea, and hiccups.
(Chlorpromazine, largactil, megatil, clozine tabs 10 mg, 25 mg, 50 mg, 100 mg, 200 mg; syrup 25 mg per 5 ml; pediatric syrup 5 mg per 5 ml; inj 25 mg per ml as 2 ml ampoules).

Clonidine hydrochloride In neonates for narcotic withdrawal: 1 µg/kg every 6–8 hr (maximum 2 µg/kg/dose every 4 hr). Children with attention deficit hyperactivity disorder: Initial 0.05 mg/d, increase by 0.05 mg/d every 3–7 days and administer in 3–4 divided doses (maximum 0.4 mg/d) or TD patch. Sedation: 4 µg/kg intranasal.

Maximum dose: 3–5 µg/kg/dose or 50–300 µg per day. Taper the dose gradually to avoid symptoms of sympathetic over-activity.

Adult dose: 0.05–0.1 mg t.i.d., gradually increase the dose every 2–3 days.

Indic: Sedation, ADHD, hypertension (except pheochromocytoma), migraine prophylaxis and Gilles de la Tourette syndrome.
(Arkamin, catapres, hyperdine tab 100 μg).

Clozapine

Indic: Treatment-resistant schizophrenia in pediatric patients aged 13 yr or more, reducing suicidal behavior in patients with schizophrenia or schizoaffective disorder.

Dose: Starting dose is 12.5 mg once daily or twice daily, increments of 25 mg to 50 mg per day, with target dose of 300–450 mg/day

C/I: A known hypersensitivity to the drug or to any of its components. It is also contraindicated in patients with uncontrolled epilepsy or a history of clozapine-induced agranulocytosis.

Adverse effects: Common adverse effects include sedation, weight gain, hypersalivation, constipation, and agranulocytosis (rare but potentially serious).
(Clozaril, denzapine, zaponex, clopine tabs 25 mg and 100 mg)

Salbutamol 0.1–0.4 mg/kg/dose q 8 hr orally.

Adult dose: 2-4 mg/dose 3–4 times/day up to maximum of 32 mg/day.

Indic: Congenital myasthenia syndrome due to DOK-7 mutation.

Adverse effects: Irritability, tremors, tachycardia, nervousness, dizziness and hypokalemia
(Asthalin, ventrolin tabs 2 mg, 4 mg; asthalin syrup 2 mg/5 ml)

Dexmedetomidine hydrochloride It is selective alpha-2 adrenergic agonist. It can be used as an adjunct with other sedatives like benzodiazepines, opioids, and propofol. >2 yr: 1–2 μg/kg intranasal half an hr before the procedure. ICU sedation: Loading dose IV 0.5–1 μg/kg/dose over 10 min, maintenance dose: 0.2–0.5 μg/kg/hr, increase by 0.1–0.3 μg/kg/hr to acheive desired level of sedation. Maximum dose 2.5 μg/kg/hr.

Adult dose: 0.2–1.0 μg/kg/hr IV infusion.
(Precedex, dexdor, dexdomitor, sileo atomizer or drops, Inj 100 μg/ml sol for IV infusion).

Diazepam 0.1–0.2 mg/kg per dose IV, IM, oral. For neonatal tetanus: 1–5 mg (maximum 2 mg/kg per dose) every 2 to 4 hr (maximum 60 mg/day) along with chlorpromazine 5–10 mg should be administered slowly intravenously every 2–4 hr, alternating with each other, so that a sedative dose is being given every 1 to 2 hr. Alternatively, 15–40 mg/kg/day continuous IV infusion can be given.

Adult dose: Anxiety 2–10 mg per day; insomnia 5–10 mg at bedtime; for muscle spasms and premedication 10–30 mg per dose oral.

Indic: Somnambulism, night terrors, status epilepticus, febrile seizures, acute seizure control at home (rectal), anxiety states, muscle spasms due to tetanus, and spasticity due to cerebral palsy.

C/I: Myasthenia gravis, acute narrow angle glaucoma.
(Valium, calmpose, placidox, anxol tabs 2 mg, 5 mg, 10 mg; calmod, paxum tab 5 mg; syrup calmpose 2 mg per 5 ml; inj calmpose, valium, paxum, anxol 10 mg per 2 ml ampoule; Direc 2 rectal solution 2 mg/ml; Rec-DZ 2.5 mg/2.5 ml and 5 mg/5 ml rectal solution, Juniz RDS rectal suppository 2.5 mg, 5 mg).

Escitalopram

It is a selective serotonin reuptake inhibitor (SSRI)

Indic: Escitalopram is indicated for the treatment of major depressive disorder and generalized anxiety disorder in pediatric patients aged 12 to 17 yr.

Dose: The recommended starting dose of escitalopram for
25 pediatric patients with major depressive disorder or generalized anxiety disorder is 10 mg once daily. The dose can be adjusted

based on response and tolerability, up to a maximum of 20 mg per day.

C/I: Escitalopram is contraindicated in patients with a known hypersensitivity to the drug or to any of its components.

Adverse effects: Common adverse effects include headache, nausea, insomnia, somnolence, and sexual dysfunction.
(Lexapro, cipralex, escitalop, esipram tabs: 5 mg, 10 mg and 20 mg; oral solution: 1 mg per mL).

Etomidate

Indic: For the induction of general anesthesia or sedation in pediatric patients.

Dose: The dose for induction of anesthesia above the age of 10 yr varies between 0.2 mg/kg and 0.6 mg/kg of body weight, and it must be individualized in each case. The usual dose for induction in these patients is 0.3 mg/kg, injected slowly over a period of 30 to 60 seconds.

C/I: A known hypersensitivity to the drug or to any of its components.

Adverse effects: Common adverse effects include pain at the injection site, apnea, laryngospasm, arrhythmias, post- operative nausea and vomiting.
(Amidate, etomidate, lipuro, hypnomidate, 2 mg/ml in 10 ml vial).

Fentanyl citrate 1–5 µg/kg/dose IV q 1–4 hr, may be administered as a continuous infusion at a rate of 1–5 µg/kg/hr. Oral transmucosal (fentanyl lozenge) and sublingual dose is 15–20 µg/kg. For more details, refer to Analgesics, Antipyretics and Anti-inflammatory drugs.

Caution: Risk of respiratory depression when co-administered with other sedatives and in infants below 3 mon.
(Inj fendrop, trofentyl, fent 50 µg/ml in 2 ml and 10 ml ampoules; oralet lozenge 200 µg, 300 µg, 400 µg).

Fluoxetine hydrochloride Children >5 yr: 5–10 mg oral once a day, maximum dose 20 mg per day.

Adult dose: 20–60 mg single daily dose.

Indic: Depression, obsessive–compulsive disorder, anxiety, panic disorder, and mood stabilizer.

(Prodep, flunil, platin caps 10 mg, 20 mg; fluxal, depzac, oxedep cap 20 mg; fludep-20 tab and fludac, exiten, flutine, prodep suspension 20 mg per 5 ml).

Haloperidol Autism spectrum disorder: 0.025–0.05 mg/kg/d; Psychotic disorder: 0.05–0.15 mg/kg/d q 8–12 hr; Nonpsychotic behavior disorder: 0.05–0.075 mg/kg/d; Agitation/hyperkinesia (chorea): 0.01–0.03 mg/kg/d q 8–12 hr; Gilles de la Tourette syndrome: 0.05–0.075 mg/kg/day in 2–3 divided doses.

Adult dose: Anxiety: 0.5 mg b.i.d, antipsychotic: 0.5–5.0 mg 2–3 doses/d (maximum 30 mg/d).

SE: Extrapyramidal and acute oculogyric effects similar to those with phenothiazines are observed and can be reversed with benztropine and diphenhydramine.

(Halopidol tabs 2 mg, 5 mg, 10 mg, 20 mg, depidol tabs 0.25 mg, 1.5 mg, 5 mg and 10 mg; depidol, halidol tabs 0.25 mg, 1.5 mg; serenace tabs 0.25, 1.5, 5 mg, 10 mg, 20 mg; serenace drops 2 mg/ml; inj serenace, salidol 5 mg/ml).

Imipramine hydrochloride Starting dose: 1.5 mg/kg/day q 8 hr oral. Increase by 1.0–1.5 mg/kg/day every 3–4 days to a maximum of 5 mg/kg/day. Adolescents: Initial 25–50 mg/day q 6–8 hr oral up to a maximum of 100 mg/day. Enuresis (>6 yr): Start with 10–25 mg oral at bedtime, increase 10–25 mg/dose at 1–2 wk intervals until maximum dose for age or desired effect is achieved. Continue for 2–3 mon, then taper slowly. When dry for 14 consecutive nights, give medication on alternate days for next 14 days. Depression: 1.5 mg/kg/day in 2–4 divided doses, increase by 1 mg/kg/day every 3–4 days up to 5 mg/kg/day.

Adult dose: 75 mg at bedtime gradually increased to 300 mg/day.

(Depsonil, microdep tab 25 mg; antidep, impramine tab 25 mg, cap 75 mg, depsol, depsin, tofranil tabs 25 mg, 75 mg).

Ketamine For IV induction, administer 0.5–2 mg/kg at a rate up to 0.5 mg/kg/min; IM, oral, rectal 3–10 mg/kg/dose; nasal and sublingual 3–5 mg/kg/dose. Continuous IV infusion @ 5–20 µg/kg/min for sedation in ventilated children. Minor procedures: 0.5–1.0 mg/kg. Sedative dose: 2 mg/kg. The concomitant use of midazolam is beneficial.

Caution: Incompatible with aminophylline, magnesium, and salbutamol.

SE: Hallucinations, bad dreams, purposeless movements of limbs, raised intracranial tension, hypertension, hypotension. Retrograde and antegrade amnesia is a desirable side effect. May increase respiratory secretions in many patients requiring co-administration of atropine 0.01 mg/kg.
(Aneket, ketalar, ketam, keta, ketamax, ketmin 10 mg per ml in 10 ml and 20 ml vials and 50 mg per ml as 2 ml and 10 ml vials).

Lithium carbonate 15–60 mg/kg/day q 6–8 hr oral to maintain blood level between 0.6 and 1.5 mEq/l (300 mg of lithium carbonate = 8.12 mEq of elemental lithium).

Adult dose: 300–600 mg q 8 hr in acute mania followed by maintenance dose of 300 mg t.d.s. or q.i.d.

Indic: Prophylaxis of maniac-depressive psychosis and treatment of maniac episodes of maniac depressive illness, bipolar disorders and depression.
(Lithocap cap 150 mg; intalith tab 150 mg; lithocarb, monolith, licab tab 300 mg).

Melatonin Children <3 yr: 1 to 2 mg, >3 yr: Administer 3 mg, 20–30 min before desired sleep time. If response is insufficient increase the dose to 6 mg after 7–10 days.

Adult dose: 6 mg one to two hr before bedtime.

Indic: Chronic sleep disturbance in those with neuro-development disabilities like cerebral palsy, autism, visual impairment or neuropsychiatric disorders.

C/I: Pregnancy, use with caution in children with epilepsy.

(Meloset 3 mg tab, eternex 3 mg tab with vitamin B6 10 mg; bioclock, gudnite tab 3 mg melatonin with 0.25 mg alprazolam).

Methylphenidate hydrochloride It is a psychostimulant drug approved for treatment of ADHD. Start with 5 mg single (sustained release) or 2 divided doses on empty stomach and gradually increase up to maximum of 60 mg/day.

Adult dose: 10 mg BD up to maximum of 60 mg/day.

Indic: ADHD and narcolepsy.

SE: Anxiety, anorexia, slow growth, tremors, tachycardia, hypertension, and seizures.
(Addwize tab 10 mg, 18 mg, inspiral and meth
10 mg and 20 mg sustained release OD).

Midazolam 0.5–0.75 mg/kg/dose oral or rectal, 0.2–0.5 mg/kg/dose nasal or sublingual, 0.05–0.15 mg/kg IV or IM. For more details, refer to Anticonvulsants.

Adult dose: For induction of anesthesia in unpremedicated patient: 0.3–0.35 mg/kg administered over 30 seconds while in premedicated patients 0.15–0.2 mg/kg is given as a loading dose. If needed, increments of 25% of initial dose may achieve therapeutic benefit.

Caution: Avoid combining it with fentanyl but it is complementary to ketamine.
(Fulsed, mezolam, midosed, shortal, benzosed, midaz 1 mg/ml in 5 ml and 10 ml vials and 5 mg/ml in 1 ml ampoule, mida nasal spray 0.5 mg/puff.

Nitrazepam 0.5–1 mg/kg/day q 12 hr or 8 hr oral dose.

Adult dose: 5–10 mg at bedtime.

Indic: Insomnia, myoclonus, infantile spasms, and partial epilepsy.

C/I: Myasthenia gravis, porphyria, and acute narrow angle glaucoma.
(Nitravet, nitrosun, nitavan, nitraplan tabs 5 mg, 10 mg; hypnotex caps 5 mg, 10 mg).

Nortriptyline For depression 6–12 yr: 1–3 mg/kg/day q 6–8 hr oral. For nocturnal enuresis: Children weighing 20–25 kg: 10 mg p.o.; 25–35 kg: 10–20 mg p.o.; 35–54 kg: 25–35 mg p.o. 30 min before bedtime.

Adult dose: 25–75 mg/d q 12 hr.

Indic: Depression, nocturnal enuresis.
(Primox, sensaril, sensival, trip tab 25 mg.)

Olanzapine Start at 2.5 to 5.0 mg/day with gradual increase in dose on weekly intervals; maximum dose 20 mg/day.

Adult dose: 10–20 mg OD.

Indic: Psychotic disorder, schizophrenia, juvenile bipolar disorder, autism spectrum disorder.

Adverse effect: Weight gain, dyslipidemia, metabolic syndrome, insulin resistance and diabetes mellitus, dry mouth, constipation, lowered seizure threshold.
(Olex, olandus, oliza, onza, olima, tolaz, olimelt, olapin tabs 2.5 mg, 5 mg, 7.5 mg, 10 mg).

Paraldehyde 0.1–0.2 ml/kg/dose deep IM or 0.3 ml/kg/dose per rectum mixed with 3 parts of coconut oil. Additional dose may be given after 30 min and then q 4–6 hr. Refractory neonatal tetanus: 0.1 mg/kg IV.

Adult dose: 1 g IM; 5–10 ml per rectal 1:10 dilution.

Indic: Refractory status epilepticus, and tetanus neonatorum.

C/I: Pulmonary and hepatic disease.

Caution: Proctitis and abscess at injection site. Ensure sterility. Use glass syringe as paraldehyde is not compatible with plastics. (Inj paraldehyde 1 g/ml in 5 ml ampoule).

Pimozide Children 12 yr age, initial dose is 1–2 mg/day in divided doses, increase the dose to get the desired effect. Maintenance 0.2 mg/kg/day or 10 mg total dose per day, whichever is less. Maximum dose 0.3 mg/kg/day or 20 mg/day.

Adult dose: 20 mg OD

Indic: Paranoid states and Gilles de la Tourette syndrome.
(Neurap, mozep, monozide, pimo, piniodac, R-zep tabs 2 mg, 4 mg; orap 2 mg, 4 mg, 10 mg).

Promethazine hydrochloride Usual antihistaminic dose is 0.2–0.5 mg/kg; sedative/hypnotic dose is 0.5–1.5 mg/kg. *See* Antihistamines for details.

Adult dose: 10–25 mg q 8–12 hr as antihistaminic and 25–100 mg as a sedative.

(Phenergan tabs 10 mg and 25 mg, avomine, phenamin, promasum, progene tab 25 mg, phenergan, phenamin syrup 5 mg per 5 ml).

Propofol

Indic: Induction of general anaesthesia for patients greater than or equal to 3 yr of age, maintenance of general anaesthesia for patients greater than or equal to 2 mon of age.

Dose: Most patients aged 3 yr through 16 yr and classified American Society of Anesthesiologists (ASA) physical status I or II require 2.5 mg/kg to 3.5 mg/kg for induction.

Anesthesia can be maintained by administering propofol by infusion or intermittent intravenous bolus injection. An initial bolus between 1–4 mg/kg, followed by subsequent administration of smaller aliquots based on patients' response (0.5–2 mg/kg). For the pediatric population, maintenance by infusion of propofol at a rate of 200 mcg/kg/min to 300 µg/kg/min should immediately follow the induction dose. Following the first half-hr of maintenance, infusion rates of 125 µg/kg/min to 150 µg/kg/min are typically needed.

C/I: Hypersensitivity to propofol, egg or soybean.

Adverse effects: Pain at the injection site, hypotension, respiratory depression, and propofol infusion syndrome (rare, but potentially serious).

(Diprivan, propoven, fresofol inj 100 mg per 10 ml (10 mg/ml), 200 mg per 20 ml (10 mg/ml), 500 mg per 50 ml (10 mg/ml), and 1,000 mg per 100 ml (10 mg/ml) single-dose vials).

Quetiapine

Indic: Treatment of schizophrenia in pediatric patients aged 13 yr or more, manic and depressive episodes of bipolar mood disorders.

Dose: The recommended starting dose of quetiapine for pediatric patients with schizophrenia is 25 mg once daily, taken at bedtime. The dose can be adjusted based on response and tolerability, up to a maximum of 800 mg per day.

C/I: A known hypersensitivity to the drug or to any of its components.

Caution: Neuroleptic malignant syndrome, tardive dyskinesia

Adverse effects: Common adverse effects include somnolence, dry mouth, dizziness, weight gain, increased cholesterol levels and transamnitis.
(Seroquel, ketipinor, quetapel, quetidin tabs: 25 mg, 50 mg, 100 mg, 200 mg, 300 mg, and 400 mg).

Risperidone Initial dose of 0.25 to 0.5 mg/day; increase by 0.25 to 0.5 mg every 2 wk.

Maximum dose: 1 mg/day in < 20 yr age and 2.5 mg/day in >20 yr age.

Indic: Aggressive, hyperactive behavior, self-injurious and disruptive behavior occurring as a comorbidity in autism spectrum disorder, conduct disorder, and psychosis.

C/I: Cardiac rhythm abnormality or other cardiovascular diseases, obesity, drug allergy, leucopenia, neutropenia.

Adverse effects: Abdominal pain, arthralgia, anxiety, headache, insomnia, somnolence, sedation, orthostatic hypotension, nausea, weight gain, extrapyramidal side effects, prolongation of Q-T interval.
(Risperdal, respidon, risdone, rispid, sizodone tabs 0.5 mg, 1 mg, 2 mg, 4 mg and syrup 1 mg/ml).

Triclofos sodium 20 mg/kg/dose for sedation orally. It is stable ester of trichloroethanol. 1–5 yr: 250–500 mg; 6–12 yr: 0.5–1.0 g.
(Pedicloryl, pedirest, silence, tricloryl, foskid syrup 500 mg per 5 ml).

Trifluoperazine hydrochloride 1 mg oral q 12–24 hr in children >6 yr of age, maximum dose 15 mg/day.

Adult dose: 5–10 mg q 12–24 hr.

Indic: Hallucinations, delusions, conduct disorder with hyperactivity.
(Manocalm tabs 2 mg, 5 mg, 10 mg; neocalm, sigmazine, trazine tabs 5 mg, 10 mg).

Trifluperidol Children 5–12 yr, initial dose 0.25 mg/day increased slowly over a few days up to a maximum of 2 mg/day. Acute psychosis: 0.5–2.5 mg IM.

Adult dose: 0.5 mg daily, gradually increased by 0.5 mg every 3–4 days up to maximum of 8 mg per day.
(Triperidol tab 0.5 mg; inj 2.5 mg per ml).

Chapter

26

Vaccines

BCG Freeze-dried live-attenuated vaccine is used within 4–6 hr after reconstitution with normal saline. Administer 0.1 ml intradermal over the top of the left upper arm by using a tuberculin syringe and 26G/27G needle. Injection site should be cleaned with sterile saline and local antiseptics should be avoided. It is given as a single dose without any boosters. Store at 2–8°C. Protect from light. Inadvertent IM administration may result in regional lymphadenitis and cold abscess.
(Tubervac SII, BCG vaccine Guindy 10, 20 dose vials).

Covid vaccines

Covaxin (Bharat Biotech): >6 yr age; each dose contains SARS age: 6 µg TLR 7/8 agonist: 15 mg 2-PE: 2.5 mg aluminium hydroxide: 0.25 mg. Dose 0.5 ml IM, 2 dose schedule at 0 and 28 days. Available as single dose vial (0.5 ml), five dose vial (2.5 ml), ten dose vial (5 ml), twenty dose vial (10 ml).

Corbevax (Biological E): >5 yr; each dose contains RBD antigen of SARS-CoV-2: 25 µg hydroxide: 750 µg CpG 1018: 750 µg. Dose 0.5 ml IM, Dose 0.5 ml IM, 2 dose schedule at 0 and 28 days. Available as single dose vial (0.5 ml), ten dose vial (5 ml), twenty dose vial (10 ml).

Covovax (SII): >12 yr; each dose (0.5 ml) contains SARS-CoV-2 spike protein 5 µg and is adjuvanted with Matrix- M-Fraction-A (42.5 µg and fraction-C (7.5 µg of Quillaja saponaria Molina extract. Dose 0.5 ml IM, 2 dose schedule at 0 and 21 days.

Available as single dose vial (0.5 ml), two-dose vial (1 ml), ten dose vial (5 ml), twenty dose vial (10 ml).

ZyCoV-D (Zydus Cadila): ≥12 yr; each dose (0.2 ml) contains DNA plasmid construct with spike protein gene region from SARS-CoV-2 virus 2 mg and phosphate buffered saline q.s. Dose 0.1 ml intradermal at two sites (total 0.2 ml), 3 dose schedule at 0, 28, 56 days. Availability 0.5 ml, 2 ml.

Covishield (SII): >18 yr of age and older. Dose 0.5 ml IM to be given as two doses at an interval of 4–12 wk. It contains ChAdOx1 nCoV-19 Coronavirus vaccine (recombinant). Available as 5 ml multidose vial.

None of the COVID vaccines should be frozen but stored at +2 to +8°C.

DT Liquid vaccine containing alum precipitated diphtheria and tetanus toxoid 0.5 ml IM. Dual antigen containing diphtheria toxoid 20–30 Lf, and tetanus toxoid 5–25 Lf.
(Dual antigen SII Td-Vac single dose ampoules, 10, 20 dose vials).

DTP (DTwP/DTaP) Liquid vaccine containing diphtheria toxoid 20–30 Lf, tetanus toxoid 5–25 Lf, wP 4 IU/aP 3 to 25 mg of 2 to 5 purified pertussis antigens. Administer 0.5 ml IM in anterolateral aspect of thigh. Store at 2–8°C. Protect from light. *Never administer any vaccine in the buttocks.*

C/I: Serious hypersensitivity, encephalopathy following previous dose of whole cell (DTwP) pertussis vaccine (collapse/shock-like state, persistent screaming episodes, temperature >40.5°C or seizures), history of uncontrolled seizures or evolving neurological disease. Progressive or evolving neurological illness is a relative contraindication to first dose of DTwP immunization. DTwP is not recommended above 7 yr, instead use dT or Tdap. *DTaP is preferred in those with severe adverse effects of DTwP or with neurological disorders, the adverse effects may still occur.*

[Triple antigen SII, Tripvac Biological Evans, Tripacel (DTaP), Daptacel (DTaP), Aventis Pasteur, Pentaxim (DTaP + Hib + IPV)

Sanofi Pasteur, Infanrix (DTaP) GSK Biological, Tetract-Hib (DTwP + Hib) Aventis Pasteur, Quadrovax (DTwP + Hib) SII, Pentavac SD (DTwP + Hep B + Hib) SII, Comvac-3 Bio Hb, Comvac-5 (DTwP + Hep B + Hib) Bharat Biotech, Kinrix (DTap + IPV), Pediarix(DTap + Hep B + IPV), Pentacel (DTap + HiB + IPV), Quadracel (DTap + IPV].

DTwP with hepatitis B 0.5 ml deep IM containing whole cell DPT and recombinant hepatitis B vaccine. Hiberix vaccine can be reconstituted with Tritanrix HB (both manufactured by GSK Biologicals) for simultaneous administration of DTwP + HBV + Hib as a single injection.
(Tritanrix HB 0.5 ml ampoules, Easy 5 (DTwP + Hep B + Hib) Panacea Biotec, Ecovac (DTwP + Hep B) by Panacea Biotec).

Hib conjugate vaccine It is given in 3 doses when initiated below 6 mon, 2 doses between 6 and 12 mon and 1 dose between 12 and 15 mon. A booster is given at 15–18 mon. Beyond 15 mon, a single dose is recommended up to 5 yr of age. The vaccine should be administered to all individuals with functional/anatomic hyposplenia irrespective of age. It can be safely administered, at a different site, along with DTP. Combination vaccines Hib + DTP, Hib + DPT + IPV, Hib + DPT + Hep B vaccines are also available.
(Hiberix, ACT-Hib, HiBest, VaximHiB, single dose vial, 0.5 ml contain 10 µg purified Haemophilus b saccharide).

Haemophilus b conjugate with DTwP or DTaP Each dose contains 12.5 Lf diphtheria toxoid, 5 Lf tetanus toxoid, 16 OPUs inactivated pertussis cells and 10 µg Hib polysaccharide. Starting at 6 wk, 3 primary doses are given IM 4–8 wk apart. One booster dose is recommended after 1 yr. Store at 2–8°C.
(Tetract-Hib, Tetramune, Tetrahibest, Easy 4, Easy 5, Comvac- B Bio Hib (Bharat Biotech), Quadrovax, QVAC 0.5 ml single dose ampoules and 10 dose 5 ml vials).

Easy Six (Panacea Biotec) contains diphtheria toxoid, tetanus toxoid, inactivated wP, Hib, r Hepatitis BsAg, inactivated salk polio virus strains of type 1, 2 and 3.

Infanrix hexa (GSK) contains diphtheria toxoid, tetanus toxoid, aP with pertussis toxoid, HBsAg, Hib, IPV containing type 1, 2, 3 polio viruses.

Hexaxim (Sanofi India) contains diphtheria, tetanus, pertussis (acellular, component), hepatitis B (rDNA), poliomyelitis (inactivated) and *Haemophilus influenzae* Type B conjugate vaccine (Adsorbed).

Hepatitis A vaccine The vaccine contains formaldehyde-inactivated hepatitis A virus (HM 175 hepatitis A virus strain) adjuvated with aluminium hydroxide. Pediatric dose 720 ELISA units/0.5 ml is given IM at 12 mon of age and second dose is given 3–6 mon later. For >18-yr-old, 1440 ELISA units are given as per above schedule.

Attenuated live hepatitis A vaccine (Biovac-A) is available and it is given as a single dose after one yr of age. It is given by subcutaneous route.

(Havrix, havpur 360, 720 units per 0.5 ml; 1440 units per 1.0 ml, Avaxim pediatric containing 80 antigen units in 0.5 ml, Biovac- A live vaccine by Wockhardt, HavShield A PFS (Abbot),Twinrix Junior (Hep A + Hep B).

Hepatitis B vaccine Purified surface antigen of hepatitis B virus (plasma derived or recombinant). It provides active protection to population at risk to develop hepatitis B and neonates born to HBsAg positive mothers when it is given within 12 hr of age (can be given up to 72 hr). Give 3 primary doses at birth, 1 mon and 6 mon. The dose is 10 μg/0.5 ml in children up to 18 yr, 20 μg/1 ml in older children and high-risk individuals.

Give IM at a site other than gluteal region. Booster dose is recommended only for immunocompromised and children having comorbidities like chronic renal disease; if the antibody levels drop below protective levels. Hepatitis B specific immunoglobulins can be given simultaneously but at a different site to individuals exposed to hepatitis B infection like neonates of e antigen positive mothers.

(Bevac, Biovac-B, Engerix-B, HBVac, Shanvac-B, Genevac-B, Enivac HB, Hepagen Plus, Revac-B, Hepaccine-B, Hepabig, Invac-B, Hepashield 1 ml ampoule contains 20 μg recombinant HBsAg. The pediatric dose of 0.5 ml contains 10 μg).
(*Tritanrix HB* (GSK Biologicals) contains diphtheria toxoid 30 i.u., tetanus toxoid 60 i.u., inactivated pertussis bacteria 4 i.u., recombinant HBsAg protein 10 μg adsorbed on aluminium salts per 0.5 ml. Available as single dose ampoule or 10 dose vials. After first dose of HBV at birth, further 2 doses of Tritanrix HB or Easy 5 or Comvac-5, Easy 6 should be given at 6 wk and 14 wk).

Human papillomavirus (HPV) vaccine Almost 100 serotypes of HPV have been identified of which 15–20 strains are oncogenic to cause cervical cancer. Gardasil (MSD) HpV4 is a mixture of L1 proteins of HPV serotypes 16, 18, 6 and 11 with aluminium containing adjuvants. It is also protective against genital warts. The vaccine is given intramuscularly over deltoid region or thigh.
Gardasil 9 HPV: Type 6: 30 μg, type 11: 40 μg, type 16: 60 μg and type 18: 40 μg type 31: 20 μg, type 33: 20 μg, type 45: 20 μg, type 52: 20 μg, type 58: 20 μg and 500 μg of aluminum 9–14 yr: Girls and boys: Two-dose (0 and 6 mon); 15–26 yr: 9vHPV (0–2– 6 mon) is recommended in a three-dose series. All immunocompromised subjects should receive a three-dose schedule.

SE: Fever, local pain, redness and swelling, rarely syncope. Observe for 15 min after vaccination.

CI: Known serious hypersensitivity to vaccine components or a previous dose.
(Gardasil (MSD), Gardasil 9, 0.5 ml pre-filled syringe, Cervavac (SII)).

Influenza vaccine Each 0.5 ml dose contains 15 μg of hemagglutinin of each of the three recommended strains (Influenza A-H1N1, H3N2 and Influenza B). Virus is inactivated after propagation in embryonated hen's eggs. Vaccine may be given to high-risk children after 6 mon of age IM or deep SC. In children below 9 yr, two primary doses are given 4 wk apart. The dose is 0.25 ml below 3 yr and 0.5 ml after 3 yr. Boosters are given once every yr before the peak influenza season. Trivalent inactivated influenza vaccine (IIV) contains the 'swine flu' or influenza A (H1N1) antigen, hence no need to vaccinate separately.

Indic: Children with chronic pulmonary, cardiac, hematologic and renal conditions, chronic liver disease, congenital and acquired immunodeficiency, long-term salicylate therapy.

C/I: Age less than 6 mon, allergy to egg, history of GBS within 6 wk following previous influenza vaccination, moderate to severe febrile illness.

FluQuadri by Sanofi Pasteur 0.25 ml and 0.5 ml in a pre-filled syringe and Fluarix tetra by GSK Biological, Aggripal by Panacea Biotec Ltd, influgen by Lupin, Influvac by Abott, Vaxiflu 4 Zydus Cadila 10 dose vial for IM use. FluQuadri by Panacea Biotec contains both seasonal flu and H1N1 viruses and is available in pre-filled 0.25 ml (<3 yr) and 0.5 ml (>3 yr) syringes.

Live-attenuated influenza vaccine (LAIV): Recommended only for children between 2 and 18 yr age, high risk individuals and pregnant women.

(Nasovac S4, Trivalent intranasal spray by Serum Institute of India Ltd).

Intranasal preparation: It should be given in a dose of 0.25–0.5 ml in each nostril. Indicated in all healthy non-pregnant individuals aged 2–49 yr of age.

C/I: Age less than 2 yr and more than 50 yr, immuno- deficiency state, chronic health problems and muscle/neurological problems that can lead to breathing or swallowing difficulties. (Nasovac Sii single dose and 5 dose inhalation device).

Japanese encephalitis vaccine Mouse brain-derived inactivated JE vaccine is currently produced by Bilological Evan (Jeev) and Bharat Biotech International Ltd (Kolar strain). Jeev (Biological Evan) is given intramuscularly (3 μg/dose in children 1–3 yr and

6 µg/dose in older children) as 2 primary doses on day 0 and 28. Jenvac (Bharat Biotech) 0.5 ml IM is given in a single dose after the age of one yr. Need for boosters is still undetermined for both of these vaccines. Efforts are being made to produce a safe recombinant JE vaccine using poxvirus vectors.

Live-attenuated JE vaccine (SA 14-14-2) by GPO MB (Sanofi Pasteur) is recommended for use in a 2 dose schedule, first at 9 mon and second at 15–18 mon of age and is administered subcutaneously. Not available for office use.

Indic: Children between 1 and 18 yr of age living in highly endemic areas and visitors to the endemic areas if duration of stay is likely to exceed 4 wk. JE vaccine is not given merely as an "outbreak" response.

SE: Fever, malaise, local pain and swelling, anaphylactic reaction and rarely acute encephalitis.

[JEN-VAC (Bharat Biotech) single dose 0.5 ml ampoules and multi-dose vials, JEEV (Biological Evan) single dose 0.5 ml 3 µg and 1.0 ml 6 µg ampoules, IMOJEV MD–live-attenuated vaccine lyophilized preparation].

Measles vaccine Live-attenuated measles vaccine containing at least 1000 TCID-50 live-attenuated measles virus (Edmonston-Zagreb strain). 0.5 ml SC single dose at 9–12 mon. Store at 2–8°C. Protect from light. Diluent is used for reconstitution at the time of administration. *Instead of isolated measles vaccine, Indian Academy of Pediatrics has recommended to administer first dose of MMR at 9 mon of age, whilst the GOI has introduced MR vaccination campaign wherein additional dose of* MR vaccine (Measles and Rubella) is administered to all children below the age of 15 yr.

(Rouvax measles vaccine single dose and 10 dose vial; M-vac Sii, Rimevax single dose vial).

Measles, mumps and rubella (MMR) Trimovax live-attenuated measles vaccine (Edmonston-Zagreb) not less than 1000 TCID-50, live-attenuated mumps vaccine (L-Zagreb strain) not less than 5000 TCID-50, live-attenuated rubella vaccine (Wistar RA 27/3 M strain) not less than 1000 TCID-50 per unit.

Priorix contains at least 1,000 TCID-50 of the Edmonston-Zagreb (measles) and RA 27/3 (rubella) strains, and 20,000 TCID-50 of the L-Zagreb (mumps) strain. 0.5 ml SC or IM is given in two doses at the age of 9 mon and 15–18 mon. No booster doses are recommended, though IAP has now recommended a 3rd dose at 4–5 yr of age. The vaccine is reconstituted with diluent at the time of administration.
[Trimovax (Aventis Pasteur), Priorix (GSK), Tresivac (Sii), Morupar, Pluserix single dose vials]

Meningococcal Purified A-C-W 135-Y polysaccharide (MPSV—meningococcal polysaccharide vaccine) of *N. meningitidis* group A 50 µg, group C 50 µg per unit. 0.5 ml SC or IM followed by boosters every 2–3 yr. Bivalent vaccines have only A and C while Quadrivalent have all four strains. MPSV should be used above 2 yr of age only. Give additional oral chemoprophylaxis during an epidemic. Store at 2–8°C. After reconstitution, the vaccine should be administered within 8 hr.

MCV (meningococcal conjugate vaccine) Menactra (for age group 9 mon – 55 yr) 9–23 mon: Two doses 3 mon apart 24 mon – 55 yr: single dose after 2 yr and MenAfriVac (age group 1–29 yr).

Indic: Give during outbreaks, close contacts and Haj pilgrims, children with terminal complement component deficiencies, functional or anatomical asplenia and HIV infection.
[Mencevaxc-bivalent (GSK) A + C single dose and 10 dose vial, meningococcal A + C Sii and Sanofi Pasteur 10 dose and 50 dose vial QuadriMenning (Biomed), Mencevac (GSK)– Quadrivalent A + C + W 135 + Y; 50 µg each; Menactra (Sanofi Pasteur), MenAfriVac monovalent conjugate vaccine by Serum Institute of India].

MMR + Varicella dual vaccine is approved for use only during 4–6 yr of age and licensed till 12 yr of age. The reconstituted vaccine can be stored between 2° and 8°C, for up to 8 hr before use. Administered as 0.5 ml SC injection. Varilrix, Priorix Tetra (GSK) contains attenuated measles virus (Schwarz strain), mumps virus (Jeryl Linn strain), rubella virus (Wistar RA 27/3 strain), varicella virus (Oka strain).

Pneumococcal vaccine Pneumo-23 is a polysaccharide vaccine (PPSV) containing 25 µg each of 23 pneumococcal serotypes. It is given as a single dose 0.5 ml SC or IM after 2 yr of age. The booster dose is not recommended as it may produce serious adverse local reactions and does not boost the immunity. Second dose may be given after 5 yr to children with asplenia or immunocompromised children.

Pneumococcal 13-valent conjugate vaccine (diphtheria CRM 197 protein) is given in a dose of 0.5 ml IM (avoid subcutaneous) at 6, 10 and 14 wk and a booster at 12–15 mon. Between 6 and 12 mon of age for catchup vaccination, 2 doses 4 wk apart followed by a booster at 12–23 mon; after one yr two doses are given 8 wk apart and after 2 yr a single dose is given.

Pneumococcal 10-valent vaccine. The primary schedule is same as PCV-13. For catchup from 1–5 yr, 2 doses 8 wk apart are given. Routine use of PCV 10/13 is not recommended after 5 yr.

PPSV should not be used alone for prevention of pneumococcal disease among high-risk individuals.

Indic: High-risk children having chronic respiratory and cardiac diseases, asplenia, splenectomy, immunocompromised children, nephrotic syndrome, CSF rhinorrhea, chronic renal failure and sickle cell disease.

(Pneumo-23, Pnu-immune 23, Pneumovax are available as single dose ampoules, Prevenar or PCV-13 (Wyeth) and Synflorix (GSK Biological) as 0.5 ml pre-filled syringe, Nucovac PCV 10 Panacea Biotech).

Polio vaccine (oral) Sabin-attenuated virus strain concentration per dose of type 1: 10^6 TCID–50, type 3: 10^6 TCID–50. Two drops are given per dose. Store at 2–4°C. Following post polio eradication, bivalent oral polio vaccine is being used containing type 1 and type 3 polio strains.

[Oral bivalent polio vaccine (Haffkine) and polio Sabin (GSK Biological). Oral bivalent polio vaccine types 1 and 3, 20 dose vials (Haffkine). Each dose is given as 2 drops of infective units of Poliovirus Type 1 10^6 $CCID_{50}$ and Type 3 10^{58} $CCID_{50}$].

Polio vaccine (parenteral) Salk inactivated virus strain 0.5 ml IM or SC per dose. It contains type 1 poliovirus (Mahoney) antigen D 40 units, type 2 (MEF-1) antigen D 8 units and type 3 (Sukett) antigen D 32 units. It is more immunogenic, less thermolabile and without any risk of vaccine-induced paralysis. It is also called eIPV (enhanced potency IPV). Three doses (instead of OPV 2 doses) can be used, if primary series is started at 8 wk. Interval between 2 doses should be 8 wk.

The Government of India, after declaration of eradication status of polio from India, has introduced intradermal fractional IPV (f IPV-1/5 th dose, i.e. 0.1 ml) in the UIP at 6 wk and 14 wk.

Indic: Immunocompromised and HIV-positive children and as a strategy after eradication of polio.

(Imovax polio vaccine (IPV) Sanofi Pasteur and Polprotec by Panacea Biotec single dose vial or 20 doses. Pentaxim can be given to provide DTaP + Hib + IPV; fIPV is given at 6 wk and 14 wk.

Rabies vaccine Inactivated rabies vaccine (*Human diploid cell vaccine*) lyophilised not less than 2.5 i.u. per ml (with diluent pre-filled in a syringe). Inactivated rabies vaccine prepared on vero cells (Verorab by Cadila and verovax-R by Pasteur-Merieux). Rabipur (Hoechst) is a purified chick embryo cell vaccine and Vaxirab is human diploid cell vaccine. All of these are called modern tissue culture vaccines (MTCVs).

Post-exposure cases: 4 doses of 1 ml each, IM (deltoid or antero-lateral thigh) on day 0, 3, 7, and 14. An optional dose on day 30 can be given in an immunocompromised child. 0.1 ml intra-dermal vaccine is considered as effective as 1.0 ml of IM dose. Rabies immunoglobulin or monoclonal antibodies 3.33 i.u./kg. Rabishield or Twinrab 40 units/kg is recommended in all category III bites along with vaccine. If a child is vaccinated previously within 3 yr, for post-exposure prophylaxis only two doses, i.e. 1 ml dose on day 0 and 3 are given. In these cases, no rabies immune globulins (RIG) is needed.

Pre-exposure prophylaxis: It is recommended in high-risk individuals like children with pets, hostelers, postmen, veterinary doctors and assistants, and wildlife handlers. Three primary doses of 1 ml each, are given IM on day 0, 7 and 21 or 28 (preferred). A booster dose is recommended for personnel at high risk every 5 yr or if the neutralizing antibody titres fall below 0.5 i.u./ml. (Worab, Meriux inactivated rabies vaccine, verorab, vaxirab, XPRab, ZuviRab, rabipur, rabivax-S contain 2.5 i.u. per 1.0 ml vials or pre-filled syringe. ThRabis (Cadila) 3-dose vaccine (0–3–7 days) is available. It contains recombinant G protein 50 µg/0.5 ml).

Rotavirus vaccine Rotarix RV-1 is available as monovalent (RIX-4414) attenuated live vaccine in a lyophilized form which should be reconstituted just before administration. It should be given orally in 2 doses at least 4 wk apart. First dose can be administered at the age of 6 wk but not later than 12 wk. Two doses should be completed by the age of 16 wk and not later than 24 wk of age. RotaTeq RV-5 is a human-bovine multiple reassortant pentavalent vaccine containing 5 rotavirus strains and is available as a liquid formulation without any need for prior reconstitution. Rotavac is attenuated 116 E rotavirus Indian strain. They are given in 3 doses 4 wk apart starting at the age of 6 wk. Vaccination should not be initiated after 15 wk of age. The last dose should not be given after 32 wk of age. (Rotarix by GSK, RotaTeq by MSD, Rotavac by Bharat Biotech and Rotasiil by serum Institute in a pre-filled oral syringe and vial).

Rubella vaccine The vaccine contains live-attenuated rubella virus Wistar RA 27/3 strain propagated on human diploid cells. 0.5 ml is given SC over deltoid region. It has been replaced by MR and MMR vaccines.
(R-vac single dose vial by Serum Institute).

Td vaccine It contains low dose diphtheria (<2 Lf) and normal dose tetanus (>40 i.u.) toxoid containing 0.01% thiomersal and >1.5 mg aluminium phosphate. It can be safely given to children above 7 yr and adults. It can safely replace monovalent tetanus toxoid (TT) vaccine even during pregnancy.
(Td-vac or dual vaccine by Sii in single dose ampoules).

Tdap vaccine provides reduced quantity diphtheria toxoid (2–2.5 Lf) with standard tetanus toxoid (5 Lf) and acellular pertussis vaccine (2.5–8 µg).

Indic: Adolescents and adults for pertussis vaccination, maternal immunization between 27 and 36 wk of gestation (to provide protection for infants who are at risk of acquiring pertussis infection within first 2–3 mon of life). Dose is 0.5 ml IM, single dose. Store at 2–8°C. Must not be frozen.

C/I: History of encephalopathy within 7 days of administration of a vaccine containing pertussis component.
(Boostrix is Tdap by GSK Biologicals, Adacel by Sanofi Pasteur).

Tetanus toxoid 5 Lf units per dose. 0.5 ml IM. Store at 2–8°C. Do not freeze. Instead of monovalent tetanus toxoid, Td/Tdap can preferably be given.
(Inj Bett, Tetvac and dual antigen single dose ampoules, 10 and 20 dose vials).

Typhoid vaccine There are either conventional heat inactivated whole cell vaccines or new generation Vi capsular polysaccharide vaccines and Vi capsular polysaccharide conjugate vaccine. Vi capsular polysaccharide parenteral vaccines. Typhim Vi, 25 µg, Typherix, Typho Vi, Vac-typho (25 µg); Tyvax-Vi (30 µg) are better than conventional vaccine. Vaccine is given to children over 2 yr, in a single dose 0.5 ml (25 µg or 30 µg) deep SC or IM. Boosters are advised every 3 yr and can also be given intradermally with minimal side effects. Vi capsular polysaccharide *S. typhi* type 2 conjugated to tetanus toxoid (Typbar-TCV) by Bharat Biotech is available which is given as a single dose at ≥6 mon.
(Typherix, Typhim-Vi, Typho-Vi, Vac-typho (25 µg); Tyvax-Vi (30 µg); Typbar-TCV, Typhoral contains 1000 million *S. typhi*, *Biovac* (*Wockhardt*), *Pedatyph* (*Biomed*), *Shantyph* (*Shantha Biotech*), *Vactyph* (*Zy. Biogen*), *Enteroshield* (*abbot*), *Zyvac TCV* (*Zydus*), *Typh BEV* (*BE*)).

Varicella virus vaccine Lyophilized, live-attenuated Oka strain of varicella zoster virus, more than 2000 PFUs per dose. The first dose is given as 0.5 ml SC at 15 mon, may be given with

MMR but at a separate site. Booster dose may be given after 4–6 yr. After 13 yr, 2 doses are given 4–8 wk apart. Store the vaccine and diluent between 2°C and 8°C.

Indic: The vaccine is specially indicated in HIV positive children with CD4 count >15% of normal, leukemia in remission for at least 3–6 mon, long-term salicylate therapy and children with chronic lung and heart disease. May protect if contacts are given vaccine within 72 hr of exposure.

Caution: The vaccination should be delayed for at least 3 mon in children who have received immunoglobulins, blood transfusion and corticosteroids. Children on chemotherapy for lymphoreticular malignancy should not be given varicella vaccine. After measles vaccine, wait for at least one mon before giving varicella vaccine. However, a combined MMR + chickenpox vaccine (Priorix Tetra) is available.

C/I: Cell-mediated immune deficiency with lymphocyte count <1200 per mm^3.

(Varivax, variped (MSD), varilrix (GSK), okavax, biovac-V (Wockhardt), nexipox (Baiko) single dose vial).

Yellow fever vaccine Attenuated live yellow fever vaccine with virus count >1000 units in 0.5 ml. It is given in a single dose after 12 mon of age SC or IM. It is mandatory vaccine before travel to select African countries. The protection lasts lifelong after a single shot (WHO).

C/I: HIV-positive, immunocompromised and elderly (>65 yr) subjects, pregnant women and infants below 9 mon.

(Stamaril by Sanofi Pasteur in a single dose 0.5 ml pre-filled syringe).

Chapter

27

Vasodilators

Captopril Venous and arteriolar vasodilator. Infants: 0.1–0.3 mg/kg/dose q 6–24 hr oral; titrate as needed (maximum 6 mg/kg/day). Children: 0.3–0.5 mg/kg/dose q 8–12 hr oral; titrate as needed (maximum 6 mg/kg/day). Monitor total leukocyte count and renal functions.

Adult dose: Initially 6.25 mg q 8 hr, titrate to a target dose of 50 mg q 8 hr.

Indic: High renin hypertension, heart failure with reduced ejection fraction, CKD to reduce proteinuria.

C/I: Aortic stenosis, severe renal impairment, porphyria, bilateral renal artery stenosis.
(Aceten, captopril tabs 12.5 mg, 25 mg; angiopril tabs 25 mg, 50 mg).

Enalapril maleate Venous and arteriolar vasodilator. Infants and children: Hypertension: Initial 0.08 mg/kg once daily (maximum 5 mg/dose); adjust dosage based on patient response. Heart failure: Initial dose 0.1 mg/kg/day q 12–24 hr, may uptitrate to a maximum of 0.5 mg/kg/day.

Adult dose: LV dysfunction: 2.5 mg q 12 hrly, titrated as tolerated to target dose of 10 mg twice daily (maximum 20 mg/day). Hypertension: 5 mg q 24 hrly; titrate at 1–2 wkly intervals up to 40 mg daily in 1–2 doses.
(Envas tabs 1.25 mg, 2.5 mg, 5 mg, canapril, enpil injection 1 ml/1.25 mg).

Hydralazine hydrochloride It is an arterial vasodilator. Heart failure (afterload reduction): Intravenous 0.1–0.5 mg/kg/dose IV 6–8 hr, maximum dose: 2 mg/kg/dose and oral 0.25–1 mg/kg/dose, maximum up to 7.0 mg/kg/day q 6–8 hr. Hypertension (chronic): 0.75 mg/kg/day in 2–4 divided doses (maximum dose 10 mg/dose), increase gradually over 3–4 wk up to maximum of 7.5 mg/kg/day in 2–4 divided doses. Hypertensive emergency/crisis: Initial 0.1 to 0.2 mg/kg/dose IV every 4–6 hr; increase as required to suggested dose range: 0.2 to 0.6 mg/kg/dose every 4–6 hr as needed. Maximum up to 20 mg/dose. Combine with a beta blocker to avoid reflex tachycardia.

Adult dose: Initial 10 mg q 6 hr gradually increased to maximum of 300 mg/day q 6–12 hrly. Combined with isosorbide dinitrate for treating adult heart failure with reduced ejection fraction; initiated at 25 mg q 8 hr and uptitrated to 75 mg q 8 hr.

C/I: Porphyria, SLE, aortic or mitral stenosis, isolated right heart failure.
(Nepresol, zinepress, tab 25 mg; apresoline tabs 25 mg, 50 mg; inj apresoline 20 mg per ml ampoule).

Isosorbide dinitrate A vasodilator used in the treatment of angina pectoris. Its action is similar to nitroglycerin but with a slower onset of action. 0.1 mg/kg/day q 6 to 8 hr oral with a maximum dose of 2 mg/kg/day. It is not recommended in children.

Adult dose: 5–10 mg sublingual; for prophylaxis 5–10 mg q.i.d. or sustained release cap 40–80 mg BD Priming dose 5–10 mg prior to activities that may provoke an angina episode.

Indic: Angina pectoris.

SE: Lupus-like syndrome; dizziness; headache.
(Sorbitrate, isordil, anzidin tabs 5 mg, 10 mg; cardicap TR cap 20 mg, 40 mg).

Isoxsuprine It is not recommended in children.

Adult dose: Oral 10–20 mg 3–4 times daily.

Indic: Cerebrovascular insufficiency, peripheral vascular disease.

SE: Hypersensitivity, and skin rash (discontinue, if skin rash appears).
(Duvadilan, perivalan, ipdilan, udilan plain and SR tabs 10 mg, 20 mg; inj 5 mg per ml as 2 ml ampoule).

Nifedipine Venous and arteriolar vasodilator. 0.25–0.5 mg/kg/day oral q 6–8 hr. Maximum dosage 3 mg/kg/day up to 120 mg/day.

Adult dose: For angina: 30–60 mg (extended release tablet) once daily (use of immediate release tablets not recommended). Maximum dose 120 mg/day.

C/I: Cardiogenic shock, acute ST-elevation myocardial infarction (STEMI).
(Calcigard, cardules, depin, myogard caps 5 mg, 10 mg; depin retard cap 20 mg; nifedine tab 10 mg).

Nitroglycerin (glyceryl trinitrate) For heart failure, continuous IV infusion 0.25–0.5 µg/kg/min, titrated every 10–15 min to a maximum of 10 µg/kg/min.

Adult dose: start at 5–10 µg/min and titrate up to a maximum of 200 µg/min.

Indic: Acute decompensated heart failure, angina.

C/I: Use of PDE5 inhibitors, increased intracranial pressure, pericardial tamponade, pure right heart failure, aortic or mitral stenosis.
(Inj nitrocin, nitroplus 5 mg/ml).

Prazosin Venous and arteriolar vasodilator. Hypertension: 0.05–0.1 mg/kg/dose oral q 8 hr (maximum 0.5 mg/kg/day in divided doses 3 times daily). Scorpion envenomation: 0.03 mg/kg/dose, subsequent doses every 3–6 hr.

Adult dose: 1 mg q 8–12 hr initially; titrate up to 20 mg daily in 2–3 divided doses.

SE: Postural hypotension, dizziness, fainting, nasal stuffiness, priapism, and intraoperative floppy iris syndrome.

(Minipress-XL gits tabs 2.5 mg, 5 mg; prazopress tabs 1 mg, 2 mg, 2.5 mg, 5 mg).

Sodium nitroprusside Venous and arteriolar vasodilator. Hypertensive crisis: 0.3–0.5 µg/kg/min (maximum 10 µg/kg/min) IV infusion, titrate every 5 min for desired effect. 50 mg is dissolved in one litre of 5% dextrose to provide concentration of 50 µg/ml.

SE: Cyanide toxicity (with prolonged dosing, or administration in a dose of more than 2 µg/kg/min), hypotension, methemoglobinemia.

C/I: Increased intracranial pressure, hypertension secondary to arteriovenous shunts or coarctation of aorta, severe hepatic impairment.
(Inj nipride, sonide 50 mg ampoule).

Tolazoline hydrochloride (alpha blocker) For pulmonary arterial hypertension in newborns with respiratory distress syndrome: 1–2 mg/kg over 10 min IV. If arterial oxygenation improves, follow it up with continuous IV infusion 0.2 mg/kg per hr. Administer through peripheral or central vein that drains into superior vena cava.

SE: Hypotension, GI bleed, thrombocytopenia, and oliguria.
(Inj priscol 25 mg per ml, 4 ml ampoule).

Chapter

28

Vitamins and Hematinics

Alfacalcidol It is 1α-hydroxycholecalciferol, the synthetic derivative of vitamin D_3. It is a prodrug which is rapidly hydroxylated in the liver to active calcitriol.

Premature infants: 0.05–0.1 μg/kg/day; <20 kg: 0.05 μg/kg/day, >20 kg: 1.0 μg/day.

Renal osteodystrophy: 0.04–0.08 μg/kg/day.

Adult dose: 1–2 μg per day.

Indic: Renal rickets, hypoparathyroidism, hypocalcemia, vitamin D resistant rickets and osteomalacia.

(Alphadol, alfacal, alfacaps, alfarich, calcit-SG, vitalpha, minroset, alphacip, alpha D_3, α-calcirol, rocaltrol, rolsical caps 0.25 μg and 1.0 μg; GR alpha and alphabond cap 0.25 μg; calvit A alphacalcidol 0.25 μg and calcium 500 mg).

Folic acid Physiological requirement: Neonates to 6 mon: 65 μg/day, 7–12 mon: 80 μg/day, 1–3 yr: 150 μg/day, 4–8 yr: 200 μg/day, 9–13 yr: 300 μg/day, 14–18 yr: 400 μg/day.

Therapeutic dose: Megaloblastic anemia: 0.5–1 mg/day for 4 wk followed by usual maintenance (up to 200 μg/day).

Hemolytic anemia: 1 mg daily.

Pregnancy: 0.4 mg per day during periconceptional period. In high-risk pregnancy (previous neural tube defects), the dose is 4.0 mg/day.

Indic: Megaloblastic anemia, tropical sprue, hemolytic anemia (thalassemia), sickle cell disease, during phenytoin therapy, prophylaxis against neural tube defects.
(Emfolic, fol-5, fol S, folacin, folfit, folimax, folite, folex, folvin, folvite, foldivit, folet, folneu, vitafol, foliz, foliden, sysfol tab 5 mg).

Iron For prophylaxis, elemental iron 1–2 mg/kg/day OD/q 12 hr oral and for treatment 3–6 mg/kg/day OD/q 12 hr oral in between meals. In preterm neonates <32 wk, begin iron supplementation by 2 wk after birth (2–4 mg/kg/day), in term infants at 4–6 mon of age; continue till 1 yr of age.
Dose of parenteral iron (IM) = 4.0 × weight in kg × Hb deficit (g/dl)
(*1 g Hb contains 3.5 mg of elemental iron; ferrous sulphate provides 20% and ferrous gluconate provides 12% elemental iron*).
(2-Her, alpiron, cheri XT, ferrikind tab provides 100 mg, fersolate tab provides 66 mg elemental iron; tonoferon pediatric syrup 80 mg per ml; orofer XT, feronia XT, ferfoz, rubired 30 mg/5 ml; vitcofol syrup 32.8 mg/5 ml; tonoferon drops provides 25 mg per ml, hemsi PD 30 mg/ml; ferronia XT, ferium XT, imax XT drops 10 mg iron and 100 µg folic acid/ml; inj Feri Max, ferryan, rubired S, iron sucrose 20 mg/5 m; inj imferon iron dextran 50 mg per ml in 2 ml, 10 ml vial; jectocos 50 mg per ml as 1.5 ml amp; imferon-F12 and jectocos plus contain folic acid and vitamin B_{12}).

Vitamin A Daily requirement 400–1000 i.u. per day (1.0 i.u. = 0.3 µg retinol).

For prophylaxis

1. Children at risk and during measles: 1,00,000 i.u. <12 mon age, 2,00,000 i.u. >12 mon age p.o. every 6 mon till 3 yr of age.
2. Prevention of BPD in neonates: 5000 i.u. intramuscular or 10,000 i.u. oral 3 days in a wk for 28 days.
3. Improvement of growth in children with HIV, malaria, or diarrheal disease:
   Infants <1 yr: 100,000 i.u./day for 2 doses, then 100,000 i.u. at 4 and 8 mon.

Children >1 yr: 200,000 i.u./day for 2 doses then 200,000 i.u. at 4 and 8 mon.

Vitamin A deficiency with xerophthalmia
<6 mon: 50,000 i.u. p.o.
6–12 mon: 100,000 i.u. p.o.
>1 yr: 200,000 i.u. p.o.
The same dose is repeated after 24 hr and 4 wk later.
The parenteral dose is one-half of the oral dose. The water-soluble formulation should be used for treatment of deficiency state.

Indic: Vitamin A deficiency states, prevention of blindness due to xerophthalmia.

Caution: Overdosage may cause anorexia, growth failure, pseudotumor cerebri, swelling and pain in long bones.
(Aquasol A cap 50,000 i.u.; vitamin A tab 50,000 i.u.; inj aquasol A 50,000 i.u./2 ml; arovit, vitamin A drops 7.5 ml 150,000 i.u./ml; AVT drops 50,000 i.u./ml.)

Vitamin B$_1$ (thiamine) Daily requirement 0.1–1.2 mg or 0.5 mg/1000 kcal diet. *Beriberi: 10–25 mg/day IM, IV; 10–50 mg/day PO for 2 wk, then 5–10 mg/day for 1 mon*, 25 mg IV slowly for collapse due to cardiomyopathy. *Metabolic disease*: 100 mg q 8 hr.

Indic: Beriberi, neuropathy, and inborn errors of metabolism.
(Benalgis, fide tab 75 mg; beneuron cap 5 mg; berin, biwon, tim tab 100 mg, cap awsom 5 mg, 10 mg, 75 mg, 100 mg, RB1 100 mg; inj berin, thiamine 100 mg/ml).

Vitamin B$_2$ (riboflavin) Daily requirement 0.1–2 mg or 1.2 mg/1000 kcal diet.

Deficiency state: 2.5–10 mg/day q OD-BD oral

Metabolic disease: 50–150 mg q 12 to 24 hr oral
(Riboseem, ribosina, riboson, robotab, ribovit tabs 5 mg; riboflavin, ribotostab tab 10 mg; ribofem tab 200 mg).

28 **Vitamin B$_6$ (pyridoxine)** 0.3–1.3 mg/kg/day oral, IM or IV.
Prevention of INH neuropathy: 10 mg per day (1 mg/kg/day).

Treatment of INH neuropathy: 50 mg every 8 hr oral.

Pyridoxine-dependent seizures: 100 mg IV over 1 min (maximum dose 400 mg) with EEG monitoring followed by maintenance dose of 50–100 mg/d.

Indic: Prevention of neuropathy due to isoniazid, pyridoxine dependent/deficiency seizures, and sideroblastic anemia.
(Mecoba alpha cap 3 mg, Abix tab, B Long tab, B Six tab 100 mg; benadon tab 40 mg, pyricontin tab 100 mg, ingavit tab, pyridox tab, perivin tab 50 mg, ingavit tab 10 mg, inj pyridox 50 mg per ml, inj bevidox, neurokem, baraplex contain 100 mg pyridoxine per 3 ml along with vitamin B_1 and B_{12}).

Vitamin B_{12} (cyanocobalamin) Physiological requirement 0.3–2 µg/day. Therapeutic dose 250 to 1000 µg IM daily or alternate day for 1 to 2 wk, then wkly until blood count is normal. Maintenance dose 1000 µg 2–4 monthly.

Indic: Megaloblastic anemia.

Caution: Depletion of iron and folic acid stores and hypokalemia.
(Inj bigvin, rejunex, mecovon, meganerv, mego, meganeuron forte, nervup, nurokind 500 µg/ml; Inj citon 1000 µg/ml, inj Alde, cobalvit , xneurocure 1500 µg/2 ml, inj bigvin, 2500 µg/ml 5000 µg; bigvin, balcobal, cobatus, methycobal, methico, neuromin, nurokind, vitcobin tab 500 µg, bvigor, mecobalamin, neurokind OD, mecofol-OD tab 1500 µg).

Vitamin C (ascorbic acid) Daily requirement: 40 mg/day in term babies, 50 mg/day for preterms, 0–6 mon: 40 mg, 6–12 mon: 50 mg, 1–3 yr: 15 mg, 3–8 yr: 25 mg, 9–13 yr: 45 mg, 14–18 yr: 65–75 mg, 40 mg/day for older children. Therapeutic dose: 100–300 mg/day oral, IV.

Indic: Methemoglobinemia, scurvy.
(Limcee, celin, cevite, chewcee, citamin, ascorbic acid, malano tab 500 mg; sukcee, redoxon,vitcee tabs 200 mg, 500 mg; cecon, celin; frutcee drops 110 mg per ml, aquasol C drops 75 mg per ml, cecon drops 100 mg per ml, pedivit C drops 100 mg per ml, inj redoxon, tildoxon 500 mg per 5 ml).

Vitamin D_3 (cholecalciferol) Maintenance dose: VLBW (<1500 g) infants: 800 i.u./day, birth to 12 mon: 400 i.u. per day, beyond 12 mon: 600 i.u./day (1.0 mg calciferol = 40,000 i.u., i.e. 10 µg = 400 i.u.).

For deficiency states: Premature neonates 1000 i.u. per day; term neonates, 1–12 mon: 2000 i.u. per dayx 90 days; 1–18 yr: 3000–6000 i.u. per day × 90 days. Alternatively treatment with large dose 30,000 i.u. fortnightly for 6 wk or 60,000 i.u. monthly × 3 doses, in 6–12 mon of age and 60,000 i.u. fornightly × 5 doses 1–18 yr of age followed by maintenance dose of 400–600 i.u. per day.

If no radiological or biochemical signs of healing is seen after 3 mon, patient should be investigated for non-nutritional rickets.

Indic: Rickets, osteomalacia.

Caution: Overdose may cause pseudotumor cerebri, hydrocephalus, nephrocalcinosis.
(Arbivit-3, nutriRight-D_3, Adferol, ultra D_3, biocitral D, D-sol, macbrite D_3, sunsip, vitamin D3 drops 400 i.u./ml; calcirol, calcikind, calcibest, calshine-P, D3-must, D-gain, vitanova, 400 i.u./0.5 ml; calcirol, D-gain, D-rise, D-power, Gen D_3, calshine K, D_3 shot, D-sol, OH-D_3 granules 60,000 i.u. per sachet; tabs/caps arachitol, calcigen D_3, adco D_3, lumid, calcirol gems, calshine K, chekbak D3 60,000 i.u.; depura, uprise D_3 60 k, vitcol D_3, 60,000 i.u./5 ml solution, inj arachitol 3,00,000 and 6,00,000 i.u. (7.5 mg), 6,00,000 (15 mg) i.u. per ml).

Vitamin E (tocopherol) Daily requirements are shown below.

Neonates: 25–50 i.u./day; Children: 1 i.u./kg/day; sickle cell anemia: 450 i.u./day; beta-thalassemia: 750 i.u./day; cystic fibrosis: 100–400 i.u./day p.o.

Indic: Prevention of anemia of prematurity, doubtful role in prevention of retinopathy of prematurity, bronchopulmonary dysplasia, and Rett syndrome.

(Evion pearls 100 mg, 200 mg, 400 mg, 600 mg; benvite, Bio E cap
28 400 i.u., vit-E cap, edge, 200 mg, 400 mg, viteolin cap 200 mg, 400 mg, evitam, covita, monovit en cap 200 mg, EEE cap 400 mg,

etoplex cap 400 mg, tocofer, evit pearls 200 mg, 400 mg; evion drops 50 mg/ml).

Vitamin K Prophylaxis against hemorrhagic disease of the newborn: 1.0 mg for term, 0.5 mg for preterm neonates IM.

Therapeutic dose: 5–10 mg/dose SC, IM or IV. Maximum single dose is 10 mg.

Indic: Hemorrhagic disease of the newborn, bleeding tendency due to liver disorder and over dose of blood thinning agents, deficiency of vitamin K-dependent clotting factors.

(Cadisper C tab, menadione sodium bisulphite 20 mg, styptindon 5 mg, Inj menadione sodium bisulphite, phytomenadione, kapilin (acetmenaphthone) 10 mg/1 ml ampoule, inj kenadion 1 mg and 10 mg/ml, inj kevit 10 mg/ml, inj reokay 10 mg/ml, kenadion tab 10 mg).

Chapter

29

Miscellaneous Agents

Albumin solution (human) 0.5–1.0 g/kg/dose IV for hypoproteinemia. Repeat every 1–2 days as needed. Each dose should be infused over 2–4 hr. Administer 0.5–1 g/kg/dose as rapid infusion for hypovolemia and shock. Do not give more than 6 g/kg in 24 hr. In case of cerebral edema: 50 to 80 ml/kg rapid infusion. Administration rate should not exceed 2 ml/min when given to hypoproteinemic patients.

Indic: Volume substitution therapy, hypoalbuminemia, before exchange blood transfusion in neonatal jaundice, nephrotic syndrome, and cerebral edema.

C/I: CHF, and severe anemia.
(Human albumin 5% 250 ml; human albumin 20% low salt content 50 ml, 100 ml; buminate 5% 250 ml, 500 ml; albuminar 20% 35 ml, 100 ml; albuminar 25% 20 ml, 50 ml, 100 ml; albudac 20% 100 ml).

Allopurinol It is a xanthine oxidase inhibitor. 10 mg/kg/day q 8 hr oral.

Adult dose: Initial 100–200 mg daily, maintenance 200–600 mg/day.

Indic: Adjuvant to chemotherapy of leukemias and malignancies, gout, Lesch-Nyhan syndrome and Duchenne's muscular dystrophy.
(Zyloric, swiloric, lodiric, aloric, ciploric, uritas tabs 100 mg, 300 mg).

Amphetamine-d 0.15–0.5 mg/kg/day before meals. Children 3–5 yr: 2.5 mg daily increase by 2.5 mg/day at weekly intervals until optimal response. Children >6 yr: 5 mg once or twice daily increase to 5 mg/d at weekly interval.

Adult dose: Start with 10 mg and increase up to 40 mg/day.

Indic: Attention deficit hyperactivity disorder.
(Dexedrine tab 5 mg, adderall XR caps 5 mg, 10 mg, 15 mg, 20 mg, 25 mg, 30 mg).

Atomoxetine 0.3 mg/kg/day q12 hr titrate over 1–3 wk to a maximum dose of 1.2–1.8 mg/kg/day.

Adult dose: 100 mg/day.

Indic: Attention deficit hyperactivity disorder.
(Axepta, attentrol tabs 10 mg, 18 mg, 25 mg, 40 mg, 60 mg).

Atorvastatin It is a lipid lowering agent. 10 mg per day up to maximum of 20 mg for children above 10 yr.

Adult dose: 10 to 40 mg (maximum 80 mg) per day, adjust dose every 2 to 4 wk.
(Atocor, atorlip, atorva, avas, caditor, lipicure, liponorm tabs 10 mg, 20 mg, 40 mg).

Atovaquone 30–40 mg/kg/d oral once for <40 kg, 750 mg/dose oral q 8 hr for 21 days for >40 kg. Administer with food.

Indic: Alternative therapy for *Pneumocystis jirovecii* pneumonia in patients intolerant to cotrimoxazole.
(Mepron suspension 750 mg per 5 ml).

Azathioprine Start with 3–5 mg/kg/day, maintenance 1–3 mg/kg/day oral once a day. For rheumatoid arthritis and systemic lupus erythematosus: 1 mg/kg/d which is gradually increased to a maximum dose of 2.5 mg/kg/d.

Indic: Prevention of rejection in renal transplant patient, severe active rheumatoid arthritis, systemic lupus erythematosus and steroid resistant nephrotic syndrome.

SE: Leukopenia, thrombocytopenia, and hepatotoxicity.

Caution: If allopurinol is administered concurrently reduce the dose by 25%.
(Imuran, zymurine, azimune, immuzat tab 50 mg; inj 100 mg vial).

Baclofen 0.75–2 mg/kg day oral q 8 hr. Maximum dose for <8 yr: 40 mg/d; >8 yr: 60 mg/d. It is useful to relieve muscle spasticity due to spinal or cerebral origin.

Adult dose: 5 mg t.i.d., increase by 5 mg every 3 days till maximum of 80 mg/d.
(Liofen, lioresal, spinofen, baclofen tabs 10 mg, 25 mg).

Betahistine dihydrochloride 8–16 mg 3 times/day after meals. Avoid below 12 yr of age.

Adult dose: 30–75 mg/d q 8 hr.

Indic: Vertigo, tinnitus, and Meniere's disease.
(Vertin tabs 8 mg, 16 mg, 24 mg).

Caffeine citrate It is more effective and safer for treatment of apnea of prematurity. It is administered in a dose of 10–20 mg/kg IV infusion slowly over 30 min. Stop the infusion, if heart rate exceeds 180/min. After 24 hr, maintenance therapy is started with a dosage schedule of 5 mg/kg oral in a single or two divided doses.
(Inj cafirate, primicef 20 mg/ml in 3 ml vial, cafirate, primicef oral solution 20 mg/ml in 1.5 ml single use vial. Capnea 20 mg/ml in 1 ml and 2 ml single use vials for oral and IV use).

Calcium gluconate 1–2 ml/kg/dose equivalent to 0.45–0.9 mEq/kg/dose, repeat if necessary. Give slowly IV by closely monitoring heart rate because it can lead to cardiac arrest. IM use may lead to local abscess. 1.0 g of calcium gluconate is equivalent to 89 mg elemental calcium or 4.46 mEq calcium. 10% solution contains 100 mg/ml of calcium gluconate equivalent to elemental calcium of 8.9 mg/ml or 0.45 mEq/ml.

Maintenance: 2–4 ml/kg/d q 6 hr or continuous IV.

29 *Hypocalcemia:* 1–2 ml/kg slow IV push.

Cardiac arrest: 0.2–0.5 ml/kg IV.

Hyperkalemia: 0.5 ml/kg over 5–10 min.

Indic: Treatment of symptomatic hypocalcemia, hyperkalemia, cardiac arrest.

SE: Hypercalcemia and bradycardia. *Concurrent use in digitalized patients may precipitate cardiac arrhythmia.* IV leakage may cause severe tissue necrosis.

Caution: Never give IV calcium gluconate to a digitalized patient and do not mix it with sodium bicarbonate solution due to precipitation of calcium carbonate.
(Inj calcium gluconate IP 10% w/v 10 ml ampoule).

Carnitine, levo 50–100 mg/kg/day up to a maximum of 3 g/day q 8–12 hr oral or maximum IV dose of 1 g.

Adult dose: Initial dose 1.0 g daily q 4 hr. The usual maintenance dose 1.0–3.0 g/day q 3–4 hr.

Indic: Myopathy, cardiomyopathy, hemodialysis, primary systemic carnitine deficiency, secondary carnitine deficiency due to inborn error of metabolism, Rett syndrome and supplement during TPN and valproate therapy.
(Carnitor tab 500 mg, carnivit-500 cap, carnivit-E cap contains carnitine 150 mg, and vitamin E 200 i.u., oral solution 500 mg/5 ml, carnit tonic 50 mg carnitine per 5 ml (with vitamin B complex), inj 500 mg/2.5 ml, 1 g/5 ml for IV use).

Cholestyramine 250–500 mg/kg/day of anhydrous cholestyramine q 8 hr after meals mixed with fruit juice or water. Avoid oral intake of other medications 2 hr before or after administration of the resin. Maximum dose 8 g/day.

Adult dose: 4 g daily 1–2 times, gradually increased up to maximum of 6 scoops in a day q 12 hr.

Indic: Hypolipoproteinemias, pruritus due to biliary obstruction.

SE: Constipation, deficiency of fat soluble vitamins.
(Questran 4 g sachet, 378 g tin, 4 g cholestyramine per 9 g sachet).

Cinnarizine Children 5–12 yr: 12.5–25 mg 2 hr before the journey, 12.5 mg q 8 hr during journey.

Adult dose: 25–50 mg 2 hr before journey, 15 mg q 8 hr during the journey.

Indic: Motion sickness and vertigo.
(Vertigon, dizikind MD, cini, cinirone, dizzigo tab 25 mg, vertigon forte, diziron forte, cinirone forte tab 75 mg; vertigil, domstal-CZ, cinirone-D, dizitac tab contains cinnarizine 20 mg and domperidone 10 mg).

Cyclophosphamide 300–750 mg/m^2 IV once 4 wkly for up to six doses as an immunomodulator.

Indic: Active flare up of dermatomyositis/polymyositis.
(Inj endoxan 200 mg, 500 mg and 1000 mg vials).

Cyclosporin Immunosuppressant for autoimmune disorders and prevention of allograft rejection. 10–15 mg/kg/d with milk or fruit juice, gradually reduce to 2–6 mg/kg/d as maintenance dose for 6 mon–1 yr. Intravenous dose is one-third of oral and is available as 0.05–0.25% solution in 5% dextrose or normal saline. Administer slowly over 2–6 hr.

SE: Nephrotoxicity, tremors, hypertension, hyperlipidemia, gingival hyperplasia and hirsutism.
(Graftin, sandimmune oral caps 25 mg, 50 mg, 100 mg; inj immusol, restasis, zymmune, sandimmune 100 mg/ml, 50 ml vial).

Cyproheptadine hydrochloride For 2–6 yr 0.25 mg/kg/day oral q 8–12 hr (maximum 12 mg/day); 7–14 yr 4 mg oral 8–12 hr up to maximum of 16 mg/day.

Indic: Migraine prohylaxis, beingn paroxysmal vertigo, antiallergic.
(Practin, ciplactin, apenorm, periatin tab 4 mg; syrup 2 mg/5 ml).

d-Penicillamine 20–40 mg/kg/day oral q 6–8 hr empty stomach. Up to 10 yr: 0.5–0.75 g/day, >10 yr: 1.0 g/day q 12 hr before meals p.o. Provide additional supplements of vitamin B_6 (25 mg/day) and zinc.

Adult dose: 125 mg 3 times/day up to maximum of 375 mg t.d.s. for arthritis; 1–3 g divided doses after food for cystinuria; 1.5–2.0 g/day before food for one yr for Wilson disease.

Indic: Heavy metal poisoning, cystinuria, rheumatoid arthritis, and Wilson's disease.

(Cupriminic, artamine tab 250 mg; distamine tabs 50 mg, 125 mg, 250 mg; pendramine tabs 125 mg, 250 mg, cilamin 250 cap 250 mg).

Deferasirox (DFO) It is an iron-chelating drug used to treat iron overload due to chronic hemolytic anemia and repeated blood transfusions. The drug binds with the circulating iron and eliminates the chelated iron via the feces. It is given in a dose of 20–35 mg/kg single oral dose on empty stomach. Children above 2 yr are given adult dose. The dose should be titrated to maintain serum ferritin level below 500 ng/ml. It is not approved for use below 2 yr of age.

(Exjade, desifer, asunra tabs 100 mg, 400 mg; defrijet, desirox tabs 250 mg and 500 mg).

Deferiprone Oral iron-chelating agent used for transfusion hemosiderosis in children with thalassemia major, hemolytic anemia, acute iron poisoning. Usual dose 50–100 mg/kg/day q 6 or 12 hr oral.

(Kelfer tabs and caps 250 mg and 500 mg).

Desferrioxamine Chelating agent for acute and chronic iron intoxication. For *acute iron intoxication*, preferred route is IM. Administer 1000 mg stat, followed by 500 mg every 4 hr for 2 doses, subsequently 500 mg every 4–12 hr depending upon clinical response (maximum 6000 mg in 24 hr). Intravenous rate of infusion should not exceed 15 mg/kg/hr for the first 1000 mg, subsequently 125 mg/hr, if needed (maximum 6000 mg in 24 hr). Chronic iron overload: 20–40 mg/kg/day SC administered over 8–12 hr, using battery driven pump. IM dose is 500–1000 mg per day. In addition, 2000 mg IV for each unit of blood transfused (separate infusion <15 mg/kg/hr). Maximum dose 1000 mg in the absence of transfusion, or 6000 mg if transfused 3 or more units of blood or packed RBCs.

Caution: The excreted iron imparts reddish color to urine.

C/I: Acute renal failure unless concomitant hemodialysis is done.
(Inj desferal 500 mg per vial).

Dextran-40 The dose is based on patient's condition.
Indic: Prevention of deep vein thrombosis, shock, cerebrovascular accident.

C/I: Fluid overload states.
(Lomodex-40: Low molecular weight dextran, 40,000 with 5% dextrose or in 0.9% saline, 10% IV infusion).

Dextran-70 The dose depends upon the patient's condition.
Indic: For short-term blood volume expansion, prevention of deep vein thrombosis.

C/I: CHF, bleeding disorder due to thrombocytopenia.
(Lomodex-70: High molecular weight dextran, 70,000 in 0.9% saline, 5% dextrose IV infusion).

Dextromethorphan 1–2 mg/kg/day q 8 hr oral up to maximum of 60 mg/day. Used as an antitussive and for nonketotic hyperglycinemia.
(Lastuss LA syrup 30 mg/5 ml, suppressa syrup 10 mg/5 ml).

Doxapram hydrochloride Start at 0.5 mg/kg/hr and increase by stepwise increments of 0.5 mg/kg/hr to a maximum of 2.5 mg/kg/hr or till control of apnea of prematurity is achieved which ever occurs earlier. Used as a constant IV infusion for apneic attacks of prematurity unresponsive to theophylline therapy. Do not mix in the drip containing sodium bicarbonate or aminophylline.

C/I: Seizure disorder, hypertension, head injury, and acute asthma.

SE: Hypotension, cerebral irritation, and convulsions.
(Dopram ampoule 20 mg per ml).

Erythropoietin-r Hu Start with 50–100 i.u./kg and give maintenance dose of 10 i.u./kg two or three times a wk IV or SC for chronic renal failure. For anemia of prematurity:
150–500 i.u./kg twice a wk SC for 8 to 12 wk. Provide iron supplements 2–3 mg/kg/day.

Adult dose: 25–50 i.u./kg three times a week, increase gradually in steps of 25 iu till weekly maintenance dose of 100–300 i.u./kg divided every 2–3 weekly injections.

(Hemax, epogen, epotin, epox, eprex 2000 i.u. and 4000 i.u. in 2 ml vials).

Estrogen (Estradiol valerate/hemihydrate) 0.5 mg p.o. daily for 6 months followed by increments of 0.5 mg p.o. every 6 months till a dose of 2 mg p.o. is reached.

Indic: Pubertal induction in hypogonadal girls.
Add a progesterone for 12–14 days every 1 to 3 mon after commencement of periods, or after 2 yr from the start of estrogen therapy.

Caution: Procoagulant state, dyslipidemia, hypertension, advancement of skeletal age.
(Estradiol hemihydrate–estrabet tabs 1 mg, 2 mg; estradiol valerate–progynova 1 mg; estova,valest, evatone tab 2 mg).

Flunarizine It is a weak calcium channel blocker that also selectively inhibits sodium channels in the brain. It is given in children above 5 yr in a dose of 5 mg once a day.

Adult dose: 10 mg single daily dose.

Indic: Prophylaxis against migraine.

SE: Sedation, dry mouth, nausea, constipation, weight gain.
(Sibelium, flunarin, nariz tabs 5 mg, 10 mg, nomigraine caps 5 mg and 10 mg).

Gamma benzene hexachloride For scabies apply to whole body below the neck, if required repeat again after a week. For pediculosis, massage over the scalp at night and cover with a cap. Morning head bath should be taken ensuring that medication does not enter the eyes.
(Ascabiol 1% emulsion; scabine 2%, gab 1% lotion).

Givinostat hydrochloride It is a histone deacetylase (HDAC) inhibitor that reduces inflammation and loss of muscle mass or sarcopenia. It is approved by FDA for treatment of patients with Duchenne muscular dystrophy (DMD) and Becker muscular dystrophy above the age of 6 years. It is the first non-steroidal drug approved to treat all genetic variants of DMD. It can be coadministered with corticosteroids.

Indic: All genetic variants of DMD and BMD, pulmonary arterial hypertension, advanced heart failure, and hematological malignancies.

Dosage: 40–60 kg: 31 mg p.o. BD, ≥60 kg: 39.9 mg p.o. BD. Shake the bottle vigorously for at least 30 seconds.

SE: Nausea, vomiting, diarrhea, fever, stomach ache, thrombocytopenia, increased triglycerides, QT prolongation and tarsades de pointes.
(Tabs duvyzat 5 mg, 10 mg, 25 mg, 50 mg).

Glucagon like peptide 1 (GLP1) receptor agonists for type 2 diabetes Approved for use as adjunct therapies in youth with type 2 diabetes mellitus >10 years of age.

Liraglutide (Inj victoza): Start with Inj. liraglutide 0.6 mg SC once a day and hike up to a maximum of 1.8 mg SC once a day.

Exenatide (Inj. bydureon): Inj. exenatide (extended release) 2 mg SC once every week.

Dulaglutide (Inj. Trulicity): Inj. dulaglutide 0.75 mg SC once every week; increase the dose to 1.5 mg once every week after 4 weeks of the initial dose.

Indic: (GLP1) agonists are approved for use in pediatric patients ≥10 years with type 2 diabetes mellitus as an adjunct to metformin.

SE: Gastrointestinal, flatulence, bloating, pain abdomen.

Caution: Pancreatitis, C-cell hyperplasia, multiple endocrine neoplasia 2 (MEN2) syndrome due to the increased risk of medullary carcinoma of the thyroid gland.
(Inj victoza pen 6 mg/ml, inj trulicity pen 1.5 mg/0.5 ml, inj bydureon pen 2 mg).

Glucagon like peptide 1 (GLP1) receptor agonists for obesity Approved for use in children aged >12 yr with obesity, i.e. BMI >30 kg/m^2 adult cut off

29 GLP-1 receptor agonists are incretins which enhance insulin secretion and increase satiety by slowing gastric emptying as

well as by their effect on the arcuate nucleus of the hypothalamus and the limbic/reward system in amygdala.

SE: Mainly gastrointestinal symptoms like nausea, vomiting, pain abdomen, bloating and diarrhea.

Caution: Pancreatitis, C-cell hyperplasia, multiple endocrine neoplasia (MEN) 2 syndrome due to the increased risk of medullary carcinoma of the thyroid gland.

(Inj saxenda (liragulide) multidose pen start at 0.6 mg SC per day for one week, increase the dose in weekly intervals till a dose of 3 mg is reached; inj wegovy (semaglutide) 2.4 mg multidose pen start at 0.25 mg SC once a week and increase dose 0.5 mg weekly after a month till 2.4 mg weekly dose is reached).

Granulocyte colony stimulating factor (G-CSF) and granulocyte mononuclear colony stimulating factor (GM-CSF) G-CSF: 5–10 µg/kg/d SC or IV. GM-CSF: 250 µg/kg as a 2-hr IV infusion or SC. It should not be administered to a patient between 14 days before and 24 hr after cytotoxic chemotherapy.

Indic: Neutropenia associated with cytotoxic therapy or after bone marrow transplantation; treatment of congenital or idiopathic neutropenia; neutropenia associated with severe HIV disease or sepsis.

(Neupogen, filgrastim (G-CSF) 300 µg per vial; sargramostim (GM-CSF) 300 µg per vial).

Hydroxyurea It is a myelosuppressive agent and is also known as hydroxycarbamide. It is credited to increase fetal hemoglobin, makes RBC's globular thus reducing the attacks of sickle cell crises and it reduces the need for blood transfusions. It is also a broad spectral anti-cancer agent. It is given in a dose of 10–15 mg/kg/day single dose p.o. The child is encouraged to take plenty of fluids.

Adult dose: 15 mg/kg/p.o. single daily dose.

Indic: Sickle cell disease, essential thrombocythemia, chronic myelogenous leukemia, polycythemia vera, and cancer of cervix in women.

SE: Anorexia, nausea, vomiting, elevation of hepatic enzymes, bone marrow suppression, neutropenia and infertility.
(Tab siklos, droxia, hydrea 100 mg, cap, cytodrox, krabinex 500 mg).

Indomethacin It is a nonsteroidal anti-inflammatory drug (NSAID). Dose in newborn: Age at dose (mg/kg) 1st 2nd 3rd <48 hr 0.2 0.1 0.1; 2 to 7 days 0.2 0.2 0.2; >7 days 0.2 0.25 0.25. Infuse over 20 to 30 min.
Compatibility with 5% dextrose, normal saline, sterile water for injection; incompatible with 10% dextrose, calcium gluconate, dopamine, dobutamine.

Indic: For closure of patent ductus arteriosus in neonates.

C/I: It is contraindicated in active bleeding, significant thrombocytopenia, coagulation defects, impaired renal function, NEC, suspected infection. Concurrent use with corticosteroids may cause gastric perforation.

SE: Hypoglycemia, oliguria, platelet dysfunction.
(Ductaclose 1 mg/vial).

Interferon alpha 2A and 2B 3 million i.u./m^2 intrathecally stat followed by 3 million unit/m^2 thrice a week SC and repeat intrathecal dose 3 million units/m^2 once a month for 6 mon.

Indic: Subacute sclerosing panencephalitis.
(Inj intalfa, pegasys, inron A 3 million/ml).

Lactase enzyme 200 FCC units are taken in 5–10 ml of EBM or formula feed, mix thoroughly and wait for 5 min. The lactase containing milk is given followed by breastfeeding or formula feed.

Indic: Lactose intolerance, infantile colic.
(Mactose, yamoo, neosmile, contains 600 FCC units of lactase per ml. Add 0.5–1.0 ml/feed. Yamoo chewable tab available).

Lactulose It is a synthetic sugar used to treat constipation. It softens the stools by absorbing water from the body. 1–2 ml/kg/day q 6 hr orally in children with hepatic coma and constipation.
Adult dose: 30–45 ml/dose q 8 hr.

SE: Dehydration, hypernatremia, and hypokalemia.

C/I: Patients who require a low galactose diet, diabetes mellitus. (Livoluk, duphalac, emty, evict, looz, totalax syrup 15 ml contains 10 g lactulose).

L-Dopa or Levodopa It is the precursor of the neurotransmitters dopamine, norepinephrine and epinephrine. Start 1 mg/kg/day, increase gradually until response or side effects appear. Maintenance dose 4–5 mg/kg/day q 8–12 hr.

Indic: Dystonia, dopa responsive dystonia, restless legs syndrome.

SE: Somnolence, dyskinesia, hallucinations, psychosis, orthostatic hypotension, GI disturbances.

(Syndopa, tidomet tab contains carbidopa 10 mg and levodopa 100 mg; syndopa, tidomet plus tab contains carbidopa 50 mg and levodopa 200 mg).

Magnesium sulfate 2–3 mEq/kg/day for PEM. Magnesium sulfate 50% solution provides 4 mEq/ml of elemental magnesium. Give 0.5–1.0 ml/kg/day q 6 hr IM. Magnesium sulfate 1% solution contains 10 mg magnesium/ml equivalent to 0.08 mEq magnesium/ml. It is given in a dose of 100 mg/kg IV. For use in asthma *see* section on Bronchodilators.

(Inj magnesium sulfate 1%, 10%, 25%, 50% 1 ml ampoules).

Mannitol (20%) 5 ml/kg initially, thereafter 2 ml/kg every 6 hr for 2 days or 0.5–3.0 g/kg/dose q 8 hr. For oliguria, give 10% of dose over 3 to 5 min and the rest during next 2–6 hr. It should be administered IV rapidly over a period of 30–60 min for relief of brain edema.

Indic: To reduce intracranial pressure, prevention and treatment of renal failure, hyponatremia and water intoxication.

(Mannitol 20% by Core Parenteral Drugs, Sipra Remedies 100 ml bottles).

Metformin It is a biguamide which effectively lowers blood glucose by decreasing glucose production in the liver, diminishing intestinal absorption and enhancing insulin sensitivity. Start with 500 twice a day daily after meals. Titrate by 500 mg every 1–2 wk, depending upon tolerability until the max tolerated dose of 1000 mg twice daily or 850 mg thrice daily of the standard metformin preparation. For sustained release tablet, start with 500 mg once a day with food at night and titrate to maximum 2000 mg once daily.

Indic: Type 2 diabetes mellitus in children ≥10 years, polycystic ovarian syndrome to normalize ovulatory abnormalities

SE: Pain abdomen, bloating, flatulence, diarrhea, lactic acidosis.

Caution: eGFR <30 mL/min/1.73 m^2, cardiac or respiratory insufficiency, or receiving radiographic contrast materials.

(Glycomet-500 SR, glycomet-850 SR, glycomet-1000 SR, gluconorm-500 SR, glyciphage SR 1 gm, gluformin 500, bigomet SR 500, bigomet SR 1000, metform SR 1000, formin SR 500, mefomin 500 SR, mefomin 1000 SR, diamet 500, exermet 500 SR prolonged release, endoformin SR 1000, exermet 500, glyciphage 500/1000, gluformin 850).

Melatonin It is a hormone produced by the pineal gland in response to night or darkness. The dose is 3 mg in children >3 yr of age, 30 min before sleep. May increase up to 6 mg after 7–10 days.

Indic: Chronic sleep disturbance in children with neurodevelopmental disorders, autism spectrum disorder, ADHD.
(Meloset tabs 3 mg and 6 mg; syrup noctura 3 mg/5 ml).

Methotrexate It is primarily used for treatment of malignant disorders. Its immunosuppressive effect is highly effective for treatment of resistant cases of juvenile rheumatoid arthritis. In JRA, the usual dose is 5–10 mg/m^2 oral on empty stomach once a week. It can be given for several years.

SE: Bone marrow suppression and hepatic dysfunction.
(Methotrexate, neotrexate, biotrexate tab 2.5 mg, imutrex, folitrax, oncotrex, remtrex tabs 2.5 mg, 5 mg, 7.5 mg and 10 mg).

Methylene blue (methylthioninium chloride). It is a thiazine dye and works by converting the ferric iron in hemoglobin to ferrous iron. It is first reduced to leucomethylene blue, which reduces heme group from methemoglobin to hemoglobin. It is given in a dose of 1 mg/kg IV over 5–30 min. If methemoglobin level remains greater than 30%, a repeat dose can be given after one hr. Along with dihydroartemisinin-piperaquine, methylene blue in an oral dose of 15 mg/kg/d for 3 days, is useful to treat artemesinin-resistant malaria and prevent transmission of gametocytes of *P. falciparum* from humans to mosquitoes.

Adult dose: 50 mg oral or IV stat.

Indic: Methemoglobinemia, falciparum malaria and ifosfamide neurotoxicity.

C/I: G6PD deficiency.

Caution: Do not refrigerate or expose to light.

SE: Headache, vomiting, excessive release of serotonin, confusion, shortness of breath, elevation of blood pressure, bluish or greenish discoloration of urine and sweat.
(Provayblue 50 mg 10 ml and bluject 100 mg/10 ml vials. Dilute in 50 ml of 5% dextrose in water).

Methylphenidate hydrochloride 0.3–1.0 mg/kg/day. Start with 5 mg orally before breakfast and lunch and increase by 5–10 mg every wk till maximum of 60 mg/day or 2 mg/kg/day. In severe cases, combine with clonidine 1–4 µg/kg/day single dose in the evening.

Adult dose: 10–20 mg BD or t.d.s. up to maximum of 60 mg.

Indic: Attention deficit hyperactivity disorder, narcolepsy, pain management.

C/I: Avoid in children below 6 yr, patients with glaucoma, and during treatment of MAO inhibitors.
(Addwize tab 10 mg, addwize OD 18 mg, ritalin, concerta, inspiral and meth OD tabs 10 mg, 20 mg as sustained release).

Mexiletine 1–8 mg/kg q 8–12 hr oral.

Adult dose: 300–1200 mg/day q 8 hr.

Indic: Congenital myotonia, myotonic dystrophy, ventricular arrhythmias.

SE: Nausea, vomiting dizziness, chest pain, tremors, breathlessness, palpitations, heartburn, light headedness.
(Mexitil caps 50 mg, 150 mg and 200 mg, inj 250 mg/10 ml).

Modafinil It is a powerful CNS stimulant belonging to amphetamine class. Avoid below 12 yr.

Adult dose: 200–400 mg once daily in the morning.

Indic: Sleep disorders and narcolepsy.

SE: Severe skin and psychiatric reactions, tremors, and tachycardia.
(Provake, modalert, modafil tabs 100 mg, 200 mg).

Olanzapine Start 2.5–5.0 mg/day with weekly increments to maximum of 20 mg/day.

Adult dose: Initial dose is 5 mg in the evening which is gradually increased to 20 mg/day, can be combined with fluoxetine for bipolar disorder.

Indic: Pyschotic disorders, juvenile bipolar disorder, autism spectrum disorder.
(Olex, olandus, oliza, onza tabs 2.5 mg, 5.0 mg, 7.5 mg, 10 mg).

Omega-3 fatty acids Health-friendly long chain polyunsaturated fatty acids namely eicosapentaenoic acid (EPA), arachidonic acid (AA) and docosahexaenoic acid (DHA). Essential for brain growth, reduces aggregation of platelets, improves lipid status and provides antioxidant effect.

Indic: Essential supplement during pregnancy and lactation, preschool children and elderly subjects at risk of cardiovascular disease and CNS disorders.
(Mega-3 cap, maxiguard cap, maxepasofgel cap containing 180 mg EPA and 120 mg DHA. Mega soft-E cap contain DHA 60 mg, EPA 90 mg, vitamin E 200 i.u., winofit, cadvion forte also contain vitamin E and other micronutrients cap thrive-G contains DHA 250 mg, EPA 90 mg, vitamin C 100 mg, vitamin E 100 i.u., zinc 15 mg, folic acid 2.5 mg and selenium 60 μg. Brainwise, docowize, brainaxo, braniest syrup contain DHA 190 mg and EPA 250 mg per 5 ml. Rapgrow and nutrokind drops provide DHA 40 mg/ml).

Oral rehydration solution (ORS) The WHO low osmolality oral rehydration solution contains sodium chloride 2.6 g, trisodium citrate 2.9 g, potassium chloride 1.5 g, glucose 13.5 g in one liter water. It provides Na+ 75 mEq/l, chloride 65 mEq/l, K+ 20 mEq/l, citrate 10 mEq/l and glucose 75 mOsm/l.
(Electral, ORS, prolyte, punarjal, walyte, electrobion, zelect, zylyte speedoral 6 g and 30 g sachets for constitution with 200 ml and 1000 ml water).

Orlistat 120 mg tds oral. It is a pancreatic lipase inhibitor that decrease the digestion and absorption of lipids from the gut (approved >12 years age with obesity).

SE: Flatulence, pain abdomen, oily stools, fecal urgency and incontinence, deficiency of fat soluble vitamins.
(Reshape, orlak tab 120 mg)

Pancuronium bromide It is an aminosteroid muscle relaxant often used for euthanasia. 0.04–0.1 mg/kg/dose q 30–60 min IV; <1 wk: 0.03 mg/kg/dose; 1–2 wk: 0.06 mg/kg/dose; 2–4 wk: 0.09 mg/kg/dose given q 4 hr, infuse over 1 min. May lead to hypertension and increased cerebral blood flow. The patient should be on ventilatory support. Neostigmine 0.025 mg/kg IV with atropine 0.02 mg/kg is effective antidote.
(Inj pancuronium 2 mg/ml; pavulon 1 mg/ml in 2 ml, 10 ml vials).

Permethrin Topical application for treatment of scabies and head lice. Permethrin 5% lotion or cream is used for treatment of scabies. After bath at night, apply to the whole body neck downward. Two applications at an interval of one wk is enough. Treat simultaneously all contacts. For head lice, shampoo the hair and towel dry. Apply 1% permethrin lotion over the scalp and rinse after 10 min. Comb with a fine metal comb. Repeat the medication after one wk and treat all contacts.
(Permite, scabper, permizo, paxib 5% cream and lotion, perlice, scablice 1% lotion for head lice).

Phentermine It is an appetite suppressant by causing prolonged feeling of fullness and satiety. Approved >16 years age for a short duration of up to 12 wk. 18.75 to 37.5 milligrams (mg) once a day, taken before breakfast or 1 to 2 hours after breakfast. Reduces the reuptake of norepinephrine thereby stimulating the pro-opiomelanocortin neurons in the hypothalamus which decreases appetite.

SE: Irritability, mood swings, insomnia, dry mouth, dizziness, headache, hypertension

C/I: Cardiovascular disease, hyperthyroidism, glaucoma and recent or concurrent use of monoamine oxidase inhibitors.
(Adipex-P, lomaira tab 37.5 mg)

Phentermine-Topiramate: Approved >12 yr age with obesity 3.75 mg phentermine/23 mg of topiramate once a day for 14 days. Doses may be increased after 14 days to maximum of 15 mg phentermine/92 mg of topiramate by 12 wk.
(Qsymia caps 3.75/23 mg, 7.5/46 mg, 11.25/69 mg, 15/92 mg).

Piracetam 40 mg/kg q 8 hr oral. Reduce the dose to half once the desired effect is obtained.

Indic: Psychomotor retardation, learning problems, psychomotor reactions, adjunct in cortical myoclonus.
(Normabrain, alcetam, cetam, neuropil, pritam, nootropil tabs 400 mg, 800 mg; susp 500 mg per 5 ml).

Polyethylene glycol It is a safe osmotic laxative and given as a single oral dose 0.75–1.5 g/kg with a glass of water.
(Laxopeg granules 17 g sachet and 255 g jar, laxopeg, looz, miraLax, syp 3.35 g).

Potassium chloride 1–2 mEq/kg/day q 8 hr oral.
Caution: Administer only when urine flow is established.
(Syrup potklor, K-sus, keylyte, potasol 15 ml provides 20 mEq (1.5 g KCl) of K^+ and potassium chloride injection 15% 10 ml ampoules provide 2 mEq of K^+ per ml).

Probenecid 25 mg/kg as oral loading dose, then 40 mg/kg/d q 6 hr.

Adult dose: 250 mg q 12 hr for a wk followed by 500 mg q 12 hr.
(Benecid, procid tab 500 mg).

Probiotics Products containing *Saccharomyces boulardii*, *Lactobacillus acidophilus*, *Lactobacillus sporogenes* with or without B complex vitamins and zinc. They displace pathogenic bacteria in the gut. One sachet or capsule is given twice a day.

Indic: Broad spectrum antibiotics, acute and persistent diarrhea, prevention of NEC, infantile eczema, gut immunity, evening colic and irritable bowel syndrome.
(Bifilac GG, darolac, gutpro, gut OK, regutol, ecoflora, econorm, G norm, binifit, laffs, stibs sachets and caps, vizylac, nutrolin-B dry powder containing lactobacilli and vitamins. Pre-prokid and darolac-zn sachets contain zinc while bifilac-zn and ViBact-zn contain zinc + glutamine).

Progesterone Oral micronized progesterone 200 to 300 mg/day for 12–14 consecutive days per month by reaching adult dose of estrogen or earlier if breakthrough bleeding occurs.

Indic: For induction of withdrawal menstrual bleeding

Caution: Fluid retention and weight gain, prothrombotic effect, androgenic effect, drowsiness and dizzines
(Gestcure 200 SR, gestcure 300 SR, susten SR 200, susten SR 400, gestofit 300 SR, gestofit 200 SR, endogest 200, nidagen-SR 200, naturogest SR 200, miprogen 400).

Prostaglandin E1 0.05–0.4 μg/kg/min by continuous infusion in a large vein or umbilical artery catheter at the level of ductus arteriosus. After the ductus is opened, the dosage can be reduced to 0.01 μg/kg/min.

Indic: Ductus-dependent congenital heart diseases.

SE: Apnea, flushing, hypotension, seizure-like activity, and platelet aggregation defect.
(Prostin VR pediatric, alprostadil 500 μg per ml ampoule).

Pyritinol hydrochloride It is a semisynthetic water soluble analog of vitamin B6. 50–100 mg q 8 hr oral.

Adult dose: 600 mg/d q 8 hr.
(Encephabol, ence tabs 100 mg, 200 mg, susp 100 mg per 5 ml). 29

Racecadotril It is a potent and specific inhibitor of enkephalinase to prevent loss of water and electrolytes from the intestines. Its therapeutic utility is controversial. 1.5 mg/kg per dose 3 times in a day.

Adult dose: 100–300 mg 3 times in a day.
(Enuff, racotil, lomorest sachets 10 mg and 30 mg, Enuff Xtra sachet 10 mg racecadotril with probiotics, enuff, racotil, redotil, zedott cap 100 mg).

Rituximab Monoclonal antibodies for immune suppression in severe autoimmune disorders. 37.5 mg/m^2 wkly for 4 doses IV or till CD19 target is achieved whichever is earlier. Premedication with hydrocortisone 1 mg/kg IV, chlorpheniramine 1 mg/kg IV and paracetamol 10 mg/kg oral is recommended before infusing rituximab.

Adult dose: 1.0 g IV 2 doses 15 days apart. May be combined with methotrexate and repeated every 24 wk.
(Reditux, mabtas 100 mg/10 ml and 500 mg/50 ml vials).

Rizatriptan benzoate A serotonin 1b,1d receptor agonist used for abortive treatment of acute migraine attack if started within 30 to 60 min . Children above 6 yr age: 5 mg for <40 kg weight and 10 mg for >40 kg weight.
(Rizan, maxalt, rizact, rizatan tabs 5 mg, 10 mg).

Sildenafil It is phosphodiesterase-5-inhibitor. 0.5–2 mg/kg/dose every 6 to 12 hr. IV loading dose 0.4 mg/kg over 3 hr followed by continuous infusion of 1.6 mg/kg/day.

Indic: Vasodilator, persistent pulmonary hypertension, erectile dysfunction and Raynaud's phenomenon.
(Alsigra, viagra, edegra, intagra, zerect, androz, penegra, caverta, silagra, target, ciidafil 50 mg, 100 mg; inj pulmosil 0.8 mg/ml, 12.5 ml vial).

Sodium bicarbonate 1–2 mEq/kg per dose IV or calculate on the basis of base deficit as follows:
29 Base deficit × weight in kg × 0.6 = mEq or ml of 7.5% solution of sodium bicarbonate required for correction of acidosis.

Indic: Correction of documented metabolic acidosis during prolonged resuscitation, bicarbonate deficit due to renal or GI losses.

SE: Local tissue necrosis, hypernatremia, and hypocalcemia.

Caution: Ensure adequate ventilation prior to infusion. Avoid bolus dose in newborn babies. Give after dilution with equal volume of distilled water or double volume of 5% dextrose.

(Inj sodium bicarbonate 7.5% 10 ml ampoules providing 0.9 mEq bicarbonate per ml).

Surfactant Intubate with appropriate size ET, check for equal breath sounds. Administer through feeding tube inserted in ET to ensure delivery of surfactant to both the lungs. Give in 4 aliquots of total dose. Ventilate using T-piece/ventilator/ resuscitation bag after each aliquot. Wait till saturation and heart rate stabilizes before administering next dose. Avoid suctioning ET 2 hours post administration.

Not receiving invasive ventilation: Insure (Intubate, give surfactant, extubate) after administration.

Indic: Respiratory distress syndrome, meconium aspiration syndrome.

SE: May cause pulmonary haemorrhage, due to fall in pulmonary artery pressure and increased lung compliance can lead to increase in left to right shunting via PDA, failure to decrease pressures post administration predisposes to air leaks.

(Survanta Beractant (Minced lung extract) 4 ml/kg (25 mg/ml) 4 ml, 8 ml vial; Curosurf Poractant alfa (Minced lung extract) 2.5 ml/kg (80 mg/ml), 1.5 ml, 3 ml vial; Neosurf Bovine Lipid Extract Surfactant (BLES) 5 ml/kg (27 mg/ml) 3 ml, 5 ml vial; Alveofact Bovine Lipid Extract Surfactant 1.2 ml/kg (45 mg/ ml) 1.2 ml, 2.4 ml vial).

Testosterone Inj testosterone enanthate 50 mg IM every 4 wk, increase the dose by 50 mg every 6–12 mon, adult dose –200 to 250 mg IM every 2 to 4 wk.

Indic: Puberal induction in hypogonadal boys.

(Testoviron depot (250 mg/ml), testoviron depot (100 mg/ml), aquaviron, testanon (100 mg/ml), sustanon (250 mg/ml), cernos depot (1000 mg/4 ml).

Triple dye Acriflavine 1.14 g, gentian violet 2.29 g, brilliant green 2.29 g and distilled water or spirit 1000 ml for topical use.

Ursodeoxycholic acid (UDCA) 10–20 mg/kg/day q 8 hr.

Adult dose: 600 mg q 12 hr.

C/I: Severe hepatic dysfunction, and complete obstruction of biliary tract.

SE: Diarrhea, abdominal discomfort.

(Urso, ursocol, udca, udcament udcoliv tab 150 mg; udihep, udiliv tabs 150 mg, 300 mg; ursoliv tab 250 mg, ursoliv cap 300 mg, suspension 125 mg/5 ml).

Zinc For deficiency, administer 0.5 mg/kg/day for infants; 10 mg/day in infants <6 mon and 20 mg/day >6 mon of age for 14 days for treatment of acute and persistent diarrhea and 6 mg/kg/d for treatment of acrodermatitis enteropathica. Maximum adult dose is 220 mg/day.

(Zevit cap elemental zinc 22.5 mg, zincolak cap 137 mg, ulceel cap 220 mg of zinc sulfate, dynazinc tab 50 mg elemental zinc; syrup zinconia, Zn 20 (zinc gluconate), zinsy (zinc acetate) provide 20 mg elemental zinc per 5 ml, zemin (zinc sulfate) 5 mg/5 ml, zevit, zincovit syrup 10 mg elemental zinc per 5 ml; drops 2.5 mg elemental zinc/ml).

Chapter

30

Specific Antidotes

Toxic agent	Antidote
1. Acetaminophen (Paracetamol) (Toxic dose 150 mg/kg)	N-acetyl cysteine (20% airborn, acetadote, fluimucil, mucare, mucomyst, mucomix 200 mg per ml in 2 ml and 5 ml vials). *Oral protocol:* 140 mg/kg loading dose of N-acetyl cysteine (NAC) orally/NG tube and then 70 mg/kg 4 hrly for additional 17 doses (diluted to 5% solution in soda or fruit juice). Repeat the dose if vomiting occurs within one hr of administration. *Intravenous protocol:* Loading dose of NAC 150 mg/kg in 5% dextrose is given over 15 min. The maintenance dose is 50 mg/kg in 5% dextrose over 4 hr followed by 100 mg/kg for 16 hr. Kings College Protocol says 50 mg/kg for 4 hr followed by 100 mg/kg for 16 hr
2. Amphetamines (Toxic dose 50 mg)	Treatment should be started if ingestion is more than 20 mg. Chlorpromazine hydrochloride 1 mg/kg IM or IV, maximum IV dose is 50 mg.
3. Anticholinergics (Atropine, belladonna)	Physostigmine 0.02 mg/kg/dose (Maximum 1 mg) or 0.5 mg IV, SC, IM every 5 min till desired effect is observed (Maximum 0.1mg/kg), then 0.5–2.0 μg/kg/min.

(Contd.)

(Contd.)

Toxic agent	*Antidote*
4. Benzodiazepines (Overdose)	Flumazenil IV in incremental doses of 0.1 mg, or (0.01 mg/kg) q1-min intervals until the desired effect is achieved. Lack of response to flumazenil at a cumulative dose of 5 mg indicates other cause for CNS depression.
5. Calcium channel blocker (nifedipine, nimodipine, verapamil)	Calcium chloride (20 mg/kg of 10% solution) (Maximum 2000 mg) or calcium gluconate (100 mg/kg of 10% calcium gluconate) IV for hypotension and bradydysrhythmias. Give glucagon, amrinone, isoproterenol, atropine and nor adrenaline or phenylephrine for hypotension unresponsive to fluids and calcium.
6. Carbon monoxide	Hyperbaric oxygen therapy. 100% oxygen, till carboxyhemoglobin level is <10%.
7. Cyanide (fatal dose 200–300 mg)	Amyl nitrite (vaporal) inhalation for 15–30 sec after every min pending IV access and then sodium nitrite 3% solution, 0.2–0.4 ml/kg IV at a rate of 2.5–5.0 ml/min (maximum dose 10 ml) followed by sodium thiosulfate 1–2 ml/kg (maximum dose 50 ml) of 25% solution over 10 min. Use lower doses, i.e. 0.2 ml/kg for children with anemia.

(Contd.)

(*Contd.*)

Toxic agent	*Antidote*
8. Digitalis (Intake of more than 4 mg of digoxin by children or >10 mg by an adult or serum digoxin level of >2 mg/ml)	Correct hypokalemia (KCl 0.5 mEq/kg/hr) and hyperkalemia (insulin, dextrose, sodium bicarbonate and kayexalate). *Never administer calcium due to risk of ventricular dysrhythmias.* Treat bradydysrhythmias with atropine (0.01–0.02 mg/kg IV) and tachydysrhythmias with phenytoin and lidocaine. Digoxin-specific immune Fab (digibind) is available in 40 mg vial. Each vial binds approximately 0.6 mg digoxin. When ingested dose or blood levels of digoxin are unknown, administer 400 mg digoxin-specific Fab IV slowly over 30 min.
9. Ethylene glycol	Ethanol 10 ml/kg 10% sol IV or 1 ml/kg of 95% sol by mouth. Maintenance dose is 1.5 ml/kg/hr 10% sol IV or 3 ml/kg/hr 10% sol IV during hemodialysis.
10. *Heavy metals*	
(a) Mercury i, iii	(i) British anti-Lewisite (BAL) 3–5 mg/kg IM every 4 hr on day 1 and 2; 2.5–3 mg/kg every 6 hr on day 3 and 4; 2.5–3 mg/kg every 12 hr for one wk. The course can be repeated after 5 days period of no therapy. Dose is same in children and adults.(BAL or dimercaprol 100 mg/ml, 3 ml ampoule).
(b) Arsenic i	(ii) EDTA (calcium disodium ethylene diamine tetra-acetic acid) 50–75 mg/kg/day in 4 divided doses IM or IV as 0.2–0.4% solution. *Adult dose*: 500 mg/m^2 (200 mg/ml ampoule).

(*Contd.*)

(*Contd.*)

Toxic agent	*Antidote*
(c) Lead i, ii, iii, iv	(iii) Symptomatic children (treat regardless of blood level) and asymptomatic children with blood level more than 70 μg/dl. Dimercaprol (BAL) 75 mg/m^2 intramuscular every 4 hr (total daily dose of 450 mg/m^2) followed by EDTA 1500 mg/m^2/24 hr by continuous infusion (start EDTA 3–4 hr after giving BAL) for a total of 5 days. BAL may be stopped once lead levels are less than 60 μg/dl. Repeated courses may be needed till blood levels are <20 μg/dl. Asymptomatic children (lead levels 45–69 μg/dl) are given EDTA 1000 mg/m^2/24 hr infusion for 5 days. (iv) d-penicillamine 20–40 mg/kg per day q 6–8 hr empty stomach orally for 5 days. (Cupriminic, cilamine 250 mg tab; distamine tabs 50 mg, 125 mg, 250 mg; pendramine tabs 125 mg, 250 mg) Oral thiamine and dimercaptosuccinic acid (DMSA) 350 mg/m^2/dose every 8 hr p.o. for 5 days, then every 12 hr for 14 days are also useful. Remove the source of lead and give supplements of calcium and iron.
11. Heparin	1 mg of protamine sulfate will neutralise 115 U of porcine heparin and 100U of low molecular weight heparin. 2.5–5.0 mg/kg followed by 1.0–2.5 mg/kg IV q 4 hrly slowly over 5 min. (Each ampoule of protamine sulfate contains 10 mg/ml). Consider time since hpa <0.5 hr = Full dose, 0.5–1 hr = 75% dose, >1 hr = 50% dose.

(*Contd.*)

(*Contd.*)

Toxic agent	*Antidote*
12. Iron (Toxic dose 35 mg/kg)	Deferoxamine 15 mg/kg/hr IV infusion up to a maximum of 80 mg/kg/day. Therapy needed for 12–36 hr till urine color becomes normal. Can be given IM in a dose of 20 mg/kg every 4–10 hr, if IV site is not available. *Adult dose:* 1 g stat IM, 0.5 g q 4 hr for 2 doses, 0.5 g q 8–12 hr till 6 g/day; Intravenous infusion is given at a rate of 15 mg/kg/hr (Desferal 500 mg/vial)
13. Isoniazid	Pyridoxine 1.0 mg IV for each 1.0 mg of isoniazid. Administer 500 mg IV over 30 min, if amount of isoniazid ingested is unknown.
14. Methemoglobinemia	Methylene blue 1–2 mg/kg IV 1% solution over 5–10 min. If needed this dose may be repeated after one hr (10 mg/ml ampoule). Maximum dose is 7 mg/kg. It may cause bluish green discoloration of urine. *Adult dose:* 65 mg thrice a day p.o.
15. Methyl alcohol	10 ml/kg of 10% solution of ethanol IV as loading dose and then 1.5 ml/kg/hr infusion (3 ml/kg/hr, if patient is on dialysis). *Oral dose:* 1 ml/kg of 95% ethanol in fruit juice over 30 min and then 0.15–0.3 ml/kg/hr as 50% ethanol in fruit juice.
16. Morphine, other opiates, and semisynthetic narcotics (meperidine, lomotil, diphenoxylate hydrochloride, heroin)	Naloxone hydrochloride 0.1 mg/kg per dose IV. Maximum dose in children is 2 mg. Repeat after 2–3 min, if needed. *Adult dose:* 0.4–2.0 mg IV, repeat every 2–3 min, if required. (Inj. adult narcan, narcotan, nex, nalox 0.4 mg/ml, narcan, narcotan 0.02 mg/ml).

(*Contd.*)

(Contd.)

Toxic agent	*Antidote*
17. Organophosphorus poisoning (Insecticides which are cholinesterase inhibitors)	Atropine sulfate 0.05 mg/kg IV; repeat every poisoning 5–10 min till secretions are dried. Once adequate atropinization is achieved, repeat doses every 30–60 min or give IV infusion 0.02–0.08 mg/kg/hr. PAM or pralidoxine 2-pyridime aldozime methiodide 25–50 mg/kg diluted to 5% in normal saline and infused over 5–30 min. May be repeated after one hr and repeat doses may be required every 6–12 hr. In severe poisoning, give infusion at a rate of 9–19 mg/kg/hr.
18. Phenothiazines and metoclopramide (extrapyramidal reactions)	Diphenhydramine hydrochloride 1–2 mg/kg IV every 30 min, may be repeated after 3 to 4 hr IM or p.o. Maximum dose 300 mg/day. (Benadryl caps 25 mg, 50 mg; syr 12.5 mg/5 ml; ampoule 50 mg/ml; vials 10 mg/ml)
19. Propranolol (beta blocker)	Atropine 0.01–0.02 mg/kg per dose SC till atropinisation occurs, maintain for 24 hr and taper in the next 24 hr. Adult dose is 0.6 mg. Glucagon 50–150 μg/kg bolus followed by 50 μg/kg/hr infusion. (Glucagon, glucagen hypokit 1 mg/ml ampoule).
20. Scorpion bite	Prazosin, the selective alpha-1-adrenergic blocking agent is true pharmacological antidote to control adrenergic effects like tachycardia, hypertension and incipient myocardial failure with pulmonary edema. Give 0.25 mg oral every 4–6 hr for 24 hr. *Adult dose:* 1 mg every 4–6 hr for 24 hr. (Prazopress tab 1 mg and 2 mg, prazopress-XL, minipress-XL Gits tab 2.5 mg and 5 mg).
21. Warfarin, dicumarol	Vitamin K 5–10 mg IM or IV (Inj kapilin 10 mg/ml)

EMERGENCY DRUGS

Adenosine 0.05–0.1 mg/kg (maximum 6 mg/dose) over 1–2 sec followed by 0.2 mg/kg/dose (maximum 12 mg/dose) every 2–5 min until SVT is terminated, up to a total dose of 0.25 mg/kg or 30 mg. Give as a rapid IV bolus, over 1–2 seconds.

Aminophylline 5–7 mg/kg IV loading dose diluted in 25 ml saline followed by 0.5–0.9 mg/kg/hr constant infusion for relief of bronchospasm.

Atropine sulfate 0.02 mg/kg/dose IV or SC, minimum dose 0.2 mg.

Calcium gluconate 1–2 ml/kg/dose of 10% solution diluted with equal volume of distilled water IV slowly over 10 min. Stop the infusion, if the heart rate drops below 100/min.

Dexamethasone 0.5 mg/kg/dose (usual dose being 4–12 mg.) q 6 hr IV for shock and cerebral edema.

Diazepam (for convulsions) Rectal: 0.5 mg/kg, IV: 0.2–0.3 mg/kg IV bolus over 1–2 min, repeat at 15 and 45 min, if seizures persist.

Dopamine or dobutamine hydrochloride 5–20 μg/kg/min as a continuous IV infusion.

Epinephrine (adrenaline) 0.01 ml/kg/dose (maximum 0.5 ml/dose) of 1:1000 solution IM. Repeat the dose after 15–20 min. For intravenous or endotracheal use for cardiac arrest: 0.1 ml/kg per dose of 1:10,000 solution. Do not use 1:1000 solution unless ten times diluted. For laryngeal edema due to anaphylaxis, 0.1 ml/kg (maximum 5 ml) of 1:10,000 solution through nebulizer. For nebulization: 0.5 ml/kg of 1:1000 solution is diluted in 3 ml normal saline.

Fentanyl citrate 1.0–5.0 μg/kg/dose q 1–4 hr IV as a continuous infusion @ 1–5 μg/kg/hr.

Furosemide 1–2 mg/kg/dose IV or p.o., up to 6 mg/kg/day q 12 hr.

Hydrocortisone sodium succinate For status asthmaticus: 25–50 mg/kg/dose every 4–6 hr IV. For endotoxic shock: 50 mg/kg initial dose followed by 50–150 mg/kg/day q 6 hr IV for 48–72 hr.

Ketamine 0.5–2.0 mg/kg/dose IV slowly or 2.5–5.0 mg/kg/dose IM.

Lignocaine hydrochloride 1 mg/kg per dose as IV bolus q 5 min up to a maximum total dose of 5 mg/kg, followed by IV infusion @ 10–50 μg/kg/min. Maximum dose 5 mg/kg/day.

Lorazepam 0.05–0.1 mg/kg/dose (maximum dose 4 mg) over 2–5 min IV or IM, may repeat after 10–15 min.

Methyl prednisolone 30 mg/kg/dose IV bolus over 10–15 min once daily for 3–5 days.

Midazolam 0.2 mg/kg IV bolus followed by continuous infusion of 0.75–10 μg/kg per min, intranasal spray 0.2 mg/kg.

Morphine sulfate 0.1–0.2 mg/kg/dose SC or IV up to a maximum dose of 15 mg q 4 hr.

Naloxone hydrochloride 0.1 mg/kg IV q 2–3 min for 3 doses up to maximum total dose of 2 mg.

Nifedipine 300–500 μg/dose sublingual.

Paraldehyde 0.1–0.2 mg/kg/dose deep IM or 0.3 ml/kg/dose per rectum mixed with coconut oil.

Phenobarbitone sodium or phenytoin sodium For seizures 15–20 mg/kg loading dose slowly IV over 20 min followed by 5–8 mg/kg/day q 12 hr.

Salbutamol 0.1–0.15 mg/kg/dose with 1.5 ml saline q 2–6 hr through a nebulizer. Injection 4–6 μg/kg/dose SC, IM or IV q 6–8 hr.

Sodium bicarbonate 1–2 mEq/kg/dose or 0.3 × kg × base deficit. Available as 7.5% solution of sodium bicarbonate which provides 0.9 mEq/ml of bicarbonate. Do not give to children with respiratory acidosis.

Index

A

D

G

H

I

N

O

P

Q

R